Clement Reeves

*Reflections and Commentary
by Rollo May*

The Psychology of Rollo May

 Jossey-Bass Publishers
San Francisco • Washington • London • 1977

THE PSYCHOLOGY OF ROLLO MAY
A Study in Existential Theory and Psychotherapy
        by Clement Reeves

Copyright © 1977 by: Jossey-Bass, Inc., Publishers
                     615 Montgomery Street
                     San Francisco, California 94111
                              &
                     Jossey-Bass Limited
                     44 Hatton Garden
                     London EC1N 8ER

Library of Congress Catalogue Card Number LC 76-50708

International Standard Book Number ISBN 0-87589-303-1

Manufactured in the United States of America

JACKET DESIGN BY WILLI BAUM

FIRST EDITION

Code 7702

The Jossey-Bass
Behavioral Science Series

THE AUTHOR

Clement Reeves is assistant professor of philosophy, University of Guelph, Ontario, Canada. He was awarded the Ph.D. degree in philosophy from the University of Ottawa, Canada, in 1974. During his postgraduate studies there, he held both a Canada Council Doctoral Fellowship and the Queen Elizabeth II Ontario Graduate Scholarship.

Reeves was awarded the B.A. degree with first class honors in philosophy and M.A. in philosophy from the National University of Ireland, University College Cork, in 1965 and 1967, respectively. During his M.A. studies, Reeves held a Postgraduate College Scholarship.

Now a member of the graduate faculty in philosophy at the University of Guelph, Reeves' principal research and teaching interests lie in the fields of medieval philosophy, contemporary European philosophy, and philosophical psychology. Reeves is married and has two daughters.

DEDICATION

To my dear friend
Dr. Jacques Croteau
in appreciation of his constant
concern and encouragement

Preface

For some years, particularly since the publication of *Existence: A New Dimension in Psychiatry and Psychology* (1958), there has been growing among psychologists in North America an intensified awareness of the need for the assimilation and effective use of philosophical understanding in psychological science in general and psychotherapeutic science in particular. Existential concepts have proved particularly fruitful in the integrational effort that such awareness has elicited and the reciprocal illumination offered by existential and psychoanalytic insights has become increasingly influential in the changing intellectual climate.

Rollo May is a leading figure in this philosophico-psychological rapprochement and a major representative of the American movement in existential psychology. In his books, and by encouraging dialogue between philosophers and psychologists sympathetic to existential psychology and psychiatry, May expresses concretely what he has believed from the time of his earliest writings—namely, that psychology needs a properly grounded, theoretically cogent, interdisciplinary approach to man.* Such an approach, he believes, can be particularly helpful in the psychotherapeutic context.

The Psychology of Rollo May is the first book to offer a systematic and comprehensive critical analysis of the theoretical foundations of May's work, together with an appreciation of the practical import of his theoretical position. I explore May's central concepts (sense of being, anxiety, love, will, intentionality, existence) and examine their development from May's earliest to his most recent work. My study focuses on the tracing of the fundamental structures of man's being to their roots in man's sense of his being and on the concrete practical understanding of human existence that such an empirico-phenomenological approach can offer. As such, this book stresses the importance of theoretical foundations and develops the proposition that the psychotherapist needs not only to understand and clarify his own presuppositions but that an adequate science of man on which to base psychotherapy requires such clarification and understanding.

It is my hope that *The Psychology of Rollo May* will be of interest in both theoretical and practical fields of endeavor. For psychologists, psychiatrists, social workers, philosophers, and some sociologists, it offers both a synthesis and critical appraisal of May's theoretical reflections and an elucidation of some ideas and theories in the field of existential psychology. Further, the *Reflections and Commentary* by May himself should be of particular interest to readers.

Useful to many readers will be the intellectual biography of May and glossary of his central terms that follow the main text. An extensively cross-referenced bibliography of May's work concludes the book.

It is a pleasant task to acknowledge my indebtedness to colleagues in philosophy at the Universities of Guelph and

---

*The author hereby takes the opportunity to point out that in this book nouns and pronouns that superficially appear to indicate masculine gender are used in the conventional sense of referring to human beings in general and are not intended to exclude the feminine gender.

Ottawa; their unfailing encouragement offered needed support in times of doubt. It is with great pleasure also that I offer my thanks to Rollo May for his interest in my project and for his generosity in writing a *Reflections and Commentary* to my book. Finally, I offer to my wife and two daughters my heartfelt appreciation of their patience, constancy, and not inconsiderable assistance.

Guelph, Ontario   Clement Reeves
December 1976

Note on Citations

Twenty-nine different works of Rollo May are cited throughout
the text. Rather than giving full bibliographic information in a
footnote at every mention, an abbreviated reference system has
been devised. Titles alone are used, and for brevity the titles—
including those of books, chapters, and articles—have been
shortened to their key words and italicized. For example, in
relation to May's chapter, "The Context of Psychotherapy"
(M. I. Stein, Ed., *Contemporary Psychotherapies*, Glencoe, Ill.:
Free Press, 1961), reference in the text is simply made to *Context*, and in this format: (*Context*, p. 89). Similarly, in relation
to May's *Man's Search for Himself*, published in 1953 (and re-
issued in paperback in 1973), just *Man's Search* is used. A list of
these abbreviated titles follows. The numbers in parentheses following the titles indicate the corresponding entries that will be
found in the full bibliography of May's works at the end of the
book. Thus, for *Context*, the reader is referred to bibliography
entry 18 (see p. 317).

For all other sources cited in the book, I have used the
last name of the author, date of publication, and page numbers

where applicable—and this information is given in parentheses after relevant material. Using this work as an example, the format is: (Reeves, 1977, p. xii).

Abbreviated Titles of May's Works

Anxiety and Values (17)
Art of Counseling (1)
Context (18)
Contributions (27)
Dangers (22)
Dreams and Symbols (12)
Emergence (29)
Existence (9)
Existential Bases (31)
Existential Psychology (10)
Existential Psychotherapy (2)
Existential Therapy (20)
Freedom and Responsibility (24)
Historical and Philosophical Presuppositions (33)
Jean-Paul Sartre (21)
Love and Will (3)
Man's Search (4)
Meaning of Anxiety (5)
Origins (38)
A Phenomenological Approach (19)
Power and Innocence (6)
Psychology and the Human Dilemma (7)
Questions (25)
Significance of Symbols (41)
Social Responsibilities (26)
Springs of Creative Living (8)
Symbolism (11)
Toward the Ontological Basis (43)
What is the Human Dilemma? (13)

Contents

The Psychology of Rollo May

*A Study in Existential Theory
and Psychotherapy*

It is essential that we clarify the *ontological* bases on which the dynamisms of psychoanalysis rest. I cannot overemphasize the importance of this enterprise, for I think such dynamisms as transference, resistance, and so forth, hang in the air and can have no lasting meaning except as their ontological basis, in man's situation as man, can be understood.

Rollo May
Psychology and the Human Dilemma

Psychotherapy seeks the most specific characteristics and events of the given individual's life—and any therapy will become weakened in vapid, unexistential, cloudy generalities which forgets this. But psychotherapy also seeks the elements of the human conflict of this individual which are basic to the perdurable, persistent qualities of every man's experience as man—and any therapy will tend to shrink the patient's consciousness and make life more banal for him if it forgets that.

Psychotherapy reveals *both* the immediate situation of the individual's "sickness" *and* the archetypal qualities and characteristics which constitute the human being as human. It is the latter characteristics which have gone awry in specific ways in a given patient and have resulted in the former, his psychological problems. . . . One of the values of living in a transitional age—an "age of therapy"—is that it forces upon us this opportunity, even as we try to resolve our individual problems, to uncover new meaning in perennial man and to see more deeply into those qualities which constitute the human being as human.

Rollo May
Love and Will

Introduction
to the Psychology
of Rollo May

In the attempted constructive therapeutic exploration of a person's existential predicament, the psychotherapist needs not only to be articulately conscious of his own philosophical presuppositions about what it is to be a human being, but he also needs an adequate science of man on which to base his psychotherapy. This is the continuing conviction animating the writings of Rollo May (1909-   ), a practicing North American psychotherapist who constantly emphasizes in his work the necessity of basing psychotherapy "on an understanding of what makes man the *human* being" (*Origins*, p. 35).

1

Since every scientific method rests on philosophical assumptions (regardless of whether the scientist acknowledges this fact), May contends that the conscientious scientist of human nature, particularly the psychotherapist, must know and understand these presuppositions, in order at least to broaden his horizon and, further, to develop and free his methods in a manner that will do justice to the richness and breadth of the human experience that he seeks to understand (*Origins,* pp. 8-9; *Emergence,* pp. 24-25, 28-30). An adequate science, of man, says May, will not fragment and destroy man's humanity as it studies him. With deceptive simplicity, May asserts that to study and understand man, to do justice to man precisely as man, we need a human model, a science of man, "a psychology that will be relevant to man's distinguishing characteristics as man" (*Emergence,* p. 48. *Questions,* pp. 182-191; *Social Responsibilities,* p. 208; also Giorgi, 1970, pp. 70, 100). We must not be content with models taken from the natural sciences, such as physics or biology. May considers inadequate, too, models taken uncritically from medicine or even from an agglomeration of the social or "human" or "cultural" sciences, such as sociology and anthropology.

Western science, asserts May, has favored an essentialist approach, that is, a search for immutable principles and laws, endeavoring to divide reality into discrete parts or aspects and tending subsequently to assume that the resultant abstractions and impressive systems of conceptualization have more reality than the given existent (*Emergence,* pp. 28-29; *Questions,* pp. 187-190). In psychology and psychotherapy, both of which have felt the attraction of such an approach, to be "scientific" in observation and the gathering of special data has tended to mean that the individual human being is seen in terms of behavior patterns, drives, forces, reflexes, and reactions. That the latter are abstractions from reality, that is, aspectual, reflective formulations derived from observation of individual human beings or even analogies applied from observation of animal behavior, may become glossed over. The special-experience methodology of quantification and measurement, born of the prescientific presuppositions of this "essentialist approach," may then, perhaps unwittingly, be assumed to be the only valid one. The person is then seen, "reduced," and understood in terms of the scientist's particular, differential, or aspectual theory. The cloth, which is the person, is cut to fit the measure, which is the theory or particular abstract formulation, and what is not susceptible of observation, measurement, quantification, and controlled experimentation may even be declared nonexistent or illusory.

While holding that such "essentialist" understanding must not be discounted—that is, that understanding gained from the aspectual formulation of human behavior, in terms of dynamisms and mechanisms, for example, must be borne in mind—May declares that psychotherapy must see such data in terms of the whole person (*Emergence,* p. 14; *Origins,* p. 13). The mechanism, for May, has meaning only in terms of the whole person, not conversely. Indeed, psychotherapy, by very reason of its one-to-one encounter of therapist and patient, must go beyond any tendency to assume uncritically the presuppositions and methods valid for the positive or natural sciences. In every understanding, says May, there is an "understander" who must, at the very least, be aware of his own philosophic presuppositions and their role in forming and guiding his understanding and, correspondingly, his methods (*Dangers,* pp. 154-155; *Love and Will,* p. 223-238). May does not, however, concern himself in his work with methods of therapy but rather with the philosophical presuppositions of and overall approach to psychotherapeutic encounter. His work does not extend to development of a precise methodology for therapy, but is concerned rather with elucidating the structures of human existence and, thereby, with understanding the philosophical approach that underlies his whole psychotherapeutic enterprise.

In his earliest book, *The Art of Counseling* (1939), May had already asserted that the wise counselor or therapist does not ignore or leave to chance such a fundamental matter, but must conscientiously and reasonably draw up his "picture of personality" and his conception of the counseling process (*Art of Counseling,* pp. 44, 74-75, 81). Later, as May's understanding of his own work deepened to include his conscious preoccupation with the very structure of human existence, he was to assert that not only did psychotherapists need to become articulately aware of their philosophical presuppositions, but that psychotherapy, to be complete, needed to clarify its own ontological bases (*Existential Therapy*, p. 134; *A Phenomenological Approach*, p. 115; *Origins*, pp. 35-36; *Emergence*, p. 9; *Existential Bases*, p. 32). Thereby, May was convinced, psychotherapy would find its theoretical foundation in a science of man that would unite the scientific understanding of man, owed chiefly to Freud, with an ontological understanding of man or an image of man that would do justice to man precisely as man (*Origins*, pp. 35-36; *Contributions*, p. 37). May himself seeks to contribute to the attainment of such a science of man by clarifying the fundamental structures of existence, or the inalienable or ontological characteristics that distinguish man precisely as man. May sees these as characteristics or "processes of the existing person," so inalienable to the being of a human being that the "omission" or absence of any one of them "would mean that we do not then have a human being" (*Existential Bases*, p. 77, see also pp. 74, 78; *A Phenomenological Approach*, p. 115).

It must be pointed out that May states himself to be aware of the etymological meaning of *ontology* as "the study of being." He uses the term with *three* ranges of meaning, that is, for him, *ontological* can mean: (1) having to do with being as such; (2) characteristic of all *living* beings; and (3) characteristic of the *human* being. The last is the meaning most frequently intended, while the first is offered more as a "general sense" or etymological meaning. In discussion (1959) of his understanding of existential psychotherapy, May offered the view that in contrast to "the narrow limits of natural science as it had been traditionally conceived," the existential approach seeks

> to find the basis for a science that will not only
> have a unity with respect to man, but will also do
> justice to the distinctive characteristics of the hu-
> man being. The methods of healing in psychother-
> apy, if they are to last, depend on such an under-
> standing.

> *This requires an approach on the ontological level. . . . By ontology here I mean something general as well as specific. The general meaning is the study of being. But the specific meaning is in asking the question, what are the characteristics which constitute the human being as human, without which he would not exist as a human being?* [Toward the Ontological Basis, *p. 5*]

From a search for clarity about his own presuppositions, May's enterprise has broadened and deepened to become a seeking of the theoretical foundations of psychotherapy in an ontological approach to man, "an approach on the ontological level" (*Toward the Ontological Basis,* p. 5), to repeat May's own words. This book seeks to trace from its earliest moments the development of May's ontological approach to man, that is, the development of his envisioning of the theoretical foundations of psychotherapy in that ontological approach. This work is not intended to pursue comparative or historical studies in psychotherapeutic theory, but rather to concentrate on the work of one living, influential psychotherapist, on his continuing reflections on the basis and meaning of his work, and to trace and examine step-by-step in internal critique the growth of his integrated understanding of the ontological basis of psychotherapy.

May believes that psychotherapy with its interaction of therapist and patient has a privileged access to the deeper understanding of human beings as human beings (*Emergence,* pp. 11-12; *Love and Will,* pp. 19-20). He asserts that the preferred method must be "to confront first of all our real experience in psychotherapy, and then find the terms . . . that will most fully express and communicate this experience" (*Emergence,* p. 45). Clearly, May's project is not the easy application of a preformulation of normal and abnormal human existence, but rather a series of attempts to study, express, and communicate what he learns and confirms of the being of man in the course of his theoretical reflections and in the psychotherapeutic encounter with the individual being of each patient. Phenomenology, for May, is the first stage in this understanding; it is the necessary and disciplined effort to clear one's mind of presuppositions and biases and to experience the data as presented in their own context, that of the particular human being (*Emergence,* pp. 20-21). May's emphasis, then, falls not on differential or aspectual theories of behavior (although these are not to be disparaged or discounted), but rather on the whole existence, the whole world outlook and on the sense of being revealed by the particular person in therapy. These May attempts to grasp and express on what he calls "the deepest levels of ontological reality" (*Emergence,* p. 9).

In seeking to communicate, understand, thematize, and interpret this experience, May chooses the terms that for him best express that reality. Many of his chosen terms come from existential philosophical thought—for example, *existence, sense of being, presence, anxiety,* and *intentionality.* He also retains such Freudian terms as *repression* and *resistance,* while insisting that their meaning must be relocated in a whole understanding of the human being *choosing* to employ such mechanisms, that is, understanding of the mechanism in terms of the person, not conversely (*Emergence,* p. 14; *Anxiety and Values,* pp. 74-75; *Context,* p. 87). May's existential emphasis is very firmly on the person, and to convey that point May employs those terms that for him capture in quintessence the deepest ontological reality of human existence.

Many and varied influences are discernible in May's terminological usages; for example, those of Paul Tillich and Alfred Adler, both of whom were May's teachers at an early stage in his development. Harry Stack Sullivan's interpersonal theories, too, cannot but have exerted a guiding influence, particularly during May's studies at the William Alanson White Institute shortly after Sullivan's ten-year presidency of that foundation had ended. May himself acknowledged the relation of his work on ontological principles in therapy to the thought of Paul Tillich and Kurt Goldstein (*Toward the Ontological Basis,* p. 5; *What is the Human Dilemma?,* pp. 10-11; *A Phenomenological Approach,* p. 127, n. 2), seeing in the latter's neurobiological work and organismic theories special data that supported and corroborated his own view of human existence, while in

Tillich's work he saw the philosophical formulation of his ontological principles. Having acknowledged the relation of his work
to theirs, May went on to add quickly that his ontological principles "arise directly out of my insights and experience in immediate psychotherapy as well as my own thinking" (*Toward the
Ontological Basis,* p. 5). While a fruitful area for further research might well be the influence exerted on May by other
contemporary writers, his brief specific mentions of their work
are usually only for the purpose of illuminating, paralleling, or
supporting a point he himself wishes to make as arising out of
his psychotherapeutic experience and his own reflective understanding. Indeed, May indicates clearly that basically he regards
clinical data as supporting and corroborating psychological and
psychotherapeutic insights (themselves based in common experience and common sense) and thereby confirming, broadening,
and integrating progress in the attainment of an overall understanding of man.

Also, May's *use* of his chosen terms would appear to owe
more to his own intuitive and reflective psychological and
psychotherapeutic understanding than to other writers. Notably, he always offers his own understanding of each term as it is
introduced, together with his own definitions, connotations,
descriptions, and formulations of the place and meaning of that
term in his whole approach to the understanding of man. With
his apparently preferred method of illustration by practical
examples, he conveys very clearly his intention of expressing
and communicating his experience as he understands and
thematizes it. In his search for the way to communicate his experience as based in common experience or everyday grasp of
existence, and to say exactly what he wants to say, his examples
range from his psychotherapeutic casebook to many fields of
human expression, particularly art and literature, while always
underscoring May's own belief in man as a finite creature whose
free, responsible, meaningful becoming is both his destiny and
his task.

While detailed comparative researches into the influence
exerted on May by other contemporary writers have already
been stated to be outside the purview of this book, it must be

clearly understood that in the cases of Freudian and Kierkegaardian thought on anxiety, and the Freudian and Platonic
conceptions of love, the matter is entirely different. Of the two
approaches in each case, that is, Freud and Kierkegaard on anxiety, and Freud and Plato on love, May asserts that they do not
represent a dichotomy but are both obviously necessary, both
clearly important to a proper understanding of the human being
and his development (*Emergence,* p. 3; *Love and Will,* p. 88).
These, then, are not merely influences, but are formative
sources in the growth of May's own understanding of both anxiety and love. As seminal in his work, therefore, they cannot but
be taken into account in a study such as this. It has, then, been
necessary to study carefully what May offers as his understanding of their thought and to examine in what manner and to
what extent May attempts to interfuse them in the development
of his own approach.

The original contribution and central purpose of this
book, however, are not in fact to compare May's thought with
that of other writers nor simply to trace formative influences on
the evolution of his thinking. Rather, this book is, to my knowledge, the first to undertake a concentrated, comprehensive,
detailed analysis of the philosophic reflections of Rollo May on
the theoretical foundations of psychotherapy. I can find no evidence of any real philosophical critique of May, neither on his
work as a whole nor on any aspect of it. Some few brief comments exist in various journals but they do not offer any extended evaluation, confining themselves to summaries and re-
statements rather than offering judgments or critique. Similarly,
in some modern manuals and histories of psychology and
psychiatry, May is occasionally briefly referred to as a leading
writer and practitioner in the American movement of existential
psychology and his principal publications are also sometimes
given mention. Since, however, no major, detailed, philosophical studies (neither comprehensive nor aspectual) of May's work
exist as yet, no quotations or supporting arguments from such
studies can be offered in this book.

To my knowledge, the only review of significance is the
brief but synoptic critical and biographical note on May written

by Herbert Spiegelberg within the context of his Chapter Five, "The American Scene: Beginnings," in his recent book *Phenomenology in Psychology and Psychiatry: A Historical Introduction* (Spiegelberg, 1972, pp. 143-168). Given the nature of Spiegelberg's enterprise, the material referring specifically to May is necessarily concise and confined to a few pages and, moreover, his book itself was not available for study by myself until this book was nearing completion. In these circumstances, I am very happy to note how frequently my own independent judgments coincide with those expressed by Spiegelberg, for example, on specific conceptions in May such as centeredness and intentionality, on the position of the book *Existence* as a watershed in May's own development and on the relevance of proper philosophic evaluation of May's work, particularly because of his position as a leading representative of the American movement in existential psychology.

The analysis and conclusions offered in this book, then, are my own original contribution in the light of the continuing responsibility of philosophical researchers to offer serious and comprehensive critique of contemporary writers, particularly those whose work is very much in evidence and socially influential. Rollo May has published a great deal and is widely read and listened to in North America. In addition to his private practice and his writing, he has lectured at universities and colleges and has been a frequent contributor to conferences and professional journals. His book *Love and Will* has become a national bestseller in America and earlier books have been reissued. A dominant figure on the American existential psychological scene, May seems to have a talent for presenting his conceptions to a wide audience, having developed a congenial style and constantly referring to art and literature or finding examples in current affairs that, in his view, help to illuminate or support his point. In his note on May, Spiegelberg states his opinion that he may well be "the most influential native American spokesman for an existential phenomenology," adding that, in his view, May has "prepared the climate for a new approach to phenomenological psychology, both creative and critical" (Spiegelberg, 1972, p. 158). He has achieved this, says Spiegelberg, not only by his own writings but also by bringing together a considerable group of American thinkers sympathetic to existential ideas. The book *Existence,* jointly edited by May, Henri F. Ellenberger, and Ernest Angel and published in 1958, offered in translation for the first time in America some notable selections from European existential psychological studies, while May's two introductory chapters presented the new movement of existential psychotherapy "in the light of his own original approach" (Spiegelberg, 1972, p. 163). Not only because of his leading position and his social influence but also because of the nature and aim of his writing, May's work warrants, and, indeed, calls for, serious study by philosophical researchers.

As the first comprehensive and detailed critique of the ontological approach of Rollo May, this book focuses on the phenomenological explication and evaluation of May's central notions and their interrelation in a whole ontological approach to man. To this end, it has been essential to allow May to speak for himself. I have sought to enter into May's own thinking, to take what May himself says and to subject it to close scrutiny for inner consistency and clarity, in a continuing effort to be faithful to the philosophic exigence of returning "to the things themselves." Every effort has been made to study May as he presents himself (that is, the phenomena or data as given in the original context) seeking of him a consistent presentation of his own views, both in general as they are integrated into a whole view, and singly in each case as they are presented with illustrations, examples, definitions, and connotations. I hope to present a conceptual clarification of the theoretical foundations that May proposes for psychotherapy, that is, his ontological approach to man, his being, characteristics, and needs. My concern is not merely clarificatory but also critical, in that I also pay continuing attention to the determination of the philosophical adequacy and grounding of May's theoretical conceptions and to their basis and meaning in the "lived" world of everyday human existence or common experience, since this world is, for May, the fundamental, essential, and inalienable context of a proper understanding of man, and hence of psychotherapy.

It follows, then, that the chosen method of this book is that of internal critique. As applied in this study, the method of internal critique issues in two fundamental phases of inquiry. These phases are not consecutive, but alternating and interwoven. They are, however, clearly distinguishable.

The first phase consists in establishing what may be called the *linguistic* (or *verbal, literal*) interpretation of May's work. At this point the questions are: What did he say? What do his statements, illustrations, examples, definitions, and so forth convey? As May and I are contemporaries and share the same mother tongue, no difficulties of translation or of archaic idiom arise. Thus, in this book, the concerns of the first moment of internal critique are the linguistic clarity and internal consistency of definitions, examples, connotations, illustrations, and so forth.

The second phase of internal critique is concerned with real (formal, objective) interpretation. In this phase there are three closely related but distinguishable aspects to the inquiry. First, it must be established what the author *intended* to say. The questions here are: What did the author *wish to convey* as compared with what was actually literally said? What does he intend or understand by a particular conception or definition, and what does he wish to convey when he offers an example, illustration, or analogy? Every effort is made here to understand the author's intention and, having indicated anything that seems unclear, inconsistent, or inappropriate, to restate, if necessary and if possible, what it seems he wished to convey.

Secondly, the focus of the inquiry then broadens, going beyond grasping the meaning and scope of a particular conception offered by the author and showing how it relates to his other conceptions and to his work as a whole, to the overall tenor of his thinking, his prereflective existential option (or dominant intentional orientation), and his reflective theoretical and practical experience. It is also sought to show how his views, singly and in general, relate to the living, everyday, common experience "fact" of human existence as individual-being-becoming-in-the-world, since this "fact" is, for May, the inalienable context of all human meaning and understanding.

Thirdly, since it is a question of ontological conceptions and of an approach to man on what May calls "the ontological level," it is necessary to determine the meaning of this designation and its extent, that is, to ascertain the meanings of *ontological* for May and whether an ultimate position is offered, and if so, whether offered explicitly or implicitly. The questions here are: can May's ontological approach be said to extend to a fully constituted theory of being, an *ontology* in the fullest sense of the term? Does he present a full understanding of the ultimate ground and goal of his approach to man, and an epistemology and an ethic integrated and consistent with this? And, finally, what is his ultimate position as he understands it? When May is found to rely on an unquestioned realism based in common experience and to effectively use the term *ontological* in such manner and for the most part to restrict its scope to the narrower meaning of "characteristic of or inalienable from the being of the being being studied, namely man," the questions become: (1) is there an ultimate position implied in his ontological conceptions, that is, can one disengage implications for an ultimate position from his central conceptions, such as the sense of being, centeredness and intentionality; and (2) whether and how clearly his stated but unexplored, essentially fiduciary assumption of realism is consistent with these ontological conceptions.

Although its phases can be abstractly considered, defined, and placed in order of widening focus, the method of internal critique as employed in the present study actually alternates and interweaves the phases in a cumulative manner, examining each conception from each angle or in each phase of that critique and establishing carefully what may be concluded from that examination.

There is in May a constant dialectic between experience and theory as he reflects on and confirms for himself what he intuits of the being of man. In the light of his pragmatic, problem-centered orientation, his criterion of truth is simply to accept as true what would be most coherent with a common-experience, realistic-synoptic view of experience, as it can be reasonably and meaningfully assented to by the individual. His findings, resulting from his realistic-integrational view—for example, the intentional character of man, his freedom and responsibility—are brought out as each central conception is examined and again in my concluding chapter. Following a recapitulation and synthesis of his position, the conclusion seeks to go further, to present a summary of the scope and meaning of that position, together with some of its limitations and psychotherapeutic implications. It is pointed out that the limits of May's achievement result precisely from the fact that he did not conduct his reflections on an absolutely or radically philosophical (or fully ontological) level, that is, the limits of his thoughts result from the ambiguity of his unquestioned realist approach and lack of epistemological foundations. Although he does explore intentionality at length and even touches on the problem of the perspectivity of perception, he does not see these as *questions* at the radically or absolutely philosophical level but simply as *facts,* the meaning and implications of which must be explored and borne in mind, particularly in the psychotherapeutic situation. For instance, in *Love and Will,* while explaining his understanding of intentionality, May uses the example of the house in the mountains to illustrate how any object can be seen (or perceived) from many different "mental" perspectives as well as physical angles (*Love and Will,* pp. 224-225). In recognizing that the meaning of the perception "comes from" both the person perceiving and the house itself, May does not question, but simply asserts, the experientially independent existence of the house. Yet he also implicitly acknowledges that for him the Cartesian dichotomy (which he seems to consider not as interpretation but as independent, existing *fact*) remains something of a problem. His practical and concrete interest and concern, however, center firmly on the personal filters of pre-constituted meaning and figure ground in the light of which each perception occurs. This discussion effectively illustrates May's recurring and predominantly, although not exclusively, concrete and practical preoccupation with the *state* of the relationship of individual and world. His theoretical concern, then, might be said to extend to understanding the fundamental structures of that relationship but not as far as the exploration of the radically ontological ground of that understanding and of the relationship itself.

It is by virtue of its task as the first comprehensive and detailed critique of the ontological approach of Rollo May that this book focuses on the phenomenological explication and evaluation of May's central notions and their interrelation in a whole ontological approach to man. It was also pointed out that to this end it is essential to allow May to "speak for himself." This book, then, centers on close scrutiny of May's own writings, details of which will be found in the first part of the bibliography, which is devoted to primary sources, that is, to May's work alone. Although not all of the titles mentioned there are actually referred to in this book, all of May's work has been taken into account in its preparation. Also, in the ordinary way, much of May's material has appeared in print more than once (in journals and accounts of conferences, for example) with peripheral changes or change of title or incorporated into books written or edited by May. For the reader, extensive cross-referencing of the material has been offered in the first part of the bibliography; the compilation and cross-referencing are unavailable elsewhere. In the Note preceding the bibliographical entries, it is pointed out that it is my considered opinion that the best and most integrated access to May's thinking is through his books and those edited by him, since all of his ideas have been dealt with more than once and in the greatest detail in these works. Accordingly, also, it might be noted in passing that it is to these publications, May's books and those edited by him, that the terminological appendix to this book confines its references, for the multiple purposes of brevity, clarity, and order.

Special mention must be made of May's recent publication, *Power and Innocence* (1972), which is referred to briefly in the final chapter. It appeared too late to have been available for detailed analysis within the present book. However, I am satisfied that this book does not in any way vitiate the analysis or conclusions of the present study but rather is an application of May's whole approach, wherein he seeks to examine and expose the distortion of the structures of existence that underlies the contemporary phenomena of violence, power, hostility, and of innocence misconstrued as ignorance or noninvolvement in direct action. The book *Power and Innocence* is greatly linked to discussion of these matters in current affairs—for example, in Vietnam, American protest movements, ghetto living, and the situation of minority groups in America. Such distortion of existential structures and its theoretical foundations were already examined in May's study of the structure of anxiety seen as underlying repression, hostility, and alienation from self and world.

I chose to exclude *The Springs of Creative Living* (1940) from detailed analysis for the following reasons. First, following *The Art of Counseling* (1939) by only a year, *Springs of Creative Living* is very similar to, and repeats, its predecessor in line, tone, content, terminology, and conclusions without offering any furthering or grounding of the ideas in *The Art of Counseling* (while repeating much of May's already stated belief in religion as essential to personality health, and his personal, early association of religion with Christianity) or anything that would change, develop, or vitiate the extensive analysis and conclusions offered in this book, both generally and with particular reference to *The Art of Counseling.* Second, *The Springs of Creative Living,* unlike *The Art of Counseling,* does not offer a "picture of personality" or systematic personal view of human being as such, nor any exploration of psychotherapeutic attitudes and encounter. *The Art of Counseling,* in addition to being May's first book, offers a more explicit and broader view of May's presuppositions in germ at their earliest stage. Thus I chose it for in-depth study as being more pertinent to the focus of this book. The reader may also be interested to learn that Dr. May stated (personal communication) that he has refused his publisher permission to reissue the book, *The Springs of Creative Living,* which is now out of print. It seems clear, then, that May himself does not wish this book to stand on equal terms with his other publications. It is noteworthy, too, in this context, that *The Art of Counseling* has recently been reissued with no change other than the omission (unacknowledged) of its original subtitle, *How to Give and Gain Mental Health.* Others of his books have also appeared in more than one edition and remain available.

May has also recently completed his personal memoir of

Paul Tillich and published it under the title *Paulus: Reminis-cences of a Friendship: A Personal Portrait of Paul Tillich* (New York: Harper & Row, c. 1973, appeared in 1975). He has also collected some of his articles on creativity in *The Courage to Create* (New York: Norton, 1975). Both books essentially re-peat May's consistent faith in the significance of the uncon-scious and the power of courageous self-affirmation and existen-tial striving to meet the challenge of existence.

It was with the publication of *Existence* (1958) that May's writings first began to evince an explicitly and con-sciously ontological approach. Indeed, his two essays in *Exis-tence* constitute a kind of watershed in May's development: *Existence* and all of his material published thereafter reflect the consciously, explicitly ontological approach that was implicitly yet clearly foreshadowed in the writings preceding *Existence*. In this book, I discuss four of the fourteen chapters of *Psychology and the Human Dilemma* (1967) in this light, because they ante-date *Existence*: Chapters Four and Five, both on anxiety, con-taining material previously examined within *The Meaning of Anxiety* (1950); Chapter Eleven, a Kafkaesque allegory on hu-man freedom repeated from *Man's Search for Himself* (1953); and Chapter Thirteen, "Questions for a Science of Man," a statement of intent, containing material that also appears in *Man's Search for Himself* and that also recalls May's introduc-tory chapters in *The Meaning of Anxiety,* particularly the mate-rial on philosophical predecessors. The reader is referred to the first part of the annotated bibliography of this book, in which a separate section is devoted to details, ordered chapter by chap-ter of the material in *Psychology and the Human Dilemma.* The remaining ten chapters of the book postdate *Existence* and have therefore been considered as such. May, however, states clearly his intention to regard the material of this book as having been carefully chosen, grouped, and integrated into a book having an organic unity, rather than as isolated essays. Nevertheless, for the convenience of the reader, my references to *Psychology and the Human Dilemma* are specially amplified with mention of the individual title and number of the chapter wherein the material referred to is to be found.

Articles and papers other than those collected and integrated into book form in *Psychology and the Human Dilemma* are listed in Part One, Section E, of the bibliography. As the annotations and cross-referencing clearly indicate, this section includes the titles of articles in books edited by May, and other titles that repeat much of the material already listed. In each entry in the bibliography as a whole, the publication data given first is that of the edition used for this book. In the case of *Existential Psychology,* the edition deemed preferable is the second edition (1969) rather than the first (1961). May says, in his foreword to the second edition, that he has "largely rewritten" his first article in this book, the article entitled "The Emergence of Existential Psychology." The rewriting consists mostly in reorganization of the material, wherein the order of sections or paragraphs was changed and some four paragraphs removed to his second article, "Existential Bases of Psychotherapy." Since May offered some new material, although brief, (on James, Laing, and Ramirez, for example) as well as reorganizing the old, I considered it more appropriate to cite from the author's own revised edition. In consequence, reference is made to the paging of the second edition only. These references, however, can be traced without great difficulty.

The introduction is followed by four chapters centering respectively on the sense of being, and the related structures of anxiety, love, and will. The original contribution of this study is to undertake a task of fundamental reconstruction and integration of May's seminal insights (that is, sense of being, anxiety, love, and will) that in his work remain, for the most part, scattered and without sustained, detailed explication, grounding, or explicit integration, whether those insights be considered separately or in terms of an integrational understanding. The structure and development of the present study, then, were neither immediately suggested by nor easily discernible in May's writings, but had to be formulated on the basis of making explicit what was only implicit throughout May's work.

Each chapter opens with a perspective on the particular conception on which the chapter focuses. In the first chapter, the perspective offers a brief survey of the emergence of the

existential attitude in psychology and psychiatry, and thereby
in psychotherapy. Such a brief survey would seem essential for
contextual understanding, because this movement is the one to
which May has been a leading contributor in North America and
is the context in which his inquiries are conducted.

Also offered for the sake of contextual understanding,
the perspectives on anxiety, love, and will, in the second, third,
and fourth chapters respectively, are my attempt to give very
brief, synoptic expression to my understanding of some strong,
contemporary, precritical trends in everyday Western thinking
on the subject of each of these structures. These trends are
merely commonly-held beliefs or misunderstandings that are
constantly found and expressed in ordinary or common experience or everyday human existence, and this is precisely the context out of which May's deliberations are born. These trends or
salient, commonly held notions are not representative in any
way of highly reflective thinking or specialist studies of these
structures (anxiety, love, and will) but are merely, in my view,
the uncritical attitudes most commonly encountered in everyday experience. Mention, then, is not made of specialist studies
nor of abstract, detailed, more reflective, rounded views, as
these would be irrelevant to the nature and purpose of the perspectives, which are not to be seen as exhaustive views of all
attitudes toward these three structures, but rather as a simple
view of the most salient and most extreme of the commonly
held misunderstandings and overemphases on the subjects of
anxiety, love, and will.

In these perspectives, some brief historical references to
the origins of these commonly held conceptions in highly reflective interpretations of existence are offered for the simple purpose of showing how, particularly in contemporary society
bombarded by printed material of all kinds, an abstract interpretation that was originally highly reflective and theoretical
can become so widely, uncritically, and simplistically accepted
as to lead a life of its own, not as interpretation or hypothesis
or premise, but rather as "indisputable fact" that "everyone
knows." For example, in the perspective on love, the ideal of
chivalric perfection or courtly love and the Freudian notion of

sexual energy as motive force are briefly shown to be such interpretations, which have been accepted by some people, in an
uncritical and oversimplified manner, as fact.

It is my firm conviction that the professional philosopher, like the psychologist and sociologist, and in a not un-
important part of his social role, bears a continuing and urgent
responsibility for the examination, elucidation, and disclosure
of the meaning, scope, limitations, and implications of such
common-experience attitudes as those mentioned in the perspectives, since these attitudes are highly influential in the formation of man's world at many levels. The particular precritical
"accepted facts" chosen for very brief summary and discussion
in the perspectives are, of course, only those that relate closely
to this book. Yet, in my view, they are also the attitudes that
seem to surface most frequently in contemporary social existence, perhaps because they are concerned with the ontological
structures of human existence itself. They are, then, fundamentally to be reckoned with in common experience and therefore also must be taken into account, however simply and
briefly, in a philosophical study such as this, focusing as it does
on a philosophical approach beginning in common experience.

The main part of each chapter consists in the internal critique of the particular conception that is the subject of each
chapter. The main part consists of two or more sections centering on how May works his way toward an ontological conception of the sense of being and each related structure in turn,
anxiety, love, and will. I seek to examine May's earliest position, its meaning, growth, change, development; and then his
mature position, its scope and implications. In the case of anxiety and love, the seminal influence of Freud, Kierkegaard, and
Plato is explored and the extent to which May interfuses them
in his own developing position is established. The fifth and final
chapter recapitulates and synthesizes May's whole position and
continues with a concluding appraisal of the scope and meaning
of that position, together with a concise statement of some limitations and psychotherapeutic implications of it.

The annotated bibliography that follows is divided into
two parts, the first dealing exclusively with primary sources or

the writings of Rollo May, the second listing secondary sources or all other authors cited in this book. As May is the author under study, the first part of the bibliography is cross-referenced in detail and presents as complete and accurate a bibliography of May's writings as possible.

Reference material necessary for proper understanding of the study is offered in two appendices, one biographical and the other terminological. This material is gathered in appendices because it is too cumbersome to be included in the body of the book and would distract the reader and interrupt the flow of the main text if included therein.

The first appendix, entitled *Rollo May: A Biographical Note,* offers an extensive biographical review that pays special attention to May's intellectual life, background, and influences. This appendix is my own original integration of biographical material on May. The discussion of influences, however brief and referential, may interest the reader particularly as this book precludes, by its very scope and method, comparative studies of influence exerted on May by his contemporaries.

For an internal critique of a particular psychotherapist's approach to the question of the philosophical foundations of psychotherapy, a rounded grasp of his central terms, their scope, meaning, connotations, and limitations, is essential. In the case of May, what is needed is not merely a list of definitions from the author himself, since his definitions do not always fully delimit the scope and meaning of his terms. Rather, what is needed is a full grasp of the connotations for him of each of his central terms, in particular any changes, developments (broader or narrower reference), or even new meanings. Hence, Appendix Two is entitled *A Comprehensive Compilation of the Definitions and Connotations of Central Terms as Given in the Writings of Rollo May.* Eighty terms, with cross-references, are comprehensively surveyed in May's most representative writings. Once again, this appendix is my original compilation and will be found to be very useful as it offers, without comment, May's own understanding of each term. It is also a comprehensive index to the location of discussion of the various terms and concepts in May's work, up to and including *Love and Will* (1969). This appendix is doubly useful as some of May's books are not indexed or only briefly so, and, in those books that are indexed, the indices do not always offer references to the philosophical terms under close examination here.

ONE

Sense of Being
as Ground and Goal

We keep searching for an embracing
whole within which the fact can be
understood as a partial phenomenon.
Ludwig Binswanger, *The Existential
Analysis School of Thought*

"The effectiveness of counseling with human beings depends
upon our understanding of what those human beings really are"
(*Art of Counseling,* p. 44; see also *Emergence,* pp. 24-25). This
statement, apparently so simple, is in fact a concise expression
of the whole project of the work of Rollo May, both in his
theoretical deliberations and practical psychotherapy. Written
in 1939, in his first book, these words underlie the quest of a
man in search of a clear formulation of his own therapeutic attitude and of his own philosophical presuppositions regarding the
nature of man. Grounded in his clinical experience, May's

inquiry seeks to contribute to the elucidation of those specific, distinguishing, that is, ontological, characteristics of man that make possible the deeper understanding and enlivening of psychotherapy.

In his first book, *The Art of Counseling,* May was already expressing the view that the wise therapist does not rely on unconscious or unwitting assumptions about what it is to be human. Instead, he must begin by examining his own presuppositions, by determining conscientiously and reasonably what his concept of personality is and, as a direct corollary, what exactly is the goal of psychotherapy.

The urgent need for this kind of inquiry was borne in on many European and American psychiatrists and psychotherapists when it was found that, as social mores in the twentieth century became more and more permissive, people did not, as expected, have fewer psychological problems (Binswanger, 1962, pp. 17-23; Ellenberger, 1967, p. 92; May, *Historical and Philosophical Presuppositions,* pp. 9-43; *Origins,* pp. 3-10). On the contrary, the number of people seeking help increased, although the incidence of repressions and inhibitions was not as high. The more prevalent problems rather seemed to be a puzzling loss of feeling and an apprehension of insecurity despite the new "freedom" of "self-expression." According to the theory of repression, the person who was not restricted or inhibited by the conformity of his "superego" to the narrow demands of social morality, should never have developed such psychological difficulties. Instinctual self-expression should have led to complete "natural" fulfillment of the needs and desires of the human organism. But this was not the case in practice. And, however helpful psychoanalysis had been and still was in disclosing theoretical explanations of the environmental factors in the etiology of the problem, the question remained one of identifying the precise meaning and character, rather than causes alone, of the patient's problem (Boss, 1963, pp. 5-27).

From the patients themselves came pretheoretical, spontaneous expressions of dismay at their own diminished ability to feel moved or enthusiastic about anything, at the continuing disappointment of loneliness, boredom, and isolation. Somehow these patients' experiences of the so-called new freedom had not lived up to their expectations. Social living, which, although no longer "constricted" by various prohibitions or superego repressions, as in Freud's day, ought to have been free and vital, had become instead a flat, dull, meaningless round of routine where nothing held even the spurious attraction of being forbidden or even disapproved for very long. These problems did not at all fit the old physical-medical analogy of finding and releasing the repressed material in the patient's past, as though lancing a psychological abscess would enable the patient to recover and live a psychologically "healthy" life. The new type of problem could not easily be categorized as repression or inhibition but seemed to be more an all-pervasive loneliness, a constantly nagging anxiety and disappointment, a kind of spiritual atrophy. In some cases it expressed itself as a sense of being swallowed up in a frantic rushing around to avoid realization of one's own boredom. Far from solving the problem of man's psychological difficulties, the new "freedoms" of affluence, sexual permissiveness, and educational and moral experimentation, seemed to have generated a whole new range of problems, from anxiety and disorientation to apathy and complete loss of interest. Patients were bringing to analysis or psychotherapy, therefore, not psychosomatic illness, nor ultimately a precisely psychological problem, but rather a philosophical question, namely, the question of meaning. For them it was and is a question of attempting to discover a constructive answer to the meaninglessness that they experience so intensely. And so, while fully accepting the importance of understanding of specific mechanisms and dynamisms and the explanatory capacity of particular systems of therapy, many psychiatrists and psychotherapists began to reexamine the presuppositions of all therapy in the hope of finding new techniques and new answers for the solution of the new problems. Their intention, which May shares, was to reinvestigate, in the light of these new problems, their own understanding of the role of psychotherapy and of the nature not primarily of abnormal or mentally ill man, but of man as such. Their hope in this investigation was to find a new, more basic structure on which all specific systems of therapy could be based, in order thereby to return to the concrete with new light on the therapeutic process in general, and on the new problems in particular. Hence, their aim was "not to be *less* but to be *more* empirical" (*Origins,* p. 8).

In the work of Rollo May, there is discernible an abiding preoccupation with the theoretical foundations of psychotherapy. Indeed, one could characterize his considerable literary output as a continuing effort to give substance and form to this basic theme. It is these theoretical foundations, May is convinced, that must be examined and explicated if psychotherapy is to become properly self-aware, that is to say, cognizant of what precisely is taking place in the therapeutic situation, of what is happening in the patient's existence, of why certain therapy is or is not effective. What is equally evident in May's work, however, is a basic commitment to the existence of the individual patient and to the concrete practice of psychotherapy. His theoretical reflections, then, are in a sense secondary and derivative, and are conducted in order to illuminate his psychotherapeutic practice. May is primarily concerned with human existence as lived, as experienced, and his theoretical deliberations on the structure of human existence are subservient to that basic concern.

When, therefore, May embarks on theoretical inquiry, there is evident an underlying practical concern, a preoccupation with its relevance for human existence in the concrete. Indeed, May is rather uneasy with theoretical projects that are not obviously and clearly rooted in the practical order, or that cannot show at each moment how they apply. For May, theoretical inquiry must be careful to avoid slipping its practical anchorage, that is, becoming dissociated from the practical concern out of which it arises and in the service of which it is undertaken. Not surprisingly, therefore, May asserts the necessity for a "*working* science of man" that will not fragment man, that will "study man scientifically and still see him whole" (*Origins,* p. 36; see also *Dangers,* p. 156; *Questions,* p. 199). On such a comprehensive scale alone can psychotherapy find a secure base.

By "science of man" May does not have in mind any of the particular human sciences, such as psychology, sociology, or anthropology, nor indeed any agglomeration of these sciences (*Questions*, p. 183). He is thinking rather of a comprehensive theory that would make possible the understanding and clarification of the essential, constitutive, defining (ontological) characteristics of man. For May, the condition of possibility for the elaboration of such a theory is to place at the source of that theory the concrete, existing human being. Only on such a foundation, May is convinced, will it be possible to conduct a study of man that does not fragment him in the process, but envisages him as a whole. With deceptive simplicity, May considers that since psychotherapy is concerned with man, it must perforce ground that concern in a human model—a model *adequate* for its purpose. With his insistence on the foundational role of the concrete, existing human being, it is not surprising that neither a medical nor a behavioristic model, for example, satisfies the criterion of adequacy (*Questions*, pp. 183-191). May, of course, does not seek to depreciate either the medical or behavioristic model nor to detract from the importance of the human sciences in general. But he is convinced that none of these separately, nor all of them collectively, can give to psychotherapy the theoretical basis it requires. For May, these particular sciences presuppose the concrete, existing human being who consciously assumes the scientific point of view, who deliberately assumes the interrogative disposition of science.

The sciences, then, are secondary and derivative: secondary, because they presuppose the existing human being; derivative, because their existence is contingent on the reflective activity of human consciousness. As reflective, conceptual elaborations, the sciences contribute to the study of man by offering limited, aspectual, causal (mechanistic, efficient) explanations. But no particular aspectual study, as May sees it, can claim to account for and offer an understanding of the human being in his uniqueness. We may throw considerable light on human behavior patterns, for example, by applying analogies from the higher primates or on human biology and physiology by comparative studies in the animal world. But such illumination is strictly analogical. For May, the reality of self-consciousness makes of man a whole new Gestalt, and therefore inaccessible in his uniqueness if approached *exclusively* with the conceptual tools of the particular sciences, whether "human" or "natural" (*Existential Bases,* p. 78; *Context,* pp. 95-96).

The study of man, as May sees it, is undoubtedly promoted by the disclosure of discrete mechanisms, the formulation of drives and concern for the reality of conditioning. May does not wish to deny "the validity of dynamisms and the study of specific behavior patterns" (*Contributions,* p. 37). He is, however, deeply convinced that the meaning and significance of mechanisms and drives must be sought ultimately in terms of the person, not conversely. It is the structure of the existence of the person that confers meaning on mechanisms, drives, and conditioning. This, of course, represents a veritable transformation in the more usual scientific approach to the study of man. It represents a direct contravention of a generally accepted principle in science, namely, that the more complex is to be understood in terms of the more simple, that organisms and activities higher on the evolutionary scale, for example, are to be explained by those lower. For May, the reverse is true: The simpler is to be understood precisely in terms of the more complex. Given the reality of self-consciousness, the human being does not merely engage in reproducing his own species, for example, but consciously assumes an attitude to his own sexuality and exteriorizes meaning through it.

The "science of man" of which May is thinking and to which his theoretical deliberations seek to contribute, is a science that refuses to confine itself to the methods of experimentation, quantification, and measurement. It is a science the favored method of which is descriptive or phenomenological. By this is meant a disciplined, experientially grounded, descriptive elucidation of those essential characteristics of man that can give to psychotherapy its theoretical basis. Such a science, while remaining rigorously empirical, extends the horizon of scientific "fact" and makes possible the understanding of those structures of human existence—for example, love and will, as experienced—that are inaccessible to the methods of the particular sciences. For May, the pursuit of this science places the scientific enterprise in a broader context.

At the source of May's contribution to this science of man lies an insight that inspires and directs his thinking. This insight is the "sense of being," or the experience of one's own existence. It is the sense of being that unifies our individual existence and makes it coherent. Hence the development of a strong sense of being must be the goal of therapy. To this fundamental insight are closely related the other defining (onto-logical) characteristics of human existence on which May's theo-retical deliberations depend, individuation and participation being the polar structure on which one's being-in-the-world and hence sense of being are built. The constitution of one's being-in-the-world is expressed quintessentially in the symbols, myths, and dreams that mediate individual and participatory meaning. The constitution by the self of its being-in-the-world may be dominated and constricted by the mode of anxiety, or the self may have succeeded in confronting anxiety and have attained a coherent constitution or sense of its being in an ordered partici-pation, in love and will. May is, then, concerned with the articu-lation of these modes of existence and their relevance to the individual in therapy. He is concerned with the relation of the individual to his own existence, or his sense of being, which is concretely grasped in the symbols that he holds most dear. At the basis of health or ill health, May believes, is the patient's ability or inability to experience his own existence as real, as worthwhile. ("The aim of therapy is that the patient *experience his own existence as real*" [*Contributions,* p. 85].) Hence, each of these insights (individuation and participation, for example), and the dominant mode of the patient's existence (anxiety, love, will) must be articulated and explored in the continuing effort to aid the patient to attain balance and integration of all of the ontological (defining, fundamental) structures that char-acterize human existence. ("The cure of symptoms—obviously a desideratum— . . . is not the chief goal of therapy. The impor-tant thing is that the person discovers his being, his *Dasein*" [*Contributions,* p. 87].) The sense of being is the integrating, unifying structure that the patient, together in encounter with the therapist, seeks to develop and to strengthen. These decisive insights and their interrelationship with the sense of being must, then, be explicated and articulated in order to throw clear light on the notion of man which, in May's view, must subtend all effective therapy.

Toward a Sense of Being

In 1958, in *Existence,* in an essay concerned with the basic theoretical contributions of existential therapy, Rollo May announced the view that the "central process" of therapy was to "help the patient recognize and experience his own existence" (*Contributions,* p. 77). To do this, the therapist would have not only to identify the individual patient's difficulties but also to understand the patient's world. Hence, the task of the therapist was not primarily to offer a technical name for the problem and an automatic, prescribed, cure, as though the patient were an automobile in need of a simple new part or an efficient tune-up or overhaul, but to find with the patient the key to his world and to understand and clarify with him the structure of his individual existence. The context, then, could not be the patient seen as a conglomeration of dynamisms and mechanisms of fixed meaning and breadth, but as a human being whose particular mode of sensing his own being was the key to his world, choices, and actions. The patient's sense of his own being was the measure of his freedom, his potentiality for forming his own future, his recognition of the limits of his possibilities and the range of his choices. Therapy, then, must be related to existence, existentially oriented, that is, it must not only be oriented toward participating and understanding *with* the patient the mode of his being-in-the-world (in all his relationships, affinities and dislikes, and daily living), but also to an experientially grounded understanding of human existence, of what it is to exist humanly in the world, of what constitutes man as man. "Psychotherapy reveals *both* the immediate situation of the individual's 'sickness' *and* the archetypal qualities and characteristics which constitute the human being as human. It is the latter characteristics which have gone awry in specific ways in a given patient and have resulted in the former, his psychological problems" (*Love and Will,* p. 20).

This was not, however, the first time that Rollo May had expressed his conviction that therapy must be existentially oriented and that technique must be subordinate to this understanding. Twenty years before the publication of *Existence,* May had already firmly stated in his first book that "personality is never static. It is alive, ever-changing, mobile" (*Art of Counseling,* p. 29). He went on to assert that, since the human being was always in a state of becoming, perfect "balance" or "equilibrium" (once considered, by analogy with physical well-being, to be "normal" as opposed to "unbalanced" or "insane") was neither attainable nor desirable since to be static was, in this instance, synonymous only with death. Personality, then, was a *continuous* achieving of states of balance, or "adjustment of tensions" to meet new situations, and the source of personality problems was the failure to make a new adjustment where such was called for by a new situation. Adjustment, however, must not be seen as mere automatic adaptation to environmental factors. It is a *creative*, free, inner process, one that takes place "within" the individual, and environment is seen as the arena or circumstances of that creative process. May rejects both Freudian instinctual determinism and Adlerian social adjustment as *ultimate* criteria of personality health, since neither of these theoretically allows for human responsibility and individuality, attributing this error to a failure to recognize the limits of the scientific method (*Art of Counseling,* p. 49). May specifically states that, since one of the first presuppositions of all therapy is that eventually the patient must assume responsibility for his own life, determinism or social pressure as ultimate criteria would work against his regaining mental health by undermining and destroying his sense of responsibility. Instead, May is firmly convinced that the individual alone has the final decision about his own attitudes.

It is clear, then, that even at this early stage in his work, May was already holding for a free, social, individual personality, a human being choosing and committing himself, controlling his own destiny even though within the limits of contin-

gency. The simple description of personality that May offers in
this his first book already contains in germ the view he will
articulate and deepen in his later work. In defining personality
as "an actualization of the life-process in a free individual who
is socially integrated and possesses religious tension" (*Art of
Counseling,* p. 45), May is setting the stage, so to speak, for a
rapprochement between psychotherapy and ontology. Although
he does not yet use the term *ontology*, it will be clearly shown
in this analysis that his earlier work grows toward the possibility
of coherent structure when it is seen to depend on the sense of
being or ontological awareness. May consistently views psychotherapy as necessarily seeking to achieve a scientific understanding of what it is to be human as such, in order thereby better to
comprehend the scope and aim of psychotherapy. It is noteworthy that while May is aware that the term *ontology* means,
etymologically, the "science of being," his use of the term,
because of the range of his particular field, has mostly, but not
exclusively, the effect of restricting its meaning to the fundamental structures of *being human*, "what it is that constitutes
man as man" (*Love and Will,* p. 290; see also *Origins,* p. 36), or
"the structures that are given to every one at every moment"
(*Love and Will,* p. 112; see also *Contributions,* p. 37). At this
point, however, it must be remembered that May's primary purpose is more immediately psychotherapeutic than radically
philosophical. His primary aim is to identify, assert, and "grasp"
the inalienable structures of human existence in their everyday
expression. Thence, he seeks to clarify and illuminate the mode
of existence of each individual patient and to aid him to a
heightened awareness of his own being and what it is to be
human.

The key word, therefore, in May's early definition of personality, is "free." Without freedom, there are only efficient,
causal, deterministic principles such as those of strictly-under-
stood Freudian or Darwinian theory (*Art of Counseling,* pp.
48-49). Human potentiality and responsibility are interdependent with ontological freedom, that is, freedom as an integral,
defining component of human existence, or as May puts it,
rather loosely at this point, freedom as a "quality of (man's)

total being" (*Art of Counseling,* p. 52). He further states that firm belief in creative willing, in possession of creative potentialities or even merely in the ability to decide *which* impulse to choose, is an essential prerequisite of therapy and the sole basis for the ultimate aim of having the patient assume responsibility for himself, for his choices and for his own actions (*Art of Counseling,* p. 52). May's thinking at this point reminds one of Allport's discussion of relative freedom as dependent on self-insight coupled with the "frame of destiny": "To state the point paradoxically, a person who harbors many determining tendencies in his neuropsychic system is freer than a person who harbors few. Thus a person having only one skill, knowing only one solution, has only one degree of freedom. On the other hand, a person widely experienced, and knowing many courses of conduct has many more degrees of freedom" (Allport, 1955, p. 85). Hence we speak of education as opening up greater possibilities, as freeing the person, and the consequences for any society of the lack of it in its political, social, and moral leaders must be obvious.

This freedom does not imply that nothing about man is determined. It is a self-evident fact that one is spatio-temporally situated, that one is, in Pascal's words, here rather than there, now rather than then. A certain time and place are allotted to each individual. Yet within the simultaneously determining factors of his existence, such as race, country, time, social rank, and financial state, each individual is free at all times to make his own choices about how he will deal with these existential data, and whether he will do *this* rather than *that*. Human freedom is precisely the capacity to relate to the historico-cultural situatedness that is the condition of human existence. Regardless of how many determining forces are at work in the life of the individual, he still possesses the creative possibility of choosing, while retaining awareness of these limiting forces, how he will mold his own existence out of the clay of heredity and environment.

Authentic realization of human freedom has two aspects that at this early stage May calls *individuation* and *social integration.* Each individual self is different from every other self and must accept himself as such before his unique "life form" can be realized. The individual "real self" is found by "uniting [the] conscious self with various levels in his unconsciousness" (*Art of Counseling*, p. 57). May here agrees with Freud and Jung in their postulation of unconscious levels and "collective unconscious." But although May asserts the unconscious to be a dynamo that produces instinctual impulses and the collective unconscious to hold material absorbed from one's national group and racial world, he holds firmly that it is the whole man, the free individual who, having accepted all of these levels or influences or factors within himself, is able, by exercising his freedom, to find and affirm his true self. The concept of "unconscious" is thus relocated within a comprehensive, ontological envisioning of human existence, not in a deterministic, biological realm alone.

To maintain his self, this free individual must be socially integrated. It is noteworthy here that May speaks of *integration*, an entirely different attitude from the Adlerian norm of social *adjustment*. While May accepts the insights of Adler into neurotic *mal*adjustment to society and the possible consequent antisocial striving for power in order to allay a fear of other people, he does not accept that the "normal" man is therefore characterized by his "successful adjustment" to society (see *Art of Counseling*, p. 198, where May points out the inadequacy of the "Adlerian social norm by itself"). May holds that the "normal" man is characterized rather by his ability to accept society and, while remaining free and individual, by his ability to find socially constructive and acceptable ways in which to express his being. Earlier, May warned against "the mischievous error" of assuming that one's own particular type is the only healthy type, whether predominantly extrovert or introvert, and is insistent that the person must "be himself." Being himself, or his individuality, is interdependent with community or participation with others. This social setting is the world in which individual personality creates and finds its meaning. In itself, then, the goal of self-realization depends both on a strong individuality and on a mature responsibility to one's world. May agrees with Alfred Adler that the healthy person "realizes and cheerfully accepts his social responsibility" (*Art of Counseling*, p. 66). The egocentric individual is not free, precisely because he has overemphasized his individuality and runs the risk of loneliness and isolation in a world of one.

Although the individual is free, and his "life form" is, in a sense, "given," freedom, individuality, and social integration are not achieved once and for all, but must be constantly renewed. This might be characterized as man's daily struggle with his fundamental nature as free, autonomous, and therefore responsible, and the call of selfish, momentary whim or the easier path of conformism. Here May rejects the reductionist, efficient causality and determinism of Freud and the rationalistic faith of Adler and Rousseau that man, if unobstructed, will grow naturally toward a state of perfection. Since May envisages human personality in an existential perspective and has already stated that personality is never static, he must reject this oversimplification and calls it "a romantic faith lacking sufficient realism" (*Art of Counseling*, p. 69).

Since the individual in his freedom has creative possibilities, he is constantly challenged not only to choose but to act. Here, entering May's "picture of personality," is a new element: This is the perception of a "gap" between what is and what could be. May speaks of this tension as religious, that is, as man's deepest moral sense, as a fundamental conviction of meaning in human life (*Art of Counseling*, pp. 69-74, 202, 212, 219-223). There is in every experience of challenge and creation an element of guilt feeling, as the aspiration toward perfection of an imperfect, existing individual, as the other aspect of challenge. However we attempt to explain this guilt feeling, as the challenge of perfection imperfectly realized, as the conflict between the unconditioned and conditioned aspects of man, May holds that no explanation can rationalize guilt feeling out of existence altogether. There is, he asserts, a normal element of guilt feeling that is not only compatible with but necessary for personality health. May posits guilt feeling as an "ultimate tension" that is, in effect, a proof of the great possibilities and destiny of man. Hence it can be positive and constructive, not necessarily morbid and destructive, as Freud affirmed it to be.

Man cannot attain a blissful state wherein no guilt feeling will ever enter to disturb his happiness, because his possibility is never exhausted in realization but remains to challenge him over and over again. The neurotic person who relapses into morbid guilt and self-defeating egocentricity in order to avoid the tension of freedom and the pain of guilt becomes static, constricted, and unproductive, while all the more crushed by guilt in his own unproductivity. The healthy individual creatively accepts his own limitations and develops the "courage of imperfection" (*Art of Counseling*, p. 141), that is, he is enabled by courage and hope to accept and affirm that he is human and therefore imperfect and capable of creating only imperfectly. He is and will remain guilty, that is, finite, always short of perfection in his living, thinking, doing, always open to error and accident. But with courage and hope, he becomes willing to walk the knife edge of insecurity.

It is clear that May already holds in this his first book that both anxiety and guilt are ontological, are inalienable, defining characteristics of man, although he does not yet explicitly use the term *ontological*. His conviction of the importance of freedom in his original definition of personality as free, individual, socially integrated, and possessing religious tension (or creative acceptance of meaning within imperfection) has been carried through to its logical conclusion in the acceptance of anxiety, imperfection, and error. The individual self affirms itself freely and constructively in encounter with other persons while accepting creatively its own limitations and imperfection. This creative acceptance or "courage of imperfection" is, in effect, the courage to live, to overcome the little fears, the everyday anxieties that confront every man in his daily life. Yet May added that, although many of the little fears and worries that hold people back from full-hearted, creative living are unnecessary and useless, there is "reason for the deep anxiety inherent in the tragic possibilities of living (*Art of Counseling*, p. 193). Implicitly, then, he already holds that anxiety is a fundamental, defining, ontological characteristic of man.

What is this creative living, this free affirmation? At this point, May speaks of it as "healthy self-expression" but he has not done much more than to give a general outline of the characteristics that are the structures of human existence. In his later work, his focus broadens to include deeper consideration of the modes of existence such as anxiety, love, and will and their symbolic expression. In *The Art of Counseling*, he has clearly already laid out the foundation for such considerations, however brief his outline of personality. In an obvious attempt to give greater content to his definition of personality, he names, somewhat belatedly, certain features of the person who has "achieved healthy self-expression" as being *spontaneity, genuineness,* and *originality* (*Art of Counseling,* pp. 190-192). It would appear that there is an overabundance of terms here, since he explains each of these characteristics in the same way, as acting with "more of one's whole self," or from the "depths" of oneself. While one may cavil at such repetition and perhaps overinsistence, it must be appreciated that May is trying to identify and describe what constitutes man's existence as specifically human and what constitutes the full "maturity" of that existence. Because of his therapeutic involvement as a counselor, this concern extends naturally to the relation between an understanding of mature free living and of neurosis as a distortion or renunciation of that mature responsibility, or as an abdication of freedom. As yet, however, May's outline of personality has not attained the unifying principle in terms of which all other ontological characteristics are interrelated and on which they depend. The articulation of the goal of integration and of the courage of maturity that are May's positive preoccupations has not yet been achieved.

The Sense of Being as Experienced

In *The Art of Counseling,* May identified freedom as the first and most essential presupposition of human personality. "For it is," he asserts, "by this characteristic that we separate human beings from animals" (*Art of Counseling,* p. 51). It was also shown in the analysis that this freedom was finite, limited— that it necessarily implied acceptance of and responsibility toward the human situation. May spoke of the realization of this limitation as instinctual, structured self-expression, a response of the total self to the worth and dignity of human existence as such. Inherent in this freedom or possession of creative possibilities was the "deep anxiety" that May mentioned only briefly here but went on to explore in detail in his book, *The Meaning of Anxiety*. Of crucial significance to that later study was May's reading of Kierkegaard's *Concept of Dread,* in which May singled out as "keystone idea . . . the relation between anxiety and freedom" (*Meaning of Anxiety,* p. 32). He noted also the new importance of the individual considered as a living, experiencing unity, whose freedom depended basically on how responsibly he related to himself. It was not a simple accretion, but depended on autonomous and responsible choices that affirmed one's individuality or "centeredness" within community. The more one was aware of one's self, the more freedom one had, the more possibilities were open, and the greater the inherent anxiety. May asserted that only when the threat was great enough to involve the total self was the experience one of anxiety, and his theoretical and clinical study resulted in his definition of anxiety as the apprehension cued by some basic threat to one's existence as a self (*Meaning of Anxiety,* p. 190; *Anxiety and Values,* p. 72).

Seeking the roots of contemporary malaise, in *Man's Search for Himself,* May first ascribed the prevailing unease to loss of believable values and goals in a rapidly changing society, values and goals that the individual held to be essential to his existence as a self. This loss of values, said May, was closely linked with the loss of the "sense of self," of the worth and dignity of the human being in general, and of one's own individual being in particular. May still held that freedom was the possession of creative possibilities, the capacity to decide and mold one's own life within the limits of one's particular existence, but now he specifically located freedom within consciousness of self (*Man's Search,* p. 138). From this point on, May related every characteristic to this consciousness of self, or sense of being, and developed a coherent view of what this sense of being is, how precisely it grounds human existence as such and, hence, why the patient's development of a strong sense of being must be the goal of therapy.

At this stage, it is important to note that while May

spoke of the "sense of self" in his earlier work, this sense is, in fact, the "sense of being" as defined in his later work. Although his definition does not change, he does refer variously to the sense of being, experiencing one's being or Dasein, sensing one's existence. Despite the seeming multiplicity of synonymous terms, the most felicitous and apparently preferred term becomes *sense of being,* and it must be stated that there is no confusion as to its import nor as to its foundational role and significance.

The stronger the sense of being and the deeper the consciousness of self, the larger the range of choices for the person. The greater his ability to "stand back" and see himself "in perspective," the more possibilities can be envisioned and examined, and the less clouded his judgment and choice. Hence, the more articulate and strong the sense of being, the more creative and responsible the person's will and decision and the greater his control of his own destiny. And so one's task must be to deepen consciousness of self, to find inner strength in order to gain control of one's life, to find new values and goals, to be spontaneous and original rather than sunk in stultifying anxiety, despair, or apathy.

May asserts that the first important step in gaining this inner strength, in becoming a person, is the realization "that it is I, the acting one, who is [sic] the subject of what is occurring" (*Man's Search,* p. 100). This interrelationship of heightened self-consciousness or self-awareness with greater aliveness is the basis of mature creative living. Not freedom now, but the capacity to have a strong sense of being, or sense of self, is here identified and affirmed as the most fundamental and uniquely human characteristic, on which freedom itself, individuation, and social integration all depend. To experience one's existence or to sense one's self, identity, center, or being is not merely to think of oneself, to feel emotions, or to be a doctor, teacher, scientist, nor is it the sum of the thinking, acting, feeling roles of one's life. The sense of being is rather "the capacity by which one *knows* he plays these roles" (*Man's Search,* p. 80). It is the capacity that is the basis for being a scientist or doctor or teacher. It is the simplest awareness of one's own identity or center, the capacity that underlies the normal, blind insistence on "being myself" or "being a person in my own right." It is beautifully illustrated in the tiny child who first speaks of himself in the third person, as "Baby," for example, or who uses his own name as though it were outside of him, and who, through interpersonal relationship, learns to speak very insistently of himself as "Me." He "preexists" his discovery of himself, to use Gabriel Marcel's phrase, but it is precisely his growing sense of himself as a self that makes possible his future development by bringing together his previous awareness of body, needs, and desires and by welding them into the composite awareness of himself as a center, of himself as his *own* self, and by extension, of his toys and dolls as *his* toys and dolls. In the sense of self or sense of being, then, is born our freedom, our conscious responsibility to and affirmation of our self. This affirmation is the constant achieving of the freedom, individuation, social integration, and religious tension of May's earliest definition of personality.

"[Man's] sense of personal identity," says May, "distinguishes him from the rest of the living or non-living things" (*Man's Search,* p. 63). May remarks also that the sense of humor that is born in the capacity to "stand outside" oneself, to see oneself in a situation, is an important means of preserving the sense of being, of retaining a healthy distance and perspective in the balance between self and world. This self-awareness is "the capacity by virtue of which we can *be scientists* in relation to nature: that is, we can think of nature 'out there,' can temporarily separate subject and object, and can think in abstract, universal laws with respect to nature" (*Man's Search,* pp. 73-84; *Questions,* p. 195).

In the achieving of consciousness of oneself, May speaks of being more alive, feeling more vividly. This, for May, means "no longer separating the body from the self" (*Man's Search,* p. 94), no longer "detaching" one's bodily existence or treating it as a means of sensation. He proposes that the self must be actively central in experiencing the body, for example, *I* feel, *I* hunger. Thus consciousness of self means *embodied* consciousness, a unitary, indivisible approach rather than an "impersonal, separated attitude," as though one could speak of "my vocal cords wanting to speak to my friend" or "my feet wanting to walk or run." It is precisely not the organ of hearing, speaking, or walking that "wants" anything, but rather the person who experiences his own wishes in a unitary, embodied awareness. It is the whole person who conceives of food for his hunger, for example, who can call certain substances momentarily tasty or repugnant. It is not the stomach alone that "wants" particular substances, but the person who in awareness of his hunger and of his own taste decides exactly what *he would like* to eat. Thus, in speaking of awareness of one's self in illness and in health, May is at pains to overcome the dichotomy or artificial separation of body and mind, which tends to the consideration of the diseased organ as a thing apart, an object for medical cure. And in his thought on love, too, for example, May identifies the modern tendency to separate sex and love as an instance of such an artificial dichotomy and therefore detrimental to the whole self.

Attaining such integration in one's self-awareness and self-expression involves making choices of values and goals. There is, therefore, a strong relation between the individual's sense of self and the values held by the individual as essential both to his being and to society. The degree of the individual's inner strength and integrity will depend on his conviction of these values. Since a man does not exist in a historical or cultural vacuum, these values will be greatly influenced by and reflective of the age and society in which he exists. Yet the measure of his self-awareness or free sense of being or self is not passive but active; it is his ethical awareness, his reflective, responsible judgment and decision. These are rooted in the person's own power to choose and affirm his values, to live by his own convictions.

Language is the means of communication, of expression of the individual's sense of his own existence, of his being-in-the-world. The loss of the sense of self, says May, is directly related to a loss of language for deeply personal meanings. He attributes this loss of effective language to the change in connotation of such basic concepts as "love," "justice" and the conse-

quent degeneration of values once commonly held. The resulting failure in interpersonal communication compounds the
disorientation and disruption felt by the individual. Language is
the expression of the capacity for self-consciousness, of the
individual's sense of being as a self and in community with
other people and in the natural world. May later identified the
linguistic expression of self-consciousness as the capacity to
symbolize, to relate to oneself and one's world in terms of
symbols, to "bridge the gap" between inner meaning and outer
existence (*Significance of Symbols,* pp. 21-22). Conscience,
then, was "*one's capacity to tap deeper levels of insight, ethical
sensitivity and awareness*" wherein traditional beliefs and one's
own experience were interrelated in a responsible, meaningful,
personal integration (*Man's Search,* p. 84). Man's ethical awareness is born in his capacity to symbolize, to affirm the worth
and dignity of the individual, and to find meaning in life in an
ultimate concern or value or goal or symbol. Hence, May defines religion as fundamentally whatever the individual takes to
be his ultimate value, as creative relation to one's existence. The
power to affirm or believe in *any* value itself depends on the
strength of one's experience of oneself as a self. May does not
deny that religious fervor, though positive in its aim, can become so constricted in its following that it issues in evil, in
hatred and violence; he cites the example of Nazi Germany,
which was founded in a "religious" surge of nationalism, but
which issued in such restriction on those eligible that only complete destruction of "enemies" could satisfy the religious exalta-
tion generated by that nationalism. Ultimately the symbol of
Nazi domination became so strong as to deny the individual his
sense of being, to submerge him and his self-expression under
the swift current of the all-important race; hence, as in the case
of the Pax Romana, the individual's sense of being had, from
the psychological viewpoint, to be reasserted or lost entirely.

It follows, then, that human time is not mere ticking of
moments, but the quality of those moments. The emphasis falls
on duration and meaning rather than on chronological passages
of time. Again, the intensity and vivid immediacy of our experience, of our present, depends on consciousness of oneself, on

the sense of being. Yet the chronological passage of time is also of fundamental importance in that man is mortal, his chronological time is limited, and he does not know what his personal limit will be. The process of ageing is a constant reminder that at every moment he is vulnerable, and his past moments cannot return. The qualitative significance of time is born precisely in man's capacity to experience his own existence and to symbolize his own end as "death." The duration and meaning of each moment are colored not only by his consciousness of it but also by his inner certainty of his own mortality. The quality of man's present, then, depends on the strength of his sense of being and is, therefore, closely related to the attaining of inner freedom and integrity.

The human being, then, must not be viewed as a "collection of static substances or mechanisms or patterns but rather as emerging and becoming, that is to say, as existing" (*Origins,* p. 12; see also *Existential Psychotherapy,* pp. 1-4). May had always held that personality was dynamic and ever-changing; now in *Existence* (1958) he deepens that view and explains that the term *existence,* from the Latin *ex sistere,* means literally to stand out, to emerge, and that for him *the term* being *is not a static noun, but an active verb participle.* The term *existence,* then, means coming into being, it means *becoming.* This orientation toward the understanding of man as being, as becoming, does not deny the importance of understanding of dynamisms and patterns but places them as subordinate in the broader context of the individual patient's own being or existence. Neurosis, then, is to be defined in terms of what destroys or inhibits man's ability to fulfill his own being. Thus, human being, for May, is always dynamic, alive, in process; that is, to be human is to become, to be continually in a state of becoming.

It follows, then, that the therapist can understand and aid another human being only as he sees what that human being is moving toward, is becoming, and not merely in terms of efficient explanations of drives and causal factors. To grasp the being of another person is quite different from knowledge of single specific facts about him, such as age, sex, race, and family circumstances. To focus on certain mechanisms, to adopt what

May calls "the theoretical view," will only isolate therapist from patient and radically distort the reality of the individual person of whom specific data are only expressions or aspects (*Contributions,* p. 38). Hence it is of the greatest importance that the psychotherapist be capable of encountering the patient or subject willingly, of entering into an understanding of the whole existence of that patient—the patient's total relationship to the world by which he constitutes his being.

To illustrate what he means by the sense of being, May cites a specific case study wherein a patient described the explicit act of contact with and acceptance of her existence and of her right to exist (*Contributions,* pp. 42-43; see also *Existential Psychotherapy,* pp. 2-4). She first sheared away the *nonessential* facts, which had dogged and haunted her existence, that at birth she was illegitimate and unwanted. The nonessential facts of her later education -through her own initiative, and her lack of family support, fell away by her relentless reduction until she was left solely with the *fact* of her existence. Since she existed, she had a right to be and could no longer be reduced or lessened with the old formula of illegitimacy or unwantedness. For the first time, the fundamental experience of her own aliveness caused her to "cease to feel like a theory toward herself," to cease to try to make up to others for her origin or to herself for her family's ill-treatment of her. The concrete, existential immediacy of her own being was, for the first time, suddenly borne in on her and that certitude became, for her, the "touchstone" of existence in general, to borrow Marcel's phrase. Hence, the bearing and direction of her life, *what* she wanted to be, could henceforth be seen concretely in relation only to the fact *that* she existed and what she herself wanted to make of that existence. The sense of being that now underlay her choices and actions could not be reduced merely to a wish to rise above miserable beginnings nor to a desire to expiate or cast off a sense of guilt about her illegitimacy. Her being was henceforth oriented toward positive fulfillment.

May emphasizes four points with regard to the experience of the sense of being (*Contributions,* pp. 44-47). First, it is not itself the solution to particular problems, but rather the precondition, the basic conviction or root on which one's choices or decisions will rest. Second, the experience cannot be encompassed *solely* in terms of transference of trust to the psychotherapist; such a transference would, more probably, minister rather to increased passivity on the part of the patient. Acceptance by the therapist should rather enable the patient to see himself as acceptable to others and should thus free him to experience his own being and to become aware of his freedom and responsibility for his own existence. May's third point is closely related to the second: The experience of one's existence cannot be reduced to a mere mirroring of social and ethical norms, since again this would tend toward rigid moralism in function of social validation rather than the conscious, responsible development of one's own ethical awareness and convictions.

May's fourth point is perhaps the most important for psychotherapy, although he does not say so. The emergence of awareness of one's being must not, says May, be identified as a mere phase in the development of "the ego." He describes the ego as relatively weak, negative, and defensive, a mirror reflection from outside, whereas the sense of being has to do with one's whole existence, conscious and unconscious. At this point, it is worthwhile to remember May's previous definition of the self as "the organizing function within the individual and the function by which one human being can relate to another" (*Man's Search,* p. 79). In *Existence,* he now categorically states that the sense of being is *not* merely the capacity to see and measure the outside world, to assess situations and people. These are precisely the organizing functions of which the self is capable; here he speaks of them as *functions of the ego.* The sense of being or sense of self as he termed it in *Man's Search for Himself,* is rather "my capacity to see myself as a being in the world, *to know myself as the being who can do these things"* (*Contributions,* p. 46). The sense of being is a necessary precondition for ego development or the organizing capacity. The sense of being or sense of oneself as an embodied, conscious whole, is experienced "prior" to the dichotomy of consciousness and body. It is precisely an artificial bifurcation, a fragmentation, that makes possible the envisioning of the human body as a determined natural object and of consciousness as solipsistic, encapsulated subject. The passive, buffeted, Freudian ego is, as May sees it, a profound symbol of that very fragmentation of man. Such fragmentation was the result of overstressing either the unconditioned, thinking aspect of man or the conditioned, determined, vulnerable bodily aspect of man. The human dilemma, as May sees it, is precisely the integration of the two aspects in a grasping or sensing of one's being as a whole, indivisible, unitary structure.

The individual's sense of his own being or existence is not merely the product of environmental conditions or social norms but is born in self-awareness, in the freedom to be purposeful and responsible for the continuous achieving of his being. The human being does not experience his being in a vacuum. His self is interrelated with his world in a dialectical relationship in that "self implies world, and world self" (*Contributions,* p. 59). In *The Art of Counseling,* May had spoken of personality as requiring a "social setting." Now he treats of "world" in far greater depth and detail. The person and his world, May believes, are a unitary, structured whole. The person is continually forming, reforming, designing his world, being influenced by it, acting, reacting. It is "openness to the world" that chiefly distinguishes man's world from the "closed" world of plants and animals. A person's world is not static and automatic, not merely a matter of adjusting and surviving. It is, rather, a dynamic process in which the individual is involved. He is in the process of forming or changing it, thus putting his specific human impress on it, while limiting factors and accidental modifications arc exerting their influence on him.

To be in the world, says May, is not primarily a spatial relation, although man is factually present in a given space *in* the world. Man's space is "oriented" space—that is, space toward which man has taken up an attitude, space that has a meaning for man and toward which he is related. Prior to any reflective plan, the structure of embodied existence constitutes a meaning for space. Man, therefore, is not merely in the world, but is related to that world. Therefore, "human" space is exis-

tentially prior to the space spoken of by the physicist, to the
space wherein man is envisioned as an object among objects. *A
priori,* man is presumed to constitute his world in a threefold
manner, which May terms the *three modes of world* (*Contributions,* pp. 55-56). After the manner of existential therapists,
May names the threefold relationship of man's being-in-the-
world Umwelt, Mitwelt, and Eigenwelt.

Environment, or Umwelt (literally, "world around"), is
only one mode of world, albeit important and influential. May
describes as the "natural world" the world of laws and cycles,
of sleeping and waking, of hunger, thirst, heat and cold, birth
and death. In delineating Umwelt as this finite, biological, determined world, May has implicitly omitted the artificial factors of
the man-made environment in which a great proportion of people live. Although May has referred briefly to the Umwelt as the
"thrown" world, he does not seem to have grasped that the
"situatedness" of a human being in his environment or surroundings involves a great deal more than the biological realm
alone. One's country of origin, one's century, place one in a
situation wherein a particular culture, language and financial circumstances condition and determine to a great extent the manner of one's existence. The complete artificiality ("man-made-
ness") of urban surroundings, the virtual absence of natural
trees, plants, grass, the ever-present artifacts, of concrete and
brick, of man-made roads and streets, of noise and speed, all
these factors, though strictly man-made, are in many cases the
everyday surroundings, and hence "natural world," of many
people. In describing Umwelt as the biological realm and in
ignoring many of the environmental factors that influence the
quality of a man's biological existence, May has implicitly reduced the comprehensiveness of meaning that Umwelt ought to
have. Hence, the interrelationship and reciprocal meaning and
influence that are the true import of being-in-the-world as Umwelt have been virtually reduced to a conception of man as
"having" biological needs such as sleep and food. May is, however, careful to insist that the *meaning* of the Umwelt for the
individual is precisely in how he relates at any given moment to
his need for sleep or food, for example. This could also be

extended to consideration of how the individual relates to the man-made world. But what May does not say, and this is a crucial consideration, is that it is not basically a matter of *how* man relates to his environment, or to his self as biological, but precisely that man *cannot not relate* at every given moment to his environment and to his condition of embodiment. It is this reciprocity of man and world that constitutes his world as Umwelt rather than mere environment or surroundings as for animals, or the mere having of the body as an instrument of sensation, as a means through which man exists.

While the categories of adjustment and adaptation to hunger, noise, and need for sleep, for example, are quite accurate in Umwelt, the category in Mitwelt (literally, "with world") is relationship. This aspect of being-in-the-world, which May calls "the world of interrelationship with human beings" (*Contributions,* p. 62), must not be confused with notions of "group influence" or "collective mind." The distinctive quality of Mitwelt is, for May, that the meaning of the group will be a meaning for each individual and will be in part constituted by his own way of relating to the others in the group and to the group as a whole. Hence, the different levels of relation between persons—for example, functional, friendly, loving—depend on the choice and commitment of the individuals involved. Adjustment or adaptation to weather, hunger, or noise, for example, is because of an objective problem or need that must be resolved or satisfied. To speak of adjustment between persons may be analogically illuminating, but cannot be the true category of Mitwelt since this would be to treat oneself or the other person as object or problem, not as a person. Relationship, says May, involves mutual awareness; in encounter, both persons are affected.

To be capable of creative relationship with other people, of social integration, as May broadly termed it in *The Art of Counseling,* the individual must be spontaneous, original, and genuine. May spoke of these traits as characteristic of the uniquely creative person who had achieved healthy self-expression. Now, in *Existence,* he identifies the third mode of world as Eigenwelt (literally, "own world") or the mode of relation-

ship to one's self. As the awareness of oneself, the capacity to
relate to oneself, Eigenwelt is even more obviously related to a
strong sense of being than either Umwelt or Mitwelt. To be
spontaneous and whole in one's responses, one needs a strong
center; hence, Eigenwelt "presupposes self-awareness" (*Contributions,* p. 63). It consists of one's relationships with oneself. It
is the "for-me" aspect of things, their meaning—their color and
smell, for example—the whole gamut of intimate likes and dislikes. The experience of isolation and alienation, which May
earlier identified as consequent to the loss of the sense of self, is
now seen to be a distortion of Eigenwelt, while abstract, arid,
unyielding intellectualism and repudiation of personal involvement are seen as submersions of Eigenwelt. Further, without a
strong Eigenwelt, interpersonal relations tend to become empty,
functional, and lacking in vitality. This is necessarily so and follows on the point made with regard to Mitwelt that relationship
is between persons. Between objects, or person and object, the
category is one of adjustment, while mere reflected appraisal of
what the other or group of others expects of one would hardly
be sufficient for full human individuation.

May insists that the three modes of world are *interrelated
and simultaneous.* Freud's genius, says May, lay in his incom-
parable study of man in the Umwelt, the mode of the biologically determined, of instincts and drives. But traditional psychoanalysis had only a shadowy, epiphenomenal, derived Mitwelt in
that some social interaction was necessitated by the positing of
libidinal drives and outlets. And the mode of Eigenwelt "was
the aspect of experience which Freud never saw" (*Contributions,* p. 64). Sullivan, too, May goes on, while opposed to mere
social conformity, went to great pains to define the self in terms
of reflected group appraisal and to argue against the concept of
the individual, thus denying Eigenwelt. May, on the other hand,
insists that the sense of being is a sense of being-in-the-world in
a simultaneously threefold manner and that its reality is lost if
one of the modes is emphasized in an attempted exclusion or
reduction of the others.

If one's being-in-the-world is continuous, emerging,
changing, developing, and becoming, then it follows that time

for the human being is not the mere chronological passage of moments all equal to each other like the ticking of a clock. As has already been pointed out, the emphasis falls rather on the quality of meaning or duration that enables the person to envisage "before" and "after" according to the significance that certain events have for him personally. Man can transcend time and space in imaginative projection of future plans, in remembering past events and former relationships. Clearly, as May sees it, this capacity to transcend time is distinctively human and wholly dependent on the capacity to know one's own existence, to have a sense of one's own being. Earlier, however, the decisive temporal ecstasy, for May, was the present, and to be aware of oneself as the experiencing "I" was a prerequisite for courageous confrontation of a vivid, immediate present. "The future," he had written, "is born out of and made by the present" (*Man's Search,* p. 229). On full realization of human being as becoming, emerging, however, he now asserted in *Existence* that personality is intelligible only as it is envisaged on a trajectory toward its future. The decisive, dominant mode of time is now the future in the light of which the human being chooses and acts. This is not to disparage the immediacy and vividness of the present, but to state that the key to the particular way in which the present is immediate and vivid is the future orientation, the purpose, that underlies human choice and action. Hence, even *"the deterministic events of the past take their significance from the present and future"* (*Contributions,* p. 69). The significance of this view for therapy is obvious. The implication of such a view of time for memory, for example, is that the selection of memories, attitudes, past influences, and events is neither purely random nor determined but is made largely on the basis of what has significance for one, or of what one wishes to become. Thus, insight is described as the sudden grasping of the meaning of some important event, the sudden dawning of a new possibility, a new orientation that will call for future decision or a change in attitude.

The capacity to transcend the given situation, to project future attitudes and plans is "exemplified in the human being's unique capacity to think and talk in symbols" (*Contributions,*

p. 73; see also *Significance of Symbols,* pp. 20-22). Symbolizing, May believes, is man's way of expressing the quintessence
of his experience as an embodied consciousness. Symbols are
the language of man's capacity to question himself, his whole
existence, to think in terms of the possible, to represent and
communicate his thoughts and experience, and to reach beyond
his individual, concrete experience and relate it to his world and
his world to his experience. Symbols are the language of man's
sense of his own being, the language of his capacity to understand and take responsibility for his own being, to care for his
own being. Symbolizing is basic to personal identity, since the
individual's sense of being is experienced both generally within
his culture and history and particularly in his own psychological
and biological world. His image of himself is born both of cultural (racial, historical, and so on) and personal (individual,
family, and so on) symbols, arising out of the capacity to envisage himself, to sense his being, to find meanings and values
that he can hold as fundamental and necessary and, as is said
colloquially and very accurately, with which he can "identify"
himself.

     Inherent, however, in the perception of possibilities and
the positing of goals and values is the knowledge of finitude, of
mortality. Anxiety is the apprehension of potentiality, of freedom, of having to make a move into the unknown or untried, of
the possibility of failure. Yet the human being who, lost in anxiety, denies himself the chance to move, to change, or does not
"live up" to his inner evaluation or image of himself, is guilty
both toward himself and toward his world. Since every choice
negates certain other possibilities (*omnis affirmatio negatio est*),
man is constantly guilty. Consistent with his view that human
freedom inheres in self-consciousness, May holds that anxiety
and guilt are ontological, that is, fundamental and defining characteristics "rooted in (man's) very existence" (*Contributions,* p.
50).

     It has been established that for May, to be is to be-in-the-
world in a simultaneously threefold manner. Man cannot choose
to remain in existence and *not* be-in-the-world. To be in the
world is necessarily to be faced with choices and decisions,

whether to implement or deny a particular possibility, whether, in a particular instance, to "throw one's weight" on the side of individuation or participation. Underlying this capacity to weigh and decide is man's capacity to envisage himself and his world, to form a sense of his own being-in-the-world. In that man must choose, he must do so in terms of values (symbols) and concern (care) for the outcome, and this, for May, implies the necessity for *commitment* (*Contributions,* p. 87). Commitment on a positive basis (toward desired goals, not merely away from undesired evils) is a prerequisite for the gaining of insight, understanding, and the power to decide. Not merely the capacity to transcend, to go beyond, to exercise one's freedom, but the *readiness* to do so, the acceptance of one's being and possibilities grounds the very perception of what those possibilities are. Deliberation and decision, then, are, for May, ontologically rooted in human freedom and in the individual's sense of his own being. Decision for its own sake is seen to be mere adjustment to external pressure, while decision in accord with one's sense of being is the root of properly integrated human action.

Hence, the therapist pays especial attention to the symbols which the individual consciously holds dear, while at the same time taking careful note of the explorative quality of the patient's dreams wherein his unconscious, and hence more direct, relation to his world, to himself and his future is expressed (*Contributions,* p. 88; see also *Existential Psychotherapy,* pp. 31-40). Again, the predominant quality of his orientation toward his existence, whether decisive or indecisive, whether insightful or blind, whether culturally conditioned or independently integrated, will be interdependent with the quality and strength of his sense of his own being, with the extent to which he takes his own existence seriously as a creature of worth and dignity.

Given this analysis of May's view of the theoretical concepts that he proposes as decisive in existential therapy—for example, modes of world, time, oriented space—it is apparent that the unifying principle underlying all of them is the sense of being. From his first tentative exploration of personality as free, individual, social, and possessing religious tension, May's thought has clearly undergone a progressive deepening and maturation. Lack of clarity has occasionally detracted from the conceptual adequacy of the comprehensive view that May seeks to attain, as in the case of Umwelt, and the belated introduction in *The Art of Counseling* of "spontaneity," and so on, as characteristic of health. The development of May's conception of human being, however, has been seen to be structurally coherent and capable of sustaining further exploration with specific regard to the modes of anxiety, love, and will and to the role of symbols.

It will be the purpose of the next section to analyze and evaluate the structure and conceptual adequacy of the processes of individuation, social integration, and so on, which, on further deliberation, May specifically organizes in an "ontological approach." In May's view, these processes, which are interdependent with the sense of being, can become the structural base of psychotherapy, and provide the "base for a science of man that will not fragmentize and destroy man's humanity as it studies him" (*Existential Bases,* p. 83).

Ontological Processes as Structural Base

Thus far, this analysis has examined the growth and development, over a period of about twenty years (*Art of Counseling,* 1939; *Existence,* 1958), of the characteristics that May holds to be specific, distinguishing—that is, ontological—characteristics of human being, and essentially related to and linked by the human being's experience of his own existence, or sense of being. In the late 1950s and early 1960s, May undertakes further consideration of the structure and relation of those characteristics or processes, naming them *centeredness, self-affirmation, participation, awareness, self-consciousness,* and *anxiety* (*Toward the Ontological Basis,* pp. 5-7; *Existential Bases,* pp. 72-83; *Context,* pp. 93-98).

In the context of discussion of these ontological principles, the meanings for May of the term *ontological* are briefly indicated in the 1959 article "Toward the Ontological Basis of Psychotherapy," where he says that for him ontology means "something general" or "the study of being," as well as "something specific" or "the question, what are the characteristics which constitute the human being as human, without which he would not exist as a human being?" The first four characteristics are spoken of as "characteristic of all *living* beings," thus providing the term *ontological,* for May, with *three* meanings: (1) pertaining to being; (2) pertaining to all *living* beings; and (3) pertaining to *human* being as such.

To be is to be centered, to be completely separate and distinct in one's own unity or identity from other beings in their separateness and distinctness. May had always held that each person is unique, that the person cannot assume any other self, and that health depends on the acceptance of one's uniqueness (*Art of Counseling,* pp. 55-57, 61). It was the function of the counselor or psychotherapist to help the patient to recognize and be his real self. Now, in the light of the principle of centeredness, May redefines neurosis, which is no longer considered a failure to adjust, but as an adjustment itself, an attempt to preserve one's center by protecting it from seemingly imminent threats (*Existential Bases,* p. 75). Neurosis, says May, is a way of refusing to cope with some aspect of one's being in order that one's center may be saved from destruction and that one may, on a reduced scale, be adequate to the demands of that center.

Centeredness, says May, is a characteristic that man shares with all living beings, such as plants and animals (*Existential Bases,* p. 74; see also *Toward the Ontological Basis,* p. 5). He does not explicitly exclude nonliving things such as rocks and stones, but seems implicitly to have done so. Although, as has been pointed out, May does understand the term *ontology* to refer "generally" to "the study of being," he seems here to confine centeredness as an ontological characteristic to *living* beings only and hence to refuse centeredness as ontological to nonliving beings. One is reminded of May's insistence on "being" as dynamic, as "becoming," emerging, as an *active* verb participle rather than a *static* noun. He seems to be unaware that he has in this instance, thereby, moved from his original conception of center or self or identity or unity to consideration of the *vital affirmation* of that center. For example, he speaks of a tree, which, having had its top pruned, "sends up a new branch from heaven knows where *to become a new center*" (*Existential Bases,* p. 74, italics mine). This is to aver that without its top, the tree is no longer centered and its new shoot somehow gives it back its centeredness. The analogy in human beings would be to assert that a person who loses a limb is no longer centered. To be centered is thus to be distinct and separate entitatively. Thus, whether the top is lopped off or not, whether the tree is visually balanced and symmetrical or not, the tree is centered. Whether the human being loses a limb or not, he is centered. Neither tree nor human being can be otherwise since they cannot both be centered and, at the same time, not be centered. Quite simply, this is what it means to say that centeredness is an ontological characteristic, in May's own terms, inalienable from the being of the person or thing being discussed.

In "The Context of Psychotherapy," May states that "all human beings are *potentially* centered in themselves." Now, as illustration of "automatic" centeredness, May proposes "a tree's centeredness—*which is marvelously developed in balance and unity,* as anyone looking at a well-grown tree can tell" (*Context,* p. 94, italics mine; see also p. 110, n. 8). A human being's centeredness, says May, is not given automatically but depends on his courage to affirm it.

If in themselves human beings are only *potentially* centered, then no human being can be completely separate or fully distinct from any other. He can never have the experience of personal identity that May earlier stated to be "the basic conviction that we all start with as psychological beings" (*Man's Search,* p. 78). If centeredness in human beings depends on the courage to affirm it, two questions arise. First, does this mean that there are two kinds of centeredness that are both ontological, the "automatic" centeredness and that dependent on courageous affirmation? Second, if centeredness in human beings is only potential, how can it ever affirm itself? If it is asserted that it *can* affirm itself, then not only must it *be* in order to affirm itself (hence it is *not* potential), but it also renders tautological

May's second ontological process, which he calls *self-affirma-tion*. It would otherwise be a case of a center endlessly center-ing *and* affirming itself.

Change, development, existing as emerging, and becoming are incomprehensible without the reality of what changes, emerges, becomes. At thirty I am greatly changed from the per-son I was at the age of five; yet I am, and am conscious of being, the same individual, who has changed and developed. The "basic conviction" of which May spoke, is indeed the awareness of identity, the sense of one's own being. Thus May, in asserting that *centeredness* can "break down" or be distorted in conflict, is confusing the nature or being of the person with the existing, becoming individual person.

With regard to the example of the tree's centeredness, its balance and unity, it seems clear that this is more appropriate to the notion of visual symmetry than to centeredness. A stunted tree is still a tree, albeit not well-grown. Again, the implication inherent in the example of the tree seen as fully centered as it is balanced and well-grown, is serious when the analogy is applied to human beings whose centeredness can be, as May sees it, dis-torted in conflict or courageously affirmed. The mentally re-tarded and physically handicapped are somehow, by implica-tion, less than centered and thus less than human; the former cannot be courageously self-affirming nor the latter fully com-plete, not having, for example, grown a new limb to complete their center. In the light of May's conviction of human freedom and the centrality of the sense of being, this position would clearly be untenable. Also, in neurosis, it is not man's nature or centeredness that is distorted in conflict, but the expression or *affirmation* of the individual person that has become distorted and conflicts with his nature or center. Even if a human being is deprived of one or more senses from an early age, as was Helen Keller, he remains a centered human being. He does not, and can never, become *other*-than-human or *non*human. A human being cannot exist in a cat way nor in a dog way; he can, how-ever, exist on a subhuman level in that he does not know and use his human powers. Nevertheless, he remains a fully cen-tered, separate, distinct, human being. He may be subjugated in

a collectivity, a primitive tribe, and may not have developed a
sense of his own individuality. Even this subjugation cannot
take away from his humanity. A human being can be *in*human,
for example, cruel or sadistic; he may even invoke his human
powers in the service of the *in*human. But he cannot be *non*-
human. It is not the human being's centeredness, then, but the
sense of that centeredness, the sense of identity, that is born in
and depends on the *quality* of that human being's affirmation
of that identity.

The courage to maintain that centeredness May calls *self-
affirmation,* or *the courage to be oneself* (*Existential Bases,* pp.
75-76). This definition is very clearly correlated with his earlier
thought on individuation in *The Art of Counseling.* In fact, it is
noteworthy here that *individuation,* the earlier term, was probably a more felicitous choice than the term *self-affirmation,*
because May has always been at pains to point out the polar
structure of a self and world in human existence. Now, if the
import of the term *self-affirmation* is reduced or contracted to
the affirmation of the self alone, the interdependence implied in
the self-world polarity is to a great extent obscured. Even the
subsequent introduction of the third ontological process under
the name of *participation* does not restore the emphasis on the
polarity. The courage to be oneself, to individuate, is one aspect
of the authentic realization of human freedom. The function of
the counselor or therapist, then, is to aid the patient to discover
this real self, to help the patient envisage his own centeredness
or identity, and to help the patient to affirm this self courageously (*Art of Counseling,* pp. 53-61).

If the self is separate, distinct, and individual, it is so precisely because of its separateness from all other beings, and
because of its distinct individuality among other individuals in
the world. Participation (*Existential Bases,* p. 76), May's third
ontological characteristic, is the more fundamental view of what
May earlier called *social integration* and later on explored in
greater detail in the formulation of his three modes of world. If
to be is to-be-in-the-world, the person is situated in participation with others in a web of interdependence and interrelationship at various levels. If either self-affirmation (that is, individ-

uation) or participation is overemphasized, the balance and perspective of the person's life becomes distorted. Such a distortion can result in neurotic symptoms of withdrawal or in neurotic symptoms of its opposite, the "outer-directed" man, as May describes him. It is precisely with the level of his participation in encounter with the therapist that the neurotic seeks to redress that balance. In order to affirm his self in a fuller way, he seeks to overcome his difficulty with participation by means of a fuller, more integrated, and more open encounter in therapy. It is the development of the integrating sense of one's being that will restore the perspective of self and world relationship.

To be in the world is not only to be a participating, self-affirming, centered self, but to be aware. *"The subjective side of centeredness is awareness,"* says May (*Existential Bases,* p. 77; see also *Context,* p. 95). Here May correlates this awareness with vigilance in animals and links it with the apprehension of attack that in human beings becomes a state of anxiety. He proceeds no further concerning awareness, but goes immediately to the fifth ontological characteristic, consciousness. Elsewhere, with specific reference to stages in therapy, May examined awareness more closely, as experience of wishes and sensations, of bodily desires and needs (*Existential Psychotherapy,* pp. 37-39; *Love and Will,* pp. 262-266). At this point in his discussion of ontological characteristics, it might have been appropriate briefly to indicate the distinction between awareness and consciousness that warranted positing these two as separate ontological characteristics. May does not do this, however, and further clouds the matter by stating that *"the uniquely human form of awareness is self-consciousness"* (*Existential Bases,* p. 77).

Awareness as the experience of sensations, of wishes, of bodily needs and desires is obviously of crucial moment in therapy, the aim of which, as May sees it, is to aid the patient to experience his own being. The person who tries to deny the needs of his body, for example, or who tries to reduce to mere physical need the human desire for loving encounter, is guilty toward himself of seeking to ignore or repress what he is, namely, embodied consciousness in the world. Awareness is also the realm of "automatic" or learned actions such as driving a car, typing, and writing, most of which suddenly become difficult when one focuses attention on the actions involved. Awareness is thus more *direct* than consciousness, that is, it consists of a more vitally immediate experience of embodied existence. The cited instances of awareness are, of course, specifically human instances. The original range of awareness that made possible the acquisition of the skills of driving, typing, and writing involved an initial selective concentration on the various actions and their sequence. The specific quality of human awareness is always, whether nearly or remotely, tempered by consciousness.

The uniquely human form of awareness, says May, is self-consciousness; May uses *self-consciousness* and *consciousness* synonymously, and occasionally even substitutes *self-awareness* and *self-relatedness* for *self-consciousness*. The fifth ontological characteristic is consciousness (*Existential Bases,* pp. 77-79; *Context,* pp. 95-96). This must not be confused with awareness. The latter, together with centeredness, individuation and participation, is characteristic of all living beings, says May. He speaks of these four as biological levels, yet holds with Teilhard de Chardin that the emergence of self-consciousness in man causes the whole Gestalt to change, and the organism to become comprehensible only in terms of the "new pattern." Thus, May undertakes almost immediately to qualify his assertion that the four characteristics are "biological levels" with the statement that the simpler biological functions must, in man, be understood in terms of the whole man, and specifically, in terms of self-consciousness. This evokes the earlier discussion of the three modes of world. Whereas plants and animals are *in* a closed world or environment, man alone has the capacity to envisage and relate to himself and his world, to his biological nature and environment. Hence, man *has* a world or Umwelt; while being *in* it, he can relate to it, transcend it, and transform it by putting a specific human "face" on it.

Again in evidence is the centrality of the sense of being, the awareness and consciousness of oneself. The emergence of consciousness of self, of the ability to envisage oneself as free, thinking subject and as limited, determined object is, for May, the specific human dilemma within which all persons must live (*What is the Human Dilemma?*, p. 9; *Art of Counseling,* p. 73). But if this dilemma is the source of our ability to come to terms with ourselves, to imagine, remember, symbolize, and create, it is also the source of the painful realization of our mortality, of our precarious existence. May identifies this apprehension of possible loss of one's being as anxiety, the "sixth and last characteristic" (*Existential Bases,* p. 81).

At this point one must take issue with the words "and last," since such characteristics as guilt, love, and will, which May earlier identified (in *Existence*) as fundamental, defining structures of human existence, have not been included in the six ontological characteristics. Now, however one may argue that love is involved in the ontological characteristic of participation, it is so by implication only, just as anxiety is already implied by consciousness, in the ability to project possibilities and to apprehend one's vulnerability. Yet May chooses to specify anxiety separately while choosing not to specify separately love, guilt, and so forth. These latter characteristics May has previously stated to be ontological, that is, fundamental, defining structures of human existence, and their absence renders redundant the inclusion of anxiety in May's list of six.

It is also noteworthy that when May treats of these ontological characteristics in *Psychology and the Human Dilemma* (*Context,* pp. 93-98; *A Phenomenological Approach,* pp. 117-127), having devoted some earlier chapters to the discussion of anxiety, he omits any mention of "six" and actually refers only to the first five characteristics. It might appear, then, that he was not entirely certain of the place of anxiety in relation to these characteristics. However, in the revised 1969 edition of *Existential Psychology,* anxiety remains specifically indicated in his second article as the "sixth and last characteristic."

There remains only the question of care, which was not mentioned in *Existential Psychology* but which seems to have been gradually emerging in May's thinking on participation, particularly as instanced in therapeutic concern and levels of encounter (*A Phenomenological Approach,* pp. 121ff.; *Contributions,* pp. 121-122). Previously, May had mentioned care in a very brief reference to Boss, Binswanger and Heidegger and had described it as man's capacity "for understanding his being and taking responsibility for it" (*Contributions,* p. 75). "Indeed, the whole existential approach is rooted in the always curious phenomenon that we have in man a being who not only *can* but *must,* if he is to realize himself, question his own being" (*Contributions,* p. 74). May's most recent exploration of love and will, which issued in his book *Love and Will,* did not reveal any fundamental changes in his envisioning of human existence, and he did now state clearly, toward the end of the book, that the structure of being-in-the-world was characterized by concern or care. Thus, a further dimension of understanding and another integrating factor comes into May's thought with the recognition of care as an ontological characteristic.

May described care as "the state in which something *does* matter; . . . the opposite of apathy" (*Love and Will,* p. 289; see also pp. 289-291). Although he is quite accurate in identifying care as the necessary or basic source of tenderness, as the joint source of both love and will, he does also rather inconsistently speak of it as being a "necessary *addition*" to Eros, and as providing the "psychological side of Eros." This is somewhat confusing since care cannot be both the source of love and a later "necessary addition." In stating that care is the source of will, however, May quite accurately adds that it is caring about a situation that involves one in *doing* something about the situation, in formulating and carrying out decisions. May shows clearly that he agrees with Heidegger's conception of care as "*ontological* in that it constitutes man as man," and, further, states that he holds care to be the ground or source of the human capacity for sympathy, concern, and involvement with other persons and things. Yet May does also speak of care as a "state," and of a person as being "in care," as opposed to sentimentality or to "not-caring." Such phrases lead one to wonder whether May does actually envisage care as coextensive with being human or whether he is more primarily oriented to considering care in terms of its psychological *expression* in particular situations.

Care as ontological is not merely something that "fights cynicism and apathy." On the contrary, even apathy and cynicism, which are psychological, are grounded in care as ontological since they are precisely manifestations of care as expressed in the desire to reduce vulnerability and to preserve one's being. The misunderstanding that would oppose care to apathy is perhaps based on the overtones which the word *care* has acquired in ordinary use and not on an understanding of care as coextensive with being human in the world, being oriented toward self and others, toward individuation and participation. It is care as ontological that is the basis or ground of caring about one's own existence as well as that of others. Hence, it is not only at the source of such self-preservative defenses as apathy, cynicism, and even hatred, but is also at the base of love, of concern for others, and of law and justice. It is also the source of individuation, participation, and the other structures that have been the fundamental elements in May's articulation of a structural base for psychotherapy. Care is also at the source of the sense of being. In *Existence,* regarding care in Heidegger's works, May spoke of it as the capacity to understand and be responsible for one's own existence. The sense of being is precisely the measure of that understanding and responsibility.

Summary

The purpose of this chapter, realized through close, documented statement and methodical examination, has been to articulate in internal critique the decisive moments of May's work and to disclose the fundamental insight that serves as the unifying principle in his envisioning of human existence. This principle, the sense of being, was shown to be the base on which is built May's "working science of man," his "structural base for psychotherapy," and his ontological approach to man. Disclosed as the touchstone of therapeutic encounter, the sense of being, in May's view, is the ground and goal of all therapy.

The need felt by many psychiatrists and psychotherapists, both in Europe and America, for reexamination of the ground and aim of therapy was briefly noted. May's conviction that the counselor must examine his own philosophical presuppositions was also noted and his rejection of specific scientific models as inadequate for psychotherapy was examined. While clearly acknowledging the explanatory capacity of behavioristic and medical models, May insisted that the ground of therapy must be comprehensive rather than aspectual and must encompass what it is to be a human being in all of the aspects of that being. May's particular orientation to finding this more comprehensive approach in a descriptive analysis of human existence was stated and its stages briefly articulated.

I undertook then to analyze his early view of personality. It was observed that he placed freedom squarely at the root of his envisioning of human existence and his emphasis on existence as changing and mobile was also noted.

Further, I sought to examine the notion of the sense of being, its first appearance in May's work as the sense of self, or experience of one's own existence, and its later articulation with regard to the modes of anxiety, love, and will; time; and the three modes of world. The expression of the sense of being was briefly noted as man's capacity to symbolize, to question and relate to his existence. The method of this section was to witness critically the unfolding of the idea of the sense of being and its centrality to the structure of existence as May envisions it.

My inquiry then centered on May's attempt to identify and articulate the structure of human existence in terms of the most fundamental characteristics. The individual conceptions of the early view of personality were seen to have been deepened and relocated and the relevance of this structural envisioning for therapy was also closely regarded. Finally, May's later assertion of care as ontological was also examined.

Through a descriptive account, then, of the psychological problems of the mid-twentieth century, May's earlier concept of personality developed quickly toward its eventual and deeper relocation within the context of considering the basic structure of human existence. His conception of therapy, which he always viewed as a process of involvement, a concerned assistance, rather than as the expert application of some automatic technique and cure, became specifically a process of loving encounter, itself made possible by the very ontological structures the expression of which had become distorted in the patient. Neurosis, which he originally viewed as failure to adjust, was now more comprehensively envisioned as precisely a protective adjustment caused by the failure properly to integrate the expression of those structures. Hence, May views as mere substitution of a new protective adaptation any therapy that would seek to "condition" the patient not to feel anxiety or guilt.

May's efforts, however, to give ontological expression to those structures that he analyzed so clearly in the psychological order, have been shown to be somewhat confused. I asserted, in the first section of this chapter, that May seems not entirely at home with theoretical concepts. It has been clearly demonstrated in the subsequent sections that May's psychological understanding of human existence is considerable precisely because he is careful to keep firmly in mind the phenomena as experienced. When, however, he attempts to examine what he identifies as the fundamental, inalienable, ontological characteristics of human existence, his analysis and examples are not unambiguous and do not always harmonize with the spirit of his psychological inquiry. The fundamental reason for this difficulty, as has been indicated, is May's insistence on human existence as emerging, as becoming. Now May is undoubtedly not mistaken when he identifies as fundamental the vital, dynamic aspects of being human. But to overemphasize the dynamic is to envision human being existentially in a manner detrimental to the envisioning of human being *essentially* (as essential nature or center) and, on the ontological level, to overemphasize the dynamic would result in as arbitrary and artificial a bifurcation (or even truncation) as the body-mind dichotomy that May is at pains to overcome.

In his insistence on envisioning human existence as emerging, becoming, in seeing "being" as an "active verb participle" rather than as a "static noun," in making the notion of centeredness dynamic to the point of meaning "center*ing*" rather than "center*ness*" or "center," May is effectively overemphasizing the dynamic. One is reminded of his early statement that "personality is never static .... Becoming static is in this realm synonymous with death" (*Art of Counseling,* p. 29). In trying to overcome the "static," however, he goes too far in his ontological reflections, in effect excluding essence (and hence the principle that makes intelligible, as distinct from describable, the being of man), which cannot finally be separated from existence. There must be something that exists, that changes, that becomes. The structure of change is precisely dependent on the response of a stable essence without which there is no change, but a totally new being.

Yet May's insistence on existence, though detrimental to essence, rings *psychologically* true because man, as self-conscious, is *essentially* constituted as a being *existentially* self-realizing. In May's terms, man's centeredness must affirm both itself and its world. In a sense, man creates himself—he is a cause of himself, a *causa sui*. Although his nature or essence is given, the personal unfolding of that nature is in his own hands to be achieved in freedom, in his response to what he is, what he wishes to be, and what he ought to be. Only a logical essence (*ens rationis*) is so fixed as to be entirely "static." Man can only become what in some way he already is. Man can only envisage and relate to his past, for example, in that it is in some way still "part of him." The movement of existential unfolding in time requires the response of a stable essence. Psychologically May recognizes this in his assertion of the limiting, determining factors of the person's existence, but in his ontological reflections, he has not made clear this same distinction, that is, between man as essential nature and man as individual existentially self-realizing.

The movement of existential, temporal unfolding is itself continuously to perceive and realize potentialities. May concentrated very early in his work on the nature and effects of anxiety as the inescapable apprehension of certain potentialities, as human foreknowledge of error, of the fact of imperfection, of contingency, of threat to the sense of being, and of anxiety as a mode of sensing one's being. Hence, the focus of the next chapter will be anxiety. For the purpose of contextual enrichment of this study, for the sake of better understanding of the common experience that is at base May's starting point, a brief perspective on some salient aspects of the twentieth-century preoccupation with anxiety will be offered. Also, the main formative influences on May's anxiety theory as seen by May himself will be separately examined. The main thrust of the chapter will be to elucidate the central importance of the sense of being in May's theory of anxiety for therapeutic achievement of the courage to face anxiety and to integrate one's existence.

TWO

Meaning of Anxiety

Uneasiness cannot be eluded, but only overcome.
> Gabriel Marcel, *Problematic Man*

It is within the context of lived, concrete, everyday experience that the human being exists. His world begins as prescientific, precritical, pretheoretical awareness. Abstraction is a "later" level made possible by consciousness of world, of fellow humans, and of self. Neither definitions nor explanations can ever encompass the total meaning of the relationship of a self with its world, in anxiety, in love, in what Gordon Allport called "oriented becoming." Man does not merely have life, he lives in various spheres of meaning; that is, he lives immediately and spontaneously within a cultural situation, interacting with

66

family, friends, and fellow citizens. The "lived world" is the encompassing world of our immediate experience. It is immediately concrete and meaningful without its meaningfulness, its concreteness being made explicit, reflected on, or conceptualized. What is found in Rollo May's theory of anxiety is a conceptualization and analysis of what is first experienced in the lived world and only later given systematic expression. His purpose is an understanding of the place of anxiety in the structure of human existence, in order thereby to return with greater possibility of aiding the individual patient in therapy.

Although it is contingent in its manifestations, anxiety is a defining characteristic of the conscious self, a characteristic incident to the perception of one's radically tenuous grip on existence. The moment one is conceived, he is old enough to die. The human self is finite, contingent, and vulnerable. Anxiety at its deepest level, then, is no mere historical phenomenon or cultural preoccupation, but is rather the dread of precisely this finiteness and contingency.

It has become almost a truism to speak of our age as one of anxiety. The essence of a truism, however, is not so much that it is hackneyed as that it is true. Yet this is an age of anxiety not because man has never been so anxious before, but rather because man seems never to have been so widely and analytically preoccupied with his own anxiety in itself. In dramatic fashion, anxiety has been portrayed as an element or product of crisis situations, as in Ibsen's plays or Bergman's films, for example. It has been disclosed and examined as an overt indication of the basic anxiety of existence and of the inalienability of man's search for meaning, as in the poetry of T. S. Eliot and W. H. Auden, for example. One might mention also the dramatists and novelists, such as Sartre, Camus, and Kafka, who seemed to have accepted as factual the contemporary feeling of meaninglessness and were concerned with analyzing the reasons for and structure of the empty futility and loneliness that for them overwhelmingly characterized modern living. On the ordinary, everyday level, what is very striking, perhaps more so than literary and highly specialized attempts to grasp and disclose the structure of contemporary anxiety and alienation, is the symptomatic, mushroom growth of such systems of "reassurance" as astrology, astroanalysis, and other transcendental, psychic sciences that promise order, meaning, integration, and fulfillment. One is uncannily reminded of the unease and unhappiness of Marlowe's Dr. Faustus. In various ways, twentieth-century man has taken his anxiety to himself with varying degrees of acceptance, some courageously exploring and seeking to understand it, others employing the stratagem of reducing awareness of contingency to specific problems with which one can cope in the practical order.

In the face of contemporary consciousness of anxiety, what remains extraordinary is man's continuing search for meaning. Even in utter bewilderment and apparent emptiness, the human self never seems to lose heart. The paradox is that even in vacuity man finds, still alive, the urge to render experience meaningful. The exploration of anxiety by philosophers and writers, the ordered fragmentation and emotionless forms of modern art are themselves part of man's fight to confront contingency, to take it into himself. Man, unlike animals, is free, although his freedom is finite, and his action, on the properly human level, born in his sense of being, is the projection and confirmation of the self that he is. Hence, man's anxiety is not an ineluctable, collective anxiety that the individual cannot control or evade. A collective is merely an *ens rationis,* a conceptual construct or logical essence, which cannot have a self, but is only the projecting-together of many individual selves. But the *expression* of the individual's anxiety necessarily goes beyond himself for language is communal. Language, born in man's capacity to symbolize his own being and his world, is the *expression* of a seeking after community, and the expression of anxiety is only understandable as a desire to overcome anxiety, to find a warmth of contact with other people that will assuage our anxiety for a time. Hence, even in anxiety, a man is not alone. From our earliest days, we exist through our relationships with other people as much as in our own center. If man's existence is coexistence, then anxiety can be characterized as a stultifying state only in its neurotic form, that is, only when the person cannot or will not accept his anxiety and go beyond it in courageous self-affirmation through participation with others.

The attempt to avoid confrontation with anxiety, to anaesthetize the pain sensed in one's own being, may become pathological anxiety, which psychologists and psychotherapists have preferred to call, after Freud, *neurotic anxiety*. Anxiety, as inalienable and inescapable, is an element within the total structure of self-affirmation, and it leads either to courage or to despair. The man who does not succeed in accepting courageously the anxiety inherent in existence can seek to avoid it by escaping into neurosis, by somehow avoiding being. The neurotic person can affirm himself only weakly and in a reduced, intensified, defensive, and therefore distorted way. Given the two aspects of self-affirmation as individuation and participation, the neurotic person may withdraw in fear and trembling to shore up his center, or may empty himself in overparticipation through fear of his own thoughts, frantically trying to catch signals from other people as to what they would like him to be. It is because of his very sensitivity to the threat of nonbeing, to the danger to his sense of being, that the neurotic evinces what one might call a "hedgehog reaction" or becomes a "social chameleon," trying to avoid what he "intuits" could hurt. His very efforts to avoid anxiety, then, are themselves characterized by anxiety and only reinforce its stranglehold on his existence. The "normal" or courageous person, on the other hand, "breaks into" his anxiety where possible by settling upon concrete objects of fear, by constituting each as a positive, singular, practical problem with which he then deals. His project of existence, then, is characterized not by anxiety, but by an integration of his perception of anxiety and the courage of self-affirmation. The neurotic, in seeking to avoid anxiety is so increasingly overwhelmed by his own foreboding that he gradually reduces the quality of his self-affirmation to a limited, intensified, "unbalanced" unreality that can ultimately destroy him by estranging him finally from himself and his world.

The line between "normal" and "neurotic" is now seen to be very thin. The average man, in a historical period of extreme anxiety, marked by events such as world war, social conflict, and racial upheaval, a period of transition from settled values and symbols into the unknown such as our own time, can cross that line if that security (values, symbols) or the way of

life that he holds dear is threatened. He can suddenly become a
fanatic in defense of the order that he has so long taken for
granted that he feels deeply and intimately threatened by any
change. This is usually the rationale behind civil strife, although
the parties may not be explicitly conscious of it.

   If indeed the person is sunk in apathy, it is precisely because of his unwillingness to come to grips with his own anxiety. Collective anxiety, which, as has been pointed out, is radically tenuous is not even a collective in the manner in which a
particular group or society or team is consciously constituted as
a collective. Collective anxiety is only an abstraction made possible by the experiencing, interacting, and projecting of many
anxious individual selves. The study of history will show that at
all times, in every century, there have been many anxiety-creating factors in the social and political sphere. Radical upheaval
and doubt are not new, nor is consciousness of death and contingency given to our century alone. Again, this is an age of
anxiety, not because man has never been so anxious as at the
present time, but because man seems never before to have been
so widely and analytically preoccupied with his own anxiety in
itself. Twenty-century man has not merely preoccupied himself
with his anxiety but he has, at times, attempted to view the
whole of life through anxious eyes, forgetting that the quality
of our anxious sensitivity to our finite condition is in direct proportion to the quality of our sensitivity to life. Our sense of
being, our affirmation of self and world, our confrontation of
the social, cultural, and political factors of our lives—these are
the measure both of our anxiety and of our sensitivity, courage,
and life orientation.

   To close oneself in anxiety is indeed to lose and reduce
oneself. Yet this anxiety cannot be evaded or even ignored since
it inheres in our very existence. Anxiety can only be transcended in courageous living. Everyone has at some time had
the direct, living experience of communicated states of mind.
Colloquially, one expresses this experience with such phrases as
"He always depresses me with his miserable outlook" or "He is
so alive and happy that to meet him cheers me up." The "lived
world" of concrete, meaningful, mutually influential interaction

and experience is directly and unequivocally grasped in such intuitive reaction and understanding.

The courage to find joy in living is not easy or automatic, but must be founded in a strong sense of something outside of oneself that is of lasting value, a symbol that is of fundamental importance to one's sense of being. The inner values and symbols of mature, integrated existence reach outward from self-preoccupation to affirm the worth of life itself and of humanity. These are inner values that, in their very expression in concrete project and everyday commitment, reinforce and strengthen the self. Hence we are again speaking of the polar structures of individuation and participation as they are expressed in common experience, in the "lived," everyday world. Thus, to be anxious is not of itself automatically to flounder in a morass of deadening constrictions. The choice remains for the individual to make, whether to surrender to anxiety in an immobilizing withdrawal of self, or to see in one's anxiety an increased sensitivity to possibility and perhaps, constructively examined and understood, a springboard to creative action.

As a practicing psychotherapist, lecturer, and writer, Rollo May, together with his colleagues in counseling, in psychology and psychiatry, has in North America been in the forefront of the continuing effort to understand and deal with human uneasiness and its effects. As a writer, May has consistently singled out the phenomenon of anxiety and its consequences for special study and structural examination. The forms that anxiety takes imply many possible interpretations of what anxiety fundamentally is, these interpretations being dependent on the presuppositions implicit in the questions asked. In devoting an entire book to the elucidation of a contemporary, comprehensive theory of anxiety, May explored first of all not only the main psychological theories of anxiety, but also the most important philosophical, biological, and cultural theories (*Meaning of Anxiety,* p. 16).

While actually preparing the book, May himself contracted tuberculosis, at a time when no drugs had yet been developed to combat the disease. He was, he says, for some considerable time in the critical position of not knowing whether he would recover fully or partially or whether he would die. During this period of personal anxiety, May says that he "read the two books on anxiety . . . up to that time, Freud's *The Problem of Anxiety* and Kierkegaard's *The Concept of Dread*" (*Existential Psychotherapy,* p. 59; see also *Emergence,* pp. 2-3). Although he could intellectually appreciate the importance of Freud's explorations, May goes on, it was Kierkegaard's description that "spoke directly" to him in that terrifying period of his illness. Freud, says May, wrote on the technical level; he knew *about* anxiety and brilliantly formulated and explored theories concerning the mechanisms of anxiety. Kierkegaard, however, knew anxiety itself, and his probing of its structure at the deepest level was, for May, immediate, concrete, and meaningful far beyond any technical theories.

May was later to hold, however, that both approaches were "obviously necessary" and do not represent a "value dichotomy" (*Emergence,* p. 3). Although Freud's theories were based on determinism, while Kierkegaard's understanding of anxiety or dread is based on his conviction of human freedom in self-awareness, May seeks an understanding that may overcome this seemingly mutual exclusivity by a new integration. May envisages the human being as emerging, becoming, and sees the sense of being as playing the foundational, integrating role. For May, anxiety is fundamental because its threat is to that very being; it strikes directly at the sense of one's own existence. Thus, the phenomenological description and philosophical formulation of anxiety by Kierkegaard, for May, offers the necessary meaning and understanding of the sense of helplessness and "objectless," overwhelming threat that Freud isolated as the experience of anxiety.

Freud, May was convinced, was an explorer of classic importance in his research into the mechanisms of anxiety and its relation to neurosis. It was, says May, principally because of Freud's work that scientific attention was focused on the inner conflicts and psychological difficulties that render some individuals capable of coping with what may, to others, seem to be a minor objective threat. It was Freud, then, who induced scientists and doctors to attend closely to the "subjective locale" or individual reference of neurotic anxiety (*Meaning of Anxiety,* p. 199). May accepts Freud's distinction between "normal" or "objective" anxiety and "neurotic" anxiety and esteems highly the explorations of Freud into the etiology and mechanics of anxiety. However, it was to Kierkegaard that he turned for a philosophical exploration of how it is that the human being can feel anxiety at all. Many years after his recovery of health, May wrote more than once of his deep regard for Freud's and Kierkegaard's studies of anxiety. Even though his book, *The Meaning of Anxiety,* had been concerned with many other writers in many fields and their various theories concerning anxiety, it is clear that the most lasting influences and seminal contributors to the formulation of May's own theory were the studies by Freud and Kierkegaard.

Hence, the purpose of the next two sections of this chapter will be to outline and evaluate May's understanding of the Freudian and Kierkegaardian theories of anxiety in order to throw light on the positive value that May draws from their respective theories in the formulation of his own understanding of anxiety. For May, human being is a whole structure in which the sense of being exercises a foundational role. In that structure, anxiety may become a predominant, constricting mode of existence or be the constructive sensitivity to possibility of creative individuality and vital, active participation. It is, then, to Freud that May turns for elucidation of the mechanics of anxiety, while it is in Kierkegaard that May finds the philosophical probing of freedom and self-awareness through which the individual can develop a strong sense of being.

Anxiety as Explained: Freud

"To study Freud on anxiety," says May, "is to become aware that his thinking on the topic was in process of *evolution* throughout his life" (*Meaning of Anxiety,* p. 113). In that evolution, May singles out two theories of anxiety as the major moments in Freud's thinking. These are: Freud's first theory, of anxiety as repressed libido, and the second theory, quite the reverse of the first, of anxiety as *cause* of repression.

With regard to the first theory, May notes that Freud distinguished first between fear (as of specific objects) that is an *expedient* warning, and the *inexpedient,* paralyzing condition of "objectless" anxiety. From his clinical work, Freud had observed that patients manifesting symptoms of various sorts, such as hostility or restlessness, for example, were remarkably free of anxiety, while those who did not clearly *manifest* such symptoms had greater, "free-floating," expectant dread. He drew the direct conclusion that anxiety must originate in repression of the cause of symptoms. Repression of libidinal impulses, the expression of which was deemed to be externally, objectively dangerous (as in the Oedipus complex), or which constituted an internal, neurotic, "imagined" danger, "automatically" caused the libido to be exchanged and discharged in anxiety.

Now, May observes that although an individual who must hold strong impulses in check may well manifest great anxiety and restlessness, it is also possible that a strong person may do so without anxiety. Yet May retains the Freudian distinction between normal anxiety as proportionate response, and neurotic anxiety as disproportionate response, to the threat of danger. One wonders how, if the object of anxiety is necessarily unknown (since Freud names fear as the *apprehension concerning a specific object*), the response can possibly be determined to be proportionate or disproportionate. May rests *his* distinction on what the individual *does,* that is, whether he moves ahead (normal) or remains defensively constricted (neurotic), and this in turn he relates to the self-strength or vulnerability of the person to anxiety-creating situations (*Meaning of Anxiety,* pp. 194, 197). But May's distinction, even adding consideration of environmental data (for example, from childhood and family relationships) still does not entirely account for the strength or vulnerability of the person in relation to anxiety.

While Freud had suggested that sexual excitation denied outlet and sexual abstinence accounted for the development of neurotic anxiety, May asserts that, in his clinical experience, many people in such situations do *not* become anxious or neurotic. In further support of his rejection of Freud's first theory as ultimate causal explanation of anxiety, May cites the contention of Hobart Mowrer that the "frank libertine . . . may be a very anxious person" (*Meaning of Anxiety,* p. 117). However, May does note approvingly that Freud's first theory has a positive value in that it recognizes the "intrapsychic locale" or subjective reference of neurotic anxiety. However, May also carefully observes that, while the neat, physicalist, analogical view of automatic conversion of libido into anxiety was very attractive, Freud himself later saw it as doubtful. Thus, he rejected it in favor of the second theory that he considered better fitted his topology of id-ego-superego, with its emerging emphasis on the organizing role of the ego.

Freud's second theory, says May, was based on his clinical observation of what he called *perception of danger by the ego,* which then repressed the dangerous impulse in order to avoid anxiety. The symptoms and inhibitions are created by the ego in the effort to avoid the situation of which anxiety is a warning. Hence, May notes that the second theory gives "anxiety as the *cause* of repressions" and says that Freud rejected his first theory as having been contradicted by his new discovery of the ego as the only seat of anxiety. Freud no longer posited neurotic anxiety as arising out of dangerous, inner, instinctual impulses but rather as arising out of the external danger of their expression, that is, the inner perception of the external danger resulted in internal conflict and anxiety. Hence, the displacement of symptom to some other "cause" (cue) of anxiety allows the neurotically anxious person to express his dread without revealing the original cause of that anxiety. Freud's theory of infantile sexuality gave him grounds for believing that much anxiety was that born of repressed and displaced longing for a socially forbidden loved one. We note, with May, that Freud's emphasis on the ego as originating the phenomenon of anxiety has taken strong hold and that the notion of libido transformation that was his original theory has gradually been eased out of prominence. Although May asserts that the conflict, even in Freud's second theory, remains one of whether or not to satisfy libidinal impulses and that it is libido that is utilized, Freud himself stated categorically in his later years that he could "no longer maintain that it is the libido itself that is turned into anxiety" (Freud, 1968b, p. 94). In fact, he declared himself to have "lost interest" in "what the material is out of which anxiety is made" (p. 85). May does not mention either that while rejecting the old instinctual anxiety and positing the ego as the only seat of anxiety, Freud now held for *two* moments or occasions of anxiety, "one as a direct consequence of the traumatic moment and the other as a signal threatening a repetition of such a moment" (pp. 94-95).

May goes on to present Freud's view of the possible origins of anxiety as the birth trauma and the fear of castration. Anxiety, for Freud, was always cued by the fear of loss, and he arrived at the conclusion through a complicated series of postulations of the specific loss feared at various stages in psychological development. In those stages, loss was feared in the form of separation from mother in the early infantile period, loss of sexual power in the period of infantile sexual development, loss of superego approval or socially derived approbation during the development of the reality-pleasure-principle balance, and, finally, loss was feared in the guise of loss of life itself. Each of these was seen as a further and more serious obstacle to reunion with the mother, and although Freud would not accept the birth experience as *literal* physical source of anxiety, he was prepared to view all anxiety as fundamentally arising out of separation from or loss of the mother. May, however, interprets this development in Freud's reasoning as taking on an increasingly symbolic meaning, and says that eventually both the birth trauma and castration fear, seen as anxieties of loss, were considered by Freud more as *symbolic* of rejection by the mother than as literal sources of anxiety. One cannot, of course, be entirely certain, says May, as to how far Freud still *inclined* to the literal interpretation; however, the stumbling block of the impossibility of applying the castration fear to women recurs in Freud's work, leading May to infer that Freud was increasingly inclined to the nonliteral, symbolic view of such origins of anxiety.

In his discussion of the trends evidenced in Freud's theories (*Meaning of Anxiety,* pp. 123-127), May singles out the decreasing role of libido, from repressed libido as *direct cause* of anxiety to repressed libido as *result or consequence* of the ego's perception of a danger or anxiety situation. May notes with great emphasis that Freud shifted his focus to the "situational" aspect of anxiety creation. As a related point, May observes that while Freud insisted on the subjective reference of the neurotic, disproportionate response to such situations, he came later to the belief that such neurotic "internal" danger was apprehended precisely in function of an external danger, such as social disapproval, punishment, and even loss of parental love. Further, May holds that, in Freud's careful relating of his anxiety theory to his topology or id-ego-superego structure (that is, helplessness in anxiety was caused by the warring of the three levels, the naming of the type of anxiety as it was deemed to have originated in one of the levels, hence, moral or superego anxiety, instinctual or id anxiety, and so on), Freud was really trying to view anxiety no longer as a purely intrapsychic process, but as arising out of the individual's whole range of environmental relationships. May concludes that Freud was prevented from pursuing this notion of relationship both by his own topology and by his libido theory.

Although rejecting Freud's conception of the individual as a "carrier" of libidinal needs that must be gratified, May accepts as positive values Freud's illumination of symptom formation, his emphasis on the subjective aspect of neurotic anxiety, and his concern with "separation" anxiety. Further, he states that, in his view, Freud's increasing concern with anxiety *situations* did not merely signal a trend toward seeing the individual in terms of relationships to others. In May's view, Freud's anxiety theory can also be shorn of its topology of id-ego-superego and of its relation to libido as a fixed quantity and reinterpreted in the light of conflicts of mutually exclusive goals and values between which the individual seeks to decide. May also holds that the person may "block off" or repress awareness of some poles of the conflict and that, in neurotic anxiety, previous conflicts are "reactivated," thus contributing to the disproportionate response that May, like Freud, sees as the difference between normal and neurotic anxiety.

It remains highly questionable whether Freud's topology

and libido theory can be totally removed from his anxiety theory, and the conflict of *freely chosen* goals and interpersonal
relationships of which May speaks substituted instead. Anxiety,
for Freud, was a psychobiological reaction to a danger, whether
real or imaginary, great or small. Freud spoke of anxiety as
"objectless," but never quite gave up the struggle to find what
object was involved. Further, for Freud, anxiety associated with
the external world was called "realistic," as compared with
anxiety originating in the superego or in the id. Anxiety, for
Freud, remained a psychobiological function of the ego, a signal
connected with the operation of the reality-pleasure principle,
with which the ego could control the id, and at the same time,
placate the superego and, though weakly, attain some measure
of intrapsychic organization.

       May's attempt here is really to dissociate Freud's descrip-
tion of anxiety from its philosophical presuppositions of determined mechanisms over which the Freudian man (*homo natura,*
as Binswanger calls him) can ultimately exercize no conscious
control. The focus of Freud's study of man is not on human
being as a whole, but is an organized view of psychological
mechanisms in their "normal" and "neurotic" manifestations.
May seeks to use the Freudian description of symptoms, the
symbol of separation or loss anxiety and the subjective reference of neurotic anxiety to grasp and illustrate *what it is that
happens* when the individual is anxious. At this point, however,
May is not discussing the question of *how* it is that an individual
can be anxious, a question that intrigued and baffled Freud.
May seeks to illuminate his own postulation of the conflicts
inherent in individuation and participation with the aid of
Freud's undoubtedly brilliant understanding of the *mechanisms
used* in anxiety. It is, however, only on the basis of jettisoning
the underlying Freudian determinism that such a rapprochement between the Freudian anxiety studies and May's conviction of the centrality of the sense of being could be said to be
effective. Here May does not speak in terms of the sense of
being, but the point remains true, because he has, from his earliest work, constantly affirmed his belief in conscious, responsible human freedom.

Further, it is in terms of what May later identifies as the ontological structure of anxiety as posing a threat to the sense of being that the distinction, to which both Freud and May subscribe, between "normal" and "neurotic" anxiety, becomes intelligible. "In greater or lesser degree, anxiety overwhelms the person's awareness of existence, blots out the sense of time, dulls the memory of the past, and erases the future—which is perhaps the most compelling proof of the fact that it attacks the center of one's being" (*Contributions,* p. 51). So far, Freud and May have both been concerned with the *response* of the individual who is anxious not with the structure of anxiety itself. It is from the work of Søren Kierkegaard that May draws the crucial insight into anxiety, seeing it as the individual confronting his freedom, and thus provides himself with another essential and integral component in the elaboration of his ontological approach, his "working science of man."

Anxiety as Understood: Kierkegaard

May notes that, for Kierkegaard, "Anxiety is the state of man ... when he confronts his freedom (*Meaning of Anxiety,* p. 33). Freedom for Kierkegaard (particularly in *The Concept of Dread,* 1969), asserts May, is possibility. It is the range of man's potentialities as they are born in his awareness of himself. It is expressed in the new experiences that man faces as he grows in individuality and independence. Yet, whenever the individual conceives a possibility, anxiety is also involved. The growth of "self-strength" progresses only with successful confrontation of this anxiety that inheres in freedom. Hence, May relates Kierkegaard's thought on anxiety to the "positive aspects of selfhood" (*Meaning of Anxiety,* pp. 232-234). For May, Kierkegaard's exploration of anxiety is basically oriented to the psychological development of the self in "enlarged self-awareness," or the heightened sense of being which May eventually identified as the distinguishing characteristic of man and the constructive goal of maturity and integrated existence. Here May did not yet use the term *sense of being* but spoke of *self-awareness* or *consciousness.*

In his study of Kierkegaard's theory of anxiety, May briefly surveys first what he considers the psychological disunity and compartmentalization of the nineteenth century. The tremendous development of the sciences, the multiple movements in art and literature all contributed to the difficulties of the person who vainly sought in the many theories a stable, whole, comprehensive view of man and of the purpose of his existence. Kierkegaard, says May, was one of those who strove to overcome the nineteenth-century rationalistic separation of man's reason and emotions, and to speak instead of the individual human being as a living, thinking, feeling, and acting unity.

May envisages Kierkegaard's intention in *The Concept of Dread* as the attempt "to describe phenomenologically the human situation" (*Meaning of Anxiety,* pp. 27-45). This, says May, Kierkegaard sees as a state of conflict born in self-awareness. Originally, the child, in a state of "dreaming innocence," is anxious only in the sense of having unspecific apprehension in learning and adventuring in new ways. The child is occupied in exploring his physical possibilities and his environment, while remaining more whim directed than decisive and hence not really exercising his freedom. It is only with the qualitative leap of the development of consciousness, of awareness of self, of good and evil, of possible crises in the process of individuation that anxiety acquires more content, "becomes reflective." Self-awareness for Kierkegaard, says May, makes possible "not only self-directed individual development, but also self-conscious historical development" (*Meaning of Anxiety,* p. 36). Thus, asserts May, Kierkegaard views man as no longer totally at the mercy of the undoubted determining natural forces of his situation or environment, but as now having the capacity for independence and choice that is born in his consciousness of himself, or his condition and possibilities. Hence, Kierkegaard holds that the greater the person's consciousness of himself, the greater his ability to will to be himself, and thus the more self or self-strength he develops.

This consciousness, however, involves anxiety. The inner conflict of choice, the immobilizing power of apprehension, and

the terrible fascination of the object of dread—of these Kierkegaard spoke in his tremendous insight into the sympathetic
antipathy and antipathetic sympathy that are characteristic of
anxious inner conflict. This ambivalence is, for Kierkegaard,
what distinguishes anxiety from fear, in which the desire is
solely to escape from the threat. Ambivalence within anxiety is
born in the apprehension of freedom both as creative possibility
and simultaneously as vulnerability to diminution or even dissolution of the self. May speaks with admiration of Kierkegaard's penetration into this phenomenon and says that such
inner conflict, such simultaneous sympathy for and dread of the
possibility of dissolution, is familiar in clinical psychology. May
cites two illustrations of such conflict: The patient severely ill
with a physical ailment is both fascinated by and dreads the
possibility of death, while the neurotic patient fears and is fascinated by his own desires, thus engendering persistent, gnaw-
ing, inner conflict.

Thus freedom is not experienced as a simple possession.
In May's words, it is not acquired in a "simple accretion"
(*Meaning of Anxiety*, p. 35). Freedom, as the apprehension by
the conscious self both of its possibility and vulnerability, is
rather a process of tension between man's consciousness of his
potentialities, his desire to retrench to the known safety and to
ignore the possible, and the simultaneous desire to reach out
and actualize the possible. The tonality of this process, then, is
anxiety. The range, strength, and actualization of one's freedom
depend on how one relates to oneself at every moment and
whether one can confront the anxiety inherent in freedom and
move ahead despite it.

At this point, says May, Kierkegaard brings in the question of responsibility and guilt as necessarily inhering in the
denial of possibility and even in the acceptance and actualization of possibility. Since every choice or creative willing means
a break with the current situation, and implies also that other
possibilities have been rejected in favor of the one chosen, guilt
is a necessary corollary of conscious choice. The more possibilities an individual has, the more creative, sensitive, and perceptive he is, the greater his burden of guilt and anxiety in the

exercise of his freedom. In May's view, sexuality, although not in itself considered by Kierkegaard or by May himself as necessarily a source of anxiety or guilt, was envisaged by Kierkegaard as a clear example of the problem of individuation in relation to community, the latter affording the context of individual creative willing and choice. Hence, for May himself, and in May's view, for Kierkegaard too, sexuality often becomes the central issue that occasions the resurgence of the anxiety of freedom.

May goes on to examine Kierkegaard's study of the uselessness of attempting to avoid anxiety or guilt, particularly by means of a belief in fate or chance. The person who seeks to avoid anxiety does so by seeking to ignore or shut out his own possibility, which was the source of his anxiety. Denial of possibility can only result in continual negation in order to avoid the guilt of denial and the anxiety that such denial and guilt generate in their turn. Thus, the person withdraws in a vicious circle of "shut-up-ness," as Kierkegaard calls it, no longer conscious, reserved, and thoughtful, as in freedom, but cowering, rigid, timorous, and unfree, wanting no contact with others, locked in neurotic, self-devouring dread of future anxious consciousness of the possible. May briefly surveys admiringly Kierkegaard's acute understanding of the reactions of such "shut-up" people, as evidenced in rigid dogmatism or fanaticism to allay anxiety of free choice, and as witnessed in activism or activity for its own sake, a macabre dance of "keeping busy" and surrounding themselves with feverish, noisy, false "life" in order to distract themselves from the pain of their anxious consciousness.

In May's view, "Kierkegaard writes in his most engaging vein about anxiety as a 'school' " (Meaning of Anxiety, p. 43). One can allay anxiety only temporarily with "artful" measures, since anxiety will return and search the inmost corners of the perceptive soul. On what May terms the negative side, education at the school of anxiety consists of frankly facing, accepting, and dealing with the human situation, the fact of death, and other aspects of contingency. On the positive side, says May, acceptance and constructive use of anxiety enables one to move through and despite anxiety-creating experiences toward fulfillment in freedom of the infinite possibilities in personality. It is Kierkegaard's belief, says May, that the individual who relates constructively to the endless limits, constrictions, difficulties, and obstacles of his contingent condition, becomes educated to inner faith, to conscious, responsible, mature "self-strength," and confidence.

Anxiety, for Kierkegaard, then, is an inner state that attacks the core of one's existence and that threatens to destroy the self. When Kierkegaard emphasized that anxiety was the "fear of nothingness" (*Meaning of Anxiety,* p. 193), says May, he was speaking of the fear of becoming nothing, the fear of the dissolution of the self. Compare Freud's assertion that anxiety, in contrast to fear, is "objectless." This, says May, is what Tillich views as the apprehension of nonbeing and may be experienced as the threat of death, that is, of physical death or psychological loss of meaning, itself spiritual death. Fear of the dissolution of the self is the terror of vulnerability, of freedom, of the possibility of loss, experienced in the awareness of finiteness that is anxiety (Tillich, 1952, pp. 32-36 on "nonbeing").

Thus, to sum up, one's sense of one's existence, or sense of being, is always inextricably linked with the sense of the vulnerability of that existence. May's study of Kierkegaard, however, emphasizes rather the positive side, the relation of anxiety to freedom, the courageous confronting of the anxiety inherent in freedom and the consequent development of self-strength and mature, conscious responsibility. It is not without significance that in May's "Summary and Synthesis of Theories of Anxiety" (*Meaning of Anxiety,* pp. 190-234), the final section is concerned with anxiety and the development of the self, of which development, in May's view, Kierkegaard's psychological exploration evinces such tremendous understanding. Clearly, then, May correlates Kierkegaard's understanding of anxiety with what May calls the "positive aspects of selfhood—freedom, enlarged self-awareness, responsibility" (*Meaning of Anxiety,* p. 233).

In the next section I will trace the development of May's own theory of anxiety and its relation to those very positive aspects, and will explicate the emergence in his thought of the importance for therapy of anxiety as ontological, as rooted in man's existence itself, as essentially and inalienably linked with the sense of being, with the challenge of courageous living as an individual-in-participation, as a being-in-the-world.

Toward an Ontology of Anxiety

In his book, *The Meaning of Anxiety,* May studied the various theories of anxiety offered by the major psychologists and sociologists and referred in some considerable detail to current biological and cultural approaches to the problem. A lengthy series of case studies in Part Two of the book parallels and offers some illustration and application of the theoretical discussion. In the final chapter of Part One, "Summary and Synthesis of Theories of Anxiety," May offers his own formulation of the problem of anxiety in the light of the other theories.

He begins to examine the nature of anxiety, the experience of threat, of uncertainty and helplessness, by asking what it is that is threatened when an individual is anxious. When the answer proves to be something essential to, or "in the core of" the person, May offers a comprehensive theoretical definition of anxiety as *"the apprehension cued off by a threat to some value which the individual holds essential to his existence as a personality"* (*Meaning of Anxiety,* p. 191). The menace, says May, may be to the person's life, such as illness, accident or the ultimate threat of death, or perhaps to those beliefs that the person holds to be synonymous with his life, such as the ability to fulfill his chosen role as a husband or a father, or as a wage-earner and supporter of a family. The threat may be to some other strongly held value or symbol, such as patriotism, social success, financial security, family or social structure, or religious or political structure; again, it is question of a value basic enough to be essential to the existence of the person.

Since, for May, a value held to be essential to one's existence is also essential to one's security as a person, or to the strength of what he later called the *sense of being,* the focus of the attack of anxiety is seen to be that security. At this point, May must, and does, distinguish between fear and anxiety.

Since fear is, as May sees it, precisely *not* an attack on the essential person nor a vague, diffuse threat, it must be said to be peripheral. The stimulus of fear can be located and dealt with by appropriate action whereas the very power of anxiety is in its uncertainty and its threat to the core or essential being.

The value threatened is the "cue" to apprehension. But what is the apprehension itself? It is, asserts May, "a subjective, objectless experience" (*Meaning of Anxiety*, p. 192), not to be confused with the danger situation that called it forth. Here we find a twentieth-century psychotherapist confirming, and supporting with clinical data in the second part of his study, the insight of Kierkegaard a hundred years before into anxiety as a psychological state (Kierkegaard, 1969, p. 82), and confirming also the assertion of Freud that "anxiety relates to the condition and ignores the object" (Freud, 1968a, p. 403). May's formulation of anxiety, however, seeks to attain a broader perspective than that of either Freud or Kierkegaard; this May seeks to do by integrating philosophical understanding and psychological theorizing with clinical data and a broad appreciation of cultural factors. Whereas Freud viewed anxiety fundamentally from the point of view of reactions and mechanisms, and whereas it was Kierkegaard who spoke of anxiety as the dread inherent in existence, May is clearly seeking, although he does not say so, to encompass both of these attempts at elucidation by grounding both in his own understanding of anxiety as cued by *any* threat that is basic enough to jeopardize the person's sense of self. In threatening the core or essence or being of the personality, anxiety, as May sees it, strikes at the very basis of the psychological structure on which one's clear perception of one's self and one's world is built. Hence, in a state of severe anxiety, the physiological reactions of blurred eyesight, tightened chest, and breathing difficulties will inhibit the individual's "physical" perception of himself and his world, while his mental confusion inhibits, distorts, or prevents his awareness of himself and his world.

This is no longer to explain the immobilizing, paralyzing quality of what Freud called "inexpedient" anxiety by referring solely to the reaction of the individual as inappropriate to the stimulus as objectively considered. This is, rather, to correlate such "inexpedience" with the understanding of anxiety as an attack on or threat to the very basis of selfhood or being, however minor or inconsequential the objective threat may appear to an observer.

Seeing anxiety, then, as at base the Kierkegaardian fear "of becoming nothing" or as the apprehension of contingency, May asserts that fear of death is a common *form* of anxiety and looks on it as normal. Furthermore, he asserts that *Urangst* (original, primitive, or "source" anxiety), or the anxiety inhering in the apprehension of human situatedness and vulnerability, does not necessarily lead to neurotic defense mechanisms except that death in some form becomes the focus or symbol of other conflicts and problems within the individual (*Meaning of Anxiety*, p. 195). It is quite clear that May does not, at this point, hold that death in itself is the direct source and prototype of all anxiety; furthermore, he is convinced that the more immediate and pressing form of anxiety is that of spiritual nonbeing, of emptiness, that is to say, the threat of meaninglessness. He recalls specifically Kierkegaard's expression "the fear of nothingness," and asserts that the loss of psychological or spiritual meaning that one identifies with one's inner self and aspirations, or holds dear as one's "reason for living," is exactly the "fear of nothing" (*Meaning of Anxiety*, p. 193).

While Freud envisioned anxiety in a mechanistic context, eventually seeing it both as a danger signal from the ego and as a reaction to the danger, May, on the other hand, sees selfhood dynamically and sees anxiety as nonbeing in various forms threatening the core of the person who, depending on the strength of his selfhood or sense of being, may react either constructively or unconstructively. Hence, for May, the self does not affirm itself *in order to evade anxiety* (which would in May's view, be a disintegrative response) but *in spite of anxiety* (which is, in May's view, an integrating, constructive response of the strong self). Implicit in this view is the possibility of conceiving of anxiety as an ontological structure, although May, in his discussion of the *forms* of anxiety, does not as yet give evidence of having explicitly and clearly attained this insight.

That the evasion of anxiety is ultimately impossible (that is to say, that anxiety is an inalienable mode of existence) is also implicit in May's distinction between "normal" and "neurotic" anxiety. It might be pointed out here that these terms are a case of transferred epithet and terminological clarification and precision would disclose that it is not the anxiety in itself that May holds to be normal or neurotic, but the method of coping with or evading it that he characterizes as normal or neurotic. Believing as he does in the subjective reference of anxiety (for example, an apparently insignificant threat, seen objectively, may stimulate an apparently inordinate response), May is concerned here with the normal or neurotic ways of behaving while in the state of anxiety.

Normal anxiety, however, May defines as reaction proportionate to the threat and not involving repression or intrapsychic conflicts, while neurotic anxiety is declared to be reaction that is *dis*proportionate to the threat and that *does* involve repression and other intrapsychic conflicts. May himself seems to sense that these definitions might seem incomplete and adds that a useful distinction between the two kinds of anxiety is *ex post facto* or made after the fact, that is, when the threat, the anxiety experienced and the resultant behavior can be objectively considered. Now, while it is true that intrapsychic conflicts are themselves responsible for the disproportionate reaction, that is, the neurotic element, it is also true that the *un*involvement of intrapsychic conflicts was precisely responsible for the proportionate reaction of the normal person. In both cases, however, whatever the threat, it was felt as a danger to the self, or it undermined what May later calls the *individual's sense of his own existence or being,* whether that being is secure and free (normal and therefore capable of coping) or insecure and constricted (neurotic and therefore defensive).

Although May seeks to distinguish closely between the "kinds" of anxiety, he does not separate them entirely and concludes that "in most persons the two kinds . . . are intermingled" (*Meaning of Anxiety,* p. 195). He attains a partial solution to this difficulty when he recognizes that people who react to relatively minor threats as if they were catastrophes are "inordinately vulnerable" to threats. But May does not explain why such people should be so vulnerable, except to refer to previous repressions or childhood conflicts. One might infinitely regress in such "explanation" and ask why the original repression had occurred. Later, however, as has been seen in Chapter One of this book, May recognizes the integrational role of the sense of being and its crucial relation to anxiety (*Contributions,* pp. 50-51). Again, in *The Meaning of Anxiety,* when he shows the strong circular relationship between neurotic anxiety and inner conflict and hostility (pp. 210-215), he has almost clarified this question. His psychological study of anxiety alone might not lead to a comprehensive envisioning of anxiety as ontological, as an inalienable mode of existence, but an ontology of anxiety already inheres implicitly in his conclusions concerning the forms of anxiety.

May now turns to the cultural and individual factors in anxiety. The individual's anxiety, he says, "is conditioned by the fact that he lives in a given culture at a particular point in the historical development of that culture" (*Meaning of Anxiety,* p. 215). While one may take exception to the strength of the term *conditioned,* which could imply a radical historical relativism, there is no doubt that each person, while remaining a free and self-determining individual, is subject to the cultural determining factors that offer both the context and some of the content of anxiety as experienced. In this sense of cultural determinants as context and content, the term *conditioned* is not incompatible with human freedom. It must, then, be taken in this sense, not only because without freedom there can be no anxiety, but also because it is clear that it is in this sense that May wishes it to be understood. "The understanding of anxiety can thus never be separated from ethical symbols, which are one aspect of the human being's normal milieu. . . . It is the essence of man's nature to interpret his values in the context of his relation to other people and their expectations" (*Anxiety and Values,* p. 76).

May distinguishes two aspects of the problem of anxiety and culture. First, the kinds or forms (occasions) of anxiety are "culturally conditioned in the respect that *the values or goals*

held by an individual to be essential to his existence as a person-
ality are largely cultural products" (*Meaning of Anxiety,* p.
215). As an example of these goals, he cites the social prestige
goal of individual competitive success and its related value of
strong individuality. Both, according to May, were originally
inherited from Renaissance individualism and strengthened by
Victorian voluntarism, and by the Spinozistic and Leibnizian
beliefs in universal reason and harmony. As all of these beliefs
are degenerating and depreciating in our present age, the time is
out of joint for the man who tries to put his trust in them. The
radical trend toward conformism is, as May sees it, a development from the loneliness and isolation of individualism overemphasized. Correspondingly, overemphasis for centuries on
social power and success at the expense of genuine, free, social
participation has often resulted in exaggerated collectivism and
in social organization that engulfs the individual in a traumatic
anonymity (for example, being seen "only" as a number) from
which he seeks to extricate himself by emphasizing his individuality once more.

May's second aspect of the problem of anxiety and culture is interdependent with the quality (or kinds) of anxiety.
"The *quantities* of anxiety experienced by a given individual are
conditioned by the degree of unity and stability in his culture"
(*Meaning of Anxiety,* p. 215; *Anxiety and Values,* pp. 72-83;
Love and Will, pp. 13-33). Given a stable culture, the individual
has time to orient himself, to step back from anxiety-creating
situations, and to regain perspective in his sense of being. Thus,
his sense of self and world are stronger, more resilient, and his
anxious reactions correspondingly less intense. If, however, the
individual's cultural milieu is in a state of traumatic change and
disunity, as in the present era, if hitherto firm values (for example, the indissolubility of marriage, the rights of the human
fetus, and the worth of the individual) are being questioned and
doubted, the individual has no recourse to society, to an
"authority," in moments of fundamental decision. He must try
to find within himself a center of courage and strength, in place
of the basic social patterns on which he depended for his security and criteria. In many cases, precisely because of over-

emphasis and overreliance on participation in collectivism, the person turns within himself only to find that he does not have a center of strength within himself.

May's next point, that "anxiety and hostility are inter-related" (*Meaning of Anxiety*, p. 222), follows directly from his discussion of anxiety and culture. Anxiety gives rise to hostility, says May, precisely because in anxiety, one's selfhood is attacked in some ultimate way and one resents the occasions of one's pain, anguish, helplessness, and inner conflict. If changes in society are at the source of one's anxiety, one will tend to resent those responsible. The current racial conflict between the supporters of integration and the supporters of segregation in America's Deep South is an example of this kind. What each side feels is threatened is its selfhood. In other words, the sense of being-in-the-world becomes dominated by a sense of being-*threatened*-in-the-world. On the segregationist side, selfhood is identified with a whole "white" way of life and a conviction of "superiority" of race, often rationalized and "justified" by "scientific" intelligence-quotient figures. On the integrationist side, selfhood is identified with attainment of equal civil rights and is threatened by social restrictions that undermine the black man's human dignity and constrict his and his children's future. Anxiety, cultural factors such as education, unequal opportunity, and repressed or even open hostility are all essential components of the situation. This is perhaps a more clear-cut case than either South Africa or Rhodesia, where recognition of black civil rights would be likely to accomplish almost immediate economic and political ruin for the tiny minority of white rulers. Self-preservation is here interpreted as necessitating segregation and is again "justified" on the basis that the majority is "incapable as yet of self-government." Economic ruin, however, would not necessarily follow integration in the Deep South but the whites would undoubtedly lose the possibility of finding confirmation in everyday existence of their belief in the "superiority" of the white race.

Individuals in a position of dependence in society, such as children, pensioners, and the infirm, may evince in their anxiety considerable hostility. In a similar way, the neurotic individual, in seeking to turn his anxiety into an objective fear rather than an objectless apprehension, may show marked hostility to the persons on whom he is most dependent. Or he may try to repress the hostility through fear of alienating such persons, and hence will generate even more anxiety (lest the hostility break through) and hostility (because "they" have made him anxious). As his awareness of his hostility and anxiety intensifies, his sense of being—his awareness of and perspective on himself and his world—becomes diminished, rendering him more helpless still in the circle of anxiety and hostility.

Anxiety is a state of such basic tension and apprehension that it must be dealt with in some way. The neurotic person, as has been described, seeks to evade it by repression, by inhibition, or by any method that will allow him not to confront his problem. May calls these the "negative methods of avoiding anxiety," which obviate the conflict by "shrinking the area of awareness" (*Meaning of Anxiety*, p. 225), or what Kierkegaard called "shut-up-ness." The "normal" person, too, may choose to avoid anxiety by affirming a rigid set of rules (whether moral, scientific, religious, or so on), which can be relied on to allay his anxiety somewhat as he relinquishes some measure of freedom and responsibility in order blindly to follow "the rules." Hence, in collectivistic societies there is an inevitable growth of a bureaucracy whose purpose is specifically to implement the rules. Again, this method sacrifices individual freedom and responsibility and allays some anxiety by shrinking the awareness of possibility, overemphasizing the participation pole of being-in-the-world and reconstituting the person's sense of being as validated by social approval.

The "normal" person is, however, free to confront his anxiety constructively and by using it as what May calls a "learning experience," or as a means of gauging possibility, is enabled to "move through it," realistically. Such positive confrontation of anxiety by courage to accept it and move ahead is dependent, says May, on the individual's subjective realization that *"the values to be gained in moving ahead are greater than those to be gained by escape"* (*Meaning of Anxiety*, p. 229). The question implicit in the original definition of anxiety as a threat to the values identified with the individual's existence has now been answered. May holds that the converse statement is the only constructive solution. The individual moves through anxiety-creating experiences without succumbing to them or seeking to evade them precisely because the values (symbols) that he identifies with his being exercise more influence over him than does the threat. This is to say that the pull exercised by firm belief in and desire to affirm a strongly held value will be greater than the threat or the attraction of security at the price of relinquishing or denying that value. This, for May, is a kind of religious affirmation, though not necessarily orthodox or denominational. Earlier, in Chapter One of this book, speaking of personality, I mentioned May's view of religious tension and of religion, which he sees as the ultimate value that the person affirms. Such "religious" affirmation is an elemental call to the deepest nature of the individual in terms of his ultimate value or concern. The choice of value or symbol will, of course, vary greatly in content and context from culture to culture, and from person to person within a given culture.

Since the individual can never be without anxiety, which inheres in human contingency and freedom, and must move through anxiety-creating experiences if he is not to constrict his individuation and development to the point of neurosis, it follows, although May does not yet assert it explicitly, that the tonality of perceived potentiality is anxiety. The ultimate tension or perception of a gap, the religious tension of May's earliest definition of personality, and the guilt feeling that inheres in such perception and tension, are now seen to depend precisely on this recognition of potentiality. Further, guilt and guilt feeling must now be construed as contingent on anxiety, while inherent in every situation of perceived possibility. It is only the neurotic who, seeking to evade anxiety, falls into *morbid* guilt. The normal person, who courageously confronts his anxiety and moves through it because of an essential value, is enabled to accept creatively his limitations and contingency, his responsibility to himself and to others, and to develop what May calls "the positive aspects of selfhood" (*Meaning of Anxiety,* p. 233). The greater the individual's capacity to bear anxiety, the more freedom he achieves and the more he enlarges the scope of his activities. This growth again increases his confidence and the strength of his sense of being. Any envisioning of the self-dynamism as solely protective May sees as an overemphasis of the negative function of anxiety. The positive aspect of anxiety, for May, is the perception of possibility, the attaining and maintaining of a strong sense of being through continuous, courageous affirmation of self and world.

It is not surprising to find May accepting a mitigated form of Otto Rank's idea of the birth trauma (*Meaning of Anxiety*, pp. 128-131). May accepts birth as symbolic of all anxiety experiences, as highly illuminative of the problem of individuation, since the element of inner conflict in anxiety may be viewed as inherent in the "breaking away" from a secure position to something new and untried. But in Rank's view, the actual experience of being born, of being "ejected" from the security and pleasure of the womb, involves such severe psychological shock and anxiety, both in the separation from the mother and in the change in state, that the intense "primal" anxiety generated must be either repressed or "abreacted" (converted and worked out). Every development in man's life, even death, is seen to be a conscious or unconscious effort to return to the womb, thus effecting a gradual catharsis of the intense primal anxiety. For Rank, anxiety inhered in individuation, because it was a special transference of the original separation experience, that is, the separation from the mother. May, however, does not accept a connection of anxiety with the literal birth of the infant, as this would imply physiological mechanisms oriented toward the satisfaction of the primary security need and would exclude existential human freedom and choice. He must also, and does, reject the postulation of anxiety as deprivation of prenatal security. May does not, however, refer to Rank's later, modified view of individuation as a series of symbolic births and rebirths, each a painful separation from the comfortable or at least accustomed past situation in order to reach out for a new potentiality, "the creation of an individual cosmos, whether it be now physically our own child, creatively our own work or spiritually our own self" (Rank, cited in

Mullahy, 1955, p. 178). A symbolic "birth" as "prototype" of all anxiety, however, May does find not only acceptable but rich in meaning and says that if it were not for some new "potentiality crying to be 'born,' we would not experience anxiety" (*Contributions,* p. 52). Yet birth is not, for May, the basic *source* of all anxiety, paradoxical as this position may seem.

Although obviously implied up to this point, man as responsible, embodied consciousness had not fully and explicitly entered into his own in May's theory of anxiety. In his second essay in *Existence,* however, entitled "Contributions of Existential Psychotherapy," May moves from the earlier exploration of the expression of anxiety to a rather brief but fundamental consideration of anxiety as an ontological structure of Dasein, of man as being-in-the-world, as a thinking-acting-feeling-living unity, to use May's words. May sees all forms of anxiety as ultimately grounded in this ontological structure, since they are recognized as particularized manifestations of this structure.

"Man," says May, "is the being who can be conscious of, and therefore responsible for, his existence" (*Contributions,* p. 41). Freedom and hence possibility or the becomingness of man are then interdependent with man's sense of his being, his consciousness of his own existence in his world. To be fully aware of oneself as existing, one must grasp also that one is becoming, and that at some unknown future moment one will cease to exist. Existence is never automatic. Not only can man choose to die, he can also choose to live. But he cannot choose *not* to die. Hence death is, paradoxically, the only absolute fact of life. Awareness of this threat gives an absolute quality to life; that is, it invests one's existence with the awareness of time, of nonbeing, or of anxiety. Thus, in May's view, anxiety is not merely a situational apprehension or an isolated affective reaction, but an ontological structure "rooted in (man's) very existence as such" (*Contributions,* p. 50; see also *Love and Will,* p. 301). For May, then, the basic *source* of all anxiety is death. Whereas birth is the *symbolic representation* of the going-outside-of-oneself in reaching for a new potentiality, the structure or source of anxiety itself is the apprehension of nonbeing, or in Kierkegaardian terms, the fear of *becoming nothing.* Such apprehension involves the whole self, whether the threat be of physical, mental, moral, or spiritual dissolution or diminution of the self. Whereas fear is a reaction among other reactions, is a specific affect like pleasure or sadness, anxiety is the individual's inner awareness that his existence can be destroyed or diminished, "that he can lose himself and his world, that he can become nothing" (*Contributions*, p. 50). His sense of being, then, is not only a sense of being-in-the-world, but also a sense of being vulnerable to total loss of that being-in-the-world.

This ontological structure is now seen to underlie both the normal and neurotic anxieties spoken of earlier. The difference, says May, lies in the vulnerability of the neurotic person, and in the increased tension and thus increased vulnerability of his self when he refuses to cope with his initial anxiety. Neurotic compulsive symptoms are a protective development by an unstable self that senses a basic threat to its being, although to an objective observer the threat may appear peripheral and minimal. Hence, normal and neurotic anxiety are now seen to be distinguishable, but not separable. The experience in both cases is an ontological one; it is the reactions that underlie the distinction. Neurotic anxiety, says May, is "the end-product of unfaced normal ontological anxiety" (*Contributions*, p. 55). Since anxiety inheres in the perception of potentiality and hence is ontological, then guilt or the denial of potentiality must also be ontological. Neurotic or morbid guilt, for May, is "the result of unconfronted, ontological guilt" (*Contributions*, p. 55).

Summary

By this fundamental shift from a psychological study of anxiety situations and reactions, and the forms or kinds of expression of anxiety, to a basic understanding of anxiety as ontological, it becomes possible to understand why anxiety is so pervasive and radical in the contemporary world and why an elucidation of its nature is absolutely essential to the psychotherapist. Anxiety, as an ontological structure of human existence, is inalienable, inevitable; the individual question is simply its form and intensity, and the resolution of anxiety situations in one's life. In a stable society or culture, the ethical symbols or values can be so widely affirmed as to provide the person with a ready bulwark, a constructive method of channeling his anxiety into action and solid content for the perception and realization of potentialities (*Significance of Symbols,* pp. 30-33; see also Heer, 1961, pp. 101-125). In a disintegrating, transitional, crisis-ridden period such as some consider ours to be, the symbols and myths of the culture, the values by which people lived before, are questioned and doubted until their unifying power and strength can be badly eroded. The defined limits of Victorian morality; the quiet, secure acceptance of a code of social ethics; the inherited Renaissance belief in strong, self-reliant individuals; the symbol of the wage earner as self-respecting—these values among others have been undermined and corroded by many changes, by the "sexual revolution," the loneliness and alienation of an increasingly computerized world, awareness of limited resources and of great need, and even by the ever-present threat of unemployment, with its corresponding soul-destroying dependence on government welfare services. Yet such developments can also give rise to new creative possibilities for independence to be seen in polar relation with dependence, generosity, and love, and computerized systems can be seen as freeing and as serving the purposes of creative men rather than as controlling them.

Men are not isolated individuals, but must live and work in community, whether through ideas or in actual, physical community. To be a self and to have a world, as has been said, are interdependent. The capacity for consciousness of self and world, the sense of one's being, is expressed through symbols that convey individual and participatory meaning. An individual's sense of being is not given, but evolves gradually as the individual grows in consciousness, grasps his cultural, biological, psychological self and takes into himself his choice of symbols. The expression of his choice will usually derive from the symbols generally accepted in his culture, and his central symbols are those that he deems essential to his existence as a self, such as religious belief, civil rights, social success, and love of his

country. The process of maturation involves a continuous transformation of the original values held, according as the process
of individuation and participation widens and deepens the existence of the person. For example, a child outgrows dependence
on a "security blanket" or favorite toy and no longer feels
threatened when it is not close at hand. Similarly, the youthful
desire to please parents by success at school gives way to a more
symbolic wish to attain social success in order to feel important
or loved, and at the same time, gradually becomes a desire to
live up to self-imposed goals or standards. Maturity is related to
the increasing capacity to orient one's existence in the light of
long-term goals that are not purely oriented toward self, but
toward expression of man's fundamental condition of being-in-
the-world, that is, toward loving participation in a world of
others, toward giving as well as receiving.

When the central symbols in a given culture are in process
of change, it is because at least some individuals in that culture
are in process of examining and reinterpreting hitherto unquestioned values. In their efforts to sense their being-in-the-world
and finding themselves unable to accept values once affirmed as
absolute, they experiment and seek to find new ways of envisaging and relating to their world. Through his participation in the
world, each self holds values that are, to some extent, "conditioned" or given content by the culture at his particular time.
His freedom in relation to this element of conditioning is precisely the freedom of choice, whether to accept or reject, to
change entirely or modify in some way the goals that culture
holds up to him as desirable or even essential. This choice he
makes in terms of his sense of his own existence, his sense of
being in the world, his place and purpose, and the ultimate goal
that is interrelated with his sense of being. The self who vali-
dates itself, or whose sense of being is built solely in terms of
conformity with everyone else, is a "radar type" who listens for
hints from the crowd around him. Such a self, in time of radical
disruption and disagreement about the basic symbols and goals,
is receiving confused signals and hence may be unable to respond decisively. In his vacillation, he experiences less and less a
sense of identity or of being, as his bewilderment increases.

Conformity, which was his main chosen method of allaying loneliness, anxiety, and uncertainty, only achieves inner emptiness and ultimate meaninglessness in a general, although perhaps gradual, diminution of the sense of being.

The challenge, then, as May sees it, is that of understanding and facing with imagination the changes and upheavals of contemporary life. The individual must learn to be open to the possibility of good in change, thus using his anxiety as constructive sensitivity rather than as constant apprehension of disaster. To have this stance is not to be an unrealistic optimist, but to open oneself to the constructive, to make the creative decision to be firm and clear in one's approach to anxiety-creating situations, and to become creatively decisive and open to new forms of participation.

Since, for May, the first practical step in tackling any problem is to understand its nature and cause, it is a necessary first step in psychotherapy, as he sees it, to examine and learn to know anxiety and to accept it as ontological, inalienable, and inevitable in human existence. Only then can the therapist enter into an understanding with the patient of the expression of anxiety in his particular existence, of its form and intensity, and help him to understand and confront it courageously.

It is, then, clearly to be seen that while May fully acknowledges the capacity of Freud's theories to throw light on *what happens in anxiety,* on what the anxious person is doing, May's own theory has a very different basis and broader reach than the mechanistic basis on which Freud's theories were constructed. Clearly, too, May's understanding owes much to the onto-psychological approach of Kierkegaard, whose insights he seeks to integrate into everyday psychotherapeutic practice. This is all the more striking as May's starting point was precisely *not* that of philosophical inquiry, but was the everyday problems and troubles of the individual patient in his psychotherapeutic practice. May's envisioning of anxiety as ontological gives depth and meaning to the situational anxieties of daily life, as these are to be understood as apprehension in "more minute form a dozen times a day" of the normal, inalienable, ontological awareness of contingency (*Emergence,* p. 3).

In man's very consciousness of the disintegration of his past symbols, there is implicit a seeking of reorientation. "We are seeking," says May, "the basis on which a morality for a new age can be founded" (*Love and Will,* p. 16). The courage to accept into himself his uncertainty and anxiety is a prerequisite of man's search for new values or bases, or a new formulation of the sense of his existence, in the light of which he can find purpose, strength, and unity. If anxiety propels us into that search, it is creative vitality or love and intentional responsible molding or will that must inform and guide it. In the acceptance of his being and his awareness of his vulnerability or nonbeing, man affirms a pattern of living creativity, a courage not merely to be but to reach out in love, to participate with other people, ideas, and things. Out of his psychotherapeutic experience, his understanding of the mechanisms explored by Freud, and his affinity with and experiential grasp of Kierkegaard's insights, May has developed a cogent philosophical inquiry into the nature of anxiety as an ontological structure of human existence, as the inner spring of man's reaching out toward the world. Since each achievement reveals new, and, in a sense, higher, possibilities and combinations, man seeks to place more and more emphasis not merely on becoming, but on *oriented* becoming, to borrow Allport's phrase. Hence, it is to love, or the creative vitality of individuation and participation, and to will, or responsible, conscious choice, that May turns as he seeks the constructive use of normal anxiety in attaining the positive aspects of selfhood.

THREE

Role
of Love

Love is an ontological concept. Its
emotional element is a consequence of
its ontological nature.
Paul Tillich, *Systematic Theology*

Our century has witnessed a tremendous upheaval in the domain of human love, one of the most discussed and widely misunderstood topics of our time. Fragmented by perspectivistic
studies, love has become a biological phenomenon, a chemical
attraction, a momentary whim. In travestied and often sensa-
tionalized form, advertisers, for example, use the human desire
to love and be loved, and more particularly, the attendant desire
to be attractive, as a means to create an ever-growing demand for
products from mouthwash to hygienic footsoap. Love has become a "sexual revolution," a best-seller, a popular song, a how-

to-do-it book, a rallying cry, and is frequently cited in support of pragmatic legislation based on popular demand.

At the level of popular experience and understanding, one can discern in this upheaval a degeneration and emasculation of ideas on love that previously exerted a powerful influence on the lives of people. In our own time, love is not generally seen to imply and encompass friendship, esteem, understanding, forbearance, compassion, joy, kindness, nor that form of altruism that is grounded in the unqualified affirmation of the being of the other as person. What *popular* experience and understanding disclose is a conception of love at once ambivalent and exaggerated. A brief exploration of a striking historical analogy may serve to bring into focus this ambivalence and exaggeration.

In the twelfth-century songs of love (chansons d'amour) of the troubadours and the courtly romances of the Grail and the Round Table, for example, we find immortalized two distinct life-styles (Heer, 1961, pp. 157-196). On the one hand, there was the cult of the unattainable and perfect, the code of courtly love or chivalry, based on the supremacy of the aristocracy, which in its later, degenerated form was so aptly delineated and lampooned by Cervantes. On the other hand, there was the opposing notion of the procreative and functional aspect of sexuality, the enjoyment of which was considered "lower" or "earthy" and which, although originally integral to love, became positively excluded from the cult of the "perfect."

Although a woman could be chosen to be an ideal or lady patroness—only a highborn lady could be chosen for such a role —she was not expected to take an active part, but to be an inspiration, a source of moral strength. However, the two modes of existence, pursuit of the perfect and ordinary sexual enjoyment, could be exercised by the one man, the first in aristocratic surroundings, the second among the peasantry, and were not at first considered to be in any way related to or influential on each other. Hence the droit de seigneur, the right of the lord of the manor to have sexual intercourse with his female vassals on their wedding night, could be considered to be a privilege of rank to be exercised on the peasantry. Later, however, the two modes came to be considered to be mutually exclusive. In the Round Table legends, for example, where the courtly quest for the Grail is an outstanding instance of chivalry as *cult*, Lancelot, whose aim was to be the Perfect Knight, can no longer be so once he has "fallen" to the level of sexual love. It is given to his son Galahad to be the Perfect Knight and to find the Grail, because Galahad has remained pure of heart, virgin, and therefore unsullied by sexual love.

With the decline of chivalrous or courtly love and the emergence of the middle or trading classes, a curious residue of the old opposition continued to influence popular experience and understanding of love and, consequently, of human relations in general. For example, emphasis was laid more and more on the contractual aspect of marriage—hitherto of grave importance mainly in political or royal marriages—wherein primacy of feeling, enjoyment, or happiness over a sound business contract was unthinkable. This attitude inevitably increased the likelihood of sexual expression outside of marriage, a state of affairs to be conducted with discretion by the husband and ignored or at least tolerated by the wife, who was not herself usually permitted such excursions. This ambivalence is evidenced, for example, in the Regency and Victorian consciousness, which could extend to allowing both for the discreet indulgence by men in a distinctively free-and-easy "bohemian" life-style and for the simultaneous requiring of unimpeachable sexual faithfulness and observance of the "proprieties" in their wives. Such ambivalence toward love was also largely responsible, for example, for the repressions and inhibitions of the "nice" women of the later nineteenth century, whose training and moral education were based on stoic acceptance of, but inner revulsion toward, the necessary bodily aspect of life. For such women, it was a question of living in a society where propriety was the cardinal virtue and where fine sensibility was shown only in accord with a strict code of etiquette.

In this atmosphere, stiflingly repressive of real feeling, where displays of emotion were frowned on and a rigid protocol subtended by a belief in the power of determination was the mode of existence of one's life, it is not surprising that at the level of popular experience and understanding the psychological insights of Freud were initially construed as shocking and ab-horrent. Nevertheless, the conception of man that underlay Freudian psychological insight was not irreconcilable with a generally accepted pragmatist ethic that drew its inspiration from the reality and promise of natural science and from a cate-gorical belief in perfectibility and progress at the source of which lay the Industrial Revolution. The very force of popular rejection of Freudian insight was itself indicative of the accu-racy with which Freud had read his society. Yet the impact of Freudianism generally precipitated recognition of a need to re-evaluate popular self-understanding. The new "freedom" of approach both to sexuality, and to human relations in general, that issued from this popular reevaluation did not tend to rehabilitate the old search for the ideal (as in the Round Table legends, for example), but, rather, served to continue the oppo-sition between "higher" love (idealistic or sublimated) and "lower" love (carnal, even marital). The old dichotomy between "ideal" and "instinctual" in the domain of human love con-tinued to exert its influence.

In the contemporary world, at the prereflective, uncriti-cal level, these two approaches have, in the area of human love, given rise to two principal opposing trends. On the one hand, there are those who advocate "freedom" in love; in its most ex-treme form, this position can mean complete abandon to instinctual whim and has issued in a growing preoccupation with techniques of erotic titillation. The absence of commit-ment and lasting personal involvement is dubbed "freedom" while responsibility is seen as a "hang-up" or inhibition or middle-class hypocrisy outmoded by a new understanding. In some cases, conformism as a result of social or group pressure operates as a collective "morality" without a true meaning matrix of belief. Out of this attitude or trend, which is the nega-tive or destructive side of the quest for meaning, grow such tell-ing phrases as "be cool" or "stay loose." The ability to remain detached is considered a sophistication. Based on a popular mis-understanding of the Freudian concept of id or all powerful unconscious, this attitude is a degenerated version of the Freud-

ian concept of libido as determined and instinctual. The pleasure principle can then become the only accepted criterion.

On the other hand, one can at the popular level also discern a tendency toward idealistic sentimentalism, which is generally associated with an intellectualist, "platonic" emphasis in
love as opposed to a carnal or "animal" or "earthy" or even
"crude" emphasis. In our own time, this has resulted in a flood
of romantic novelettes, "soap operas," songs, and films that, at
their worst, glorify love as moonlight and roses and seem to por-
tray life as happening on a movie set complete with eighty-piece
orchestra to underscore one's moods. Viewed as entertainment,
this is pure escapism, and as such, has its place; but it can only
be a relaxing interlude. Yet in its vapid sentimentalism it is curiously considered "higher" by the popular mind, which seems to
categorize it as unsullied by "crude" emphasis on sexuality, and
therefore "better" and even more virtuous.

Neither of these two extreme, common-experience trends
or attitudes, which might respectively be characterized as detached, pleasure seeking, and "sophisticated," as compared with
sentimentalist, "idealistic," and "pure," can do justice to the
whole human person in his embodied existence. Since both in
their extreme form are exaggerations, neither attitude can encompass all meaningful manifestations of love in a meaningful
way, for to exaggerate one aspect is necessarily to prejudice an
adequate envisioning of the whole. Furthermore, neither of
these attitudes can come close to giving holistic expression to
man's fundamental needs, the need for self-affirmation, for participation with others in an integrated order of existence. In a
word, neither of these two popular extremes implies a holistic,
comprehensive, integral understanding of being human. Both of
them imply a rejection or at the very least a nonacceptance of
some aspect of embodied consciousness.

Although the former trend or common-experience view is
associated in popular understanding with the name of Freud
and with impulses from an inexorable unconscious, together
with a "scientific" rejection of the ontological as an erroneous
notion belonging to a previous stage of human evolution in
understanding, and although the latter or second extreme view

is ordinarily associated with idealistic or "platonic" love or union of souls (as essentially unsullied by corporality), the conceptions of the nature of love in the writings of Freud and Plato are more basic and meaningful than is popularly imagined or understood. For his part, far from conceiving of the two approaches as in opposition, Rollo May believes that "not only are the two compatible, but that they represent two halves both of which in a human being's psychological development are required" (*Love and Will*, p. 88). As early as 1939, May rejected the envisioning of human reality as "caught between two worlds" (that is, as spiritual nature somehow "superadded" to animal nature), and went on to say that "it is in reality not a matter of *two* worlds, but of two aspects of the same world" (*Art of Counseling*, p. 73). This is to assert that man's nature is *simultaneously* conditioned and unconditioned and any envisioning of human existence must needs respect the tension or polarity between the two.

To reduce love to a fixed quantity of sexual energy requiring release from tension and to subsume all other manifestations of human existence under the rubric of "aim-inhibited" or "sublimated" sexual energy or instinctual vitality, is arbitrarily to "detotalize" man. Such a characterization does not offer explanation of the fundamental human tendencies disclosed by phenomenological analyses, to reach out to other people in authentic altruism, to seek the beautiful, to equate the mind with the plenitude of being. Man is embodied consciousness. Hence, a purely physicalist explanation of love can never be entirely adequate. Neither can love as a manifestation of *embodied consciousness* be considered higher insofar as it seeks progressively to disengage itself from corporeal influence nor when it is construed as specified by and oriented to more rarefied contemplation of abstract forms, relationships and beauty absolute. To construe love thus would be to denigrate *embodied* consciousness by arbitrarily and artificially raising consciousness to a separate and higher level. As May sees it, it is question of a judicious integration of the two aspects of love, the corporeal and the conscious. May contends that both aspects are needed in the psychological development of a human being. He envisages them as regressive and progressive aspects and subsumes both into an integrated, basic, intentional structure for which he prefers the term *Eros*. The regressive aspect, for May, is correlated with Freud's concept of love and the progressive with Plato's concept. Their relevance, according to May, lies not in their opposition but in their interrelationship. An understanding of his view of their interrelationship is of prime importance, because it constitutes the ground out of which derives May's own perspective on love as a fundamental mode of human existence.

Regressive Aspect: Freudian Eros

In his discussion of the Freudian concept of love (*Love and Will*, pp. 81-98), Rollo May distinguishes between three levels at which that concept must be considered. These are (1) the popular influence of Freud's work, (2) the concept of libido as sexual energy requiring release, and (3) the concept of libido as life instinct or Eros. This section therefore examines May's understanding of Freud's theory of love and explicates the positive value that May draws from his understanding of that theory.

With regard to the first of these levels, May states that, in the main, Freudian concepts such as "libido" and "drive" have, when taken literally, tended to be popularly misunderstood and misapplied. Such misunderstanding and literalist misapplication have then, as May sees it, tended to contribute greatly to the common-experience separation of sex from love. Attempt has already been made in the first section of this chapter to outline some salient aspects and extreme implications of the everyday exaggeration of this separation and mistaken opposition. May is not, however, concerned solely here with the separation and opposition as such, but also with what he considers the resulting banalization of love in our own time. He is especially concerned with the relation of the popular misunderstanding to over-emphasis and misuse of specific Freudian concepts.

The second level, as May sees it, is that of Freud's use of the terms *sexual instinct, drive,* and *libido* in order to posit a model of sexual love or libido as a fixed or determinate quantity of energy in every person. This energy, when denied sexual expression, was considered by Freud to be inhibited in aim and to be accordingly sublimated to find another outlet. The libido could be directed away from oneself to another object (altruism), in which case one's narcissistic or self-oriented libido (egoism) was deemed to be proportionately reduced in quantity. Both terms, *altruism* and *egoism,* are here mentioned specifically and only in the restricted sense in which Freud uses them (Freud, 1968a, pp. 424-425). Attainment of pleasure was achieved by release of tension or expression of sexual energy (Freud, 1968a, pp. 312-328; pp. 329-347).

Freud, says May, "struggled valiantly to reduce love to libido" (*Love and Will,* p. 81) since libido as a fixed quantity of sexual energy could be located and encompassed within the physicalist paradigm to which Freud was committed. May, on the other hand, does not accept the foundational notion of libido as fixed quantity nor, correspondingly, the interrelated notion of a quantitative loss of self-esteem (egoism) in the transfer of a quantity of libido to an object other than the ego. In fact, May poses as analogy the *neurotic fear* of the loss or diminution of one's being in falling in love. Further, he states that, in his clinical experience, the *normal* individual, although simultaneously anxious because of his new sensitivity and vulnerability, becomes *more* assured and self-confident when he loves someone else. May sees as inadequate the "explanation" of this self-assurance solely in terms of a "return gift" from the beloved of a quantity of libido that would replace the expended libido. Further, he believes that the heightened inner sense of worth does not essentially depend on whether the love is returned or not. He states himself to be in agreement, however, with Freud's observation, made in 1912, that "the psychical value of the erotic (sexual) needs is reduced as their satisfaction becomes easy" (*Love and Will,* p. 84). It is the later development of this seminal insight on Freud's part that May indicates to be the third level for discussion and, further, declares to be the most interesting and important.

This third level coincides with the development of Freud's controversial death-instinct theory (1920). Freud opposed the sexual instincts to the death instinct, whose function he identified as that of reducing the organic once again to an inanimate state. Since the goal of the sexual instincts was pleasure by means of reduction of tension, the sexual instincts, or *Eros*, as Freud now preferred to call them, were ultimately serving the aim of the death instinct. Since the death instinct by definition could not be the producer of fresh tensions, Freud theorized that it must be Eros that, taking the form of instinctual needs, introduced new tensions and thus maintained the level that release of tension in expenditure of libido would have lowered (Freud, 1967, p. 89, 105-106n).

As May rightly observes, this is remarkable, for this new concept of Eros as life instinct comes in to rescue the sexual instincts from the unwitting self-destruction that would be the result of their unintended aid to the death instinct. Since Freud did not posit this new view of Eros (in *The Ego and the Id,* 1923) until after he had recognized (in *Beyond the Pleasure Principle,* 1920) that the sexual instincts or libido, while in operation to attain the maximum possible pleasure by release of tension, were ultimately self-defeating, May concludes that this Eros, as the introducer of fresh tensions, does represent something genuinely new. He is convinced that Freud's "Eros" is not only more powerful than, but also very different from Freud's "libido," and identifies as "inconsistencies" only the continuing efforts of Freud to force his new conception of Eros to fit in with his old energy system and still to identify this Eros with the sexual instincts. May is further convinced that Freud believed that love was basic to all human experience, involved in every action, and a fundamental source of motivation. May goes on to assert that although the Freudian Eros is a "push from behind," a life force issuing out of the chaotic, undifferentiated energy sources and, at its worst, a "radically solipsistic, schizoid system," he is of opinion that the *meaning* of Freud's concept goes far beyond a literal understanding or "strict application of the concept" (*Love and Will,* pp. 88, 90). He holds, further, that Eros as the life instinct includes the irrational and that Freud believed that control and discipline of Eros was fundamental both in cultural development and in the development of strong character.

For May, then, the Freudian Eros not only has its source in sexual energy but also, as disciplined, controlled, and sublimated, is basic to cultural vitality and development. This view raises the question of whether vitality is ultimately reducible to sexual energy, regardless of its being envisaged as fixed and quantified or not. One thing is clear, however: May is convinced that if the ultimate aim of that life energy or vitality is solely release of tension, the culture or civilization built by it must fall since, even in Freudian theory, mere release of tension without regeneration of tension would ensure the ultimate triumph of the death instinct. The question remains, however, whether Freud's concept of Eros can accommodate the meaning and value that May would like to attribute to it.

On introducing the notion of sexual instincts or life instincts, Freud declared that his concept of the libido of sexual instincts harmonized with the Eros of poetry and philosophy in its capacity to bind all things together (Freud, 1967, pp. 89, 92, 106n). He also stressed the libidinal character of the self-preservative instincts (or narcissistic libido) because of his recognition of the sexual instincts or Eros, and he pondered the problem of whether all instincts were libidinal. His conclusion was to transform the old opposition of ego instincts and sexual instincts into one between the life instincts or Eros and the death instincts. All instincts, then, other than the destructive aggression of the death instinct, which could indeed appropriate libido and operate through masochism and sadism, were ultimately reducible to an undifferentiated, chaotic life force or libido.

This formulation excludes both freedom and choice. Here love is necessarily envisaged solely in terms of sexual energy, at first undifferentiated and later channeled toward a particular object. Indeed, in his *General Introduction to Psychoanalysis,* Freud firmly asserted that "we speak of 'love' when we lay the accent *upon the mental side of the sexual impulses* and disregard, or wish to forget for a moment, the demands of the fundamental physical or 'sensual' side of the impulses" (Freud, 1968a, p. 339, italics mine). And, in *The Ego and the Id,* Freud identified his "Eros" and the "sexual instincts" and spoke of "desexualized Eros" as "displaced libido" or "sublimated energy" that would still have the same purpose as the original

Eros of uniting and holding together. Freud even maintained that the activity of thinking was itself produced by sublimation of sexual energy or erotic forces (Freud, 1962, p. 35).

It is not our purpose here to argue for or against the insights of Freud, but merely to point out that his concept of Eros as life instinct is not the fundamental notion. The fundamental notion remains the sexual drive that Freud chooses to call *Eros*. This Eros can also be desexualized and sublimated, and hence becomes, by extension, the life force that produces all of those actions that tend to continue or stimulate life. There is here no all-embracing, integrated concept of love, no understanding of friendship or authentic concern for the being of another, no possibility of intersubjectivity except as a function of sexuality, however that sexuality is manifested, that is, whether directly expressed or displaced and sublimated. The object—we note Freud does not speak of *person*—becomes important because of the amount of libido that is attached to it. The object does not "generate" the libido, since the libido is a "fixed" substance already present; it merely provides the outlet for expression of a quantified amount of libido. The "producer of fresh tensions," Eros or the life force, does its work within the subject's id-ego-superego structure. Contact with others, even after the introduction of the notion of Eros, remains at the level of object. Thus the notion of sexual energy requiring release is clearly retained.

Moreover, it is to be remembered that the Freudian Eros was posited as part of a polar structure; love, or the life instinct, was in polarity with death as force striving against force, and death was the inevitable winner of this unequal struggle. In a permanent interplay of erotic and destructive forces, Eros or the life instinct acted to preserve the self and the race, losing only individuals to death, but continuing the race, while the death instinct acted to reduce biological complexity to simple components and ultimately triumphed in death. Neither Eros nor the death instinct was reducible to the other. Freud remained committed to a dualist position.

May insists, however, that sexuality as "basic to the ongoing power of the race . . . surely has the *importance* Freud gave it, if not the *extension*" (*Love and Will,* p. 38), and states his belief that every human experience of authentic love has some element of sexuality in it. Without free and conscious orientation, however, as May sees it, this would indeed remain a radically solipsistic, schizoid system. Were the Freudian Eros to be the sole basis for May's understanding of love, it would remain radically egoistic without possibility of real participation in any world other than the biological Umwelt. Although esteeming highly Freud's investigation of the origin of emotions that May identifies as the regressive aspect of love, May holds that emotions are never exclusively a "push from the rear" but are always pointing *toward* something. The Freudian study is considered by May to be an unparalleled understanding of the effect on emotions of past experiences, an unequaled insight into the instinctual element linked with past experience, causally determined and in some way conditioned by environmental factors. But May, unlike Freud, holds for the fundamental freedom of the human being, and more, for the ability of the human being to *know* himself to be free, to have a sense of his being and to express that sense symbolically. Hence, May envisages the Freudian Eros as incomplete, as bound to the biological order or Umwelt, with only a shadowy, uncertain glimpse of others in an epiphenomenal social structure. To supply and illustrate the aspect of purpose, motivation, and reaching out to others, May turns to what he considers the progressive aspect of love, which for him is correlated with the Plato's concept of Eros as formulated in the *Symposium.*

Progressive Aspect: Plato's Concept of Eros

"What Freud does have in common with Plato," writes May, "is that both believed that love is fundamental in human experience, love pervades all actions, and is a deep, broad, motivating force" (*Love and Will,* p. 88). It has already been shown, however, that Freud's concept of Eros is limited by his insistence on a quantified libidinal energy and by his envisaging of the loved person or thing as object given value by the transfer of libido. Because of its inherent limitations, the Freudian Eros has been seen to be inadequate as a comprehensive theory of love. May proposes that Plato's concept can be seen to complement Freud's concept and that together the two concepts are like two sides of a coin, completing each other. For May, not only are the two concepts compatible but both are also *required* for the proper psychological development of a human being (*Love and Will,* pp. 88, 91-92). Hence it will be necessary first to examine May's understanding of Plato's concept of love and to disclose its role in May's envisioning of normal psychological development and later to examine his view of the compatibility of the two concepts.

In his references to Plato's concept (*Love and Will,* pp. 72-98), May first distinguishes in Greek thought three forms of the concept of Eros, the earliest one being the powerful, original, creative force and the later one, the mischievous, chubby cupid or playing child. May identifies Plato's Eros as a middle form of the concept, standing between the other two in meaning. He sees Plato's Eros not merely as the creative urge or vitality of all things but also as man's ability to take hold of that creativity from within, or the imaginative freedom of human beings to explore possibilities. This middle form May calls *Eros the mediator,* envisaging it as the force that gives men motivation to act, the desire to attain goals, to actualize possibilities. Whereas May correlated Freud's Eros with determinism, he correlates Plato's concept with future and purpose, and hence with freedom. Whereas Freud's Eros, in being determined and instinctual, was linked with causal factors in the past (efficient causality), Plato's Eros is, for May, correlated with future and so brings us to a different kind of causality, final causality. This, says May, is action undertaken for an end or goal and proceeding from a deliberate will. It implies an awareness, a consideration and choice of possibilities, and hence also implies an imaginative freedom to form the future. This process of "active loving" May considers the progressive aspect of emotions, that is, the reflectively intended and meaning-oriented aspect of emotion.

The progressive aspect of emotions, says May, begins in the present and relates to the future (*Love and Will,* pp. 77-81;

pp. 91-105). This he correlates with Plato's concept of Eros as formulated in the *Symposium* and says that the difference between Freud's and Plato's concepts arises precisely from this orientation or "pointing-toward" that is central to Plato's concept. May understands Plato's Eros to be a yearning for union, a capacity to relate to new forms of experience, the creative spirit in man, and power thrusting toward generation and creation. For May, then, this concept comprehends both the biological reproductive drive and the yearning for knowledge. The biological, for Plato, asserts May, is not denied, but is incorporated and transcended in Eros, as the self is continuously nourished and regenerated. Physical creation produces bodily children, while creation of the soul produces, for example, poetry, art, and law.

The creative force that is Eros is "the binding element . . . the bridge between being and becoming" (*Love and Will*, p. 79, see also pp. 223-231), the desire to attain unity and meaning. May understands Plato to mean that one already participates to some extent in or knows in some way the loved object, because one is drawn by it. Hence Plato's Eros seeks, through the commitment of love, the form or unique essence of the loved person or thing, in order to unite itself with it. This oriented search May correlates with his own notion of intentionality as the structure that lies at the source of the meaning of all experience. He does not identify Eros with intentionality but states that they "have much in common" in that both are oriented toward union. Plato's Eros seeks self-fulfillment, but is not to be confused with egocentric whim in a passive world. It is a seeking of objective loveliness, a recognition of the attraction and vitality of the thing or person loved.

When one examines Plato's formulation of Eros as given in the *Symposium* (Plato, 1953, pp. 479-555), one finds rather a more involved concept than May has delineated. Love, for Plato, is not merely desire of the good, although it does seek the good. It is intermediate between wisdom and ignorance and must be so, says Plato, since if ignorant it could not know what to seek, and if wise it would already be in possession of the good. Thus, love is the desire everlastingly to remain in possession of the good and the beautiful (*kalokagatha*) to know it more fully. Since men are mortal, part of that desire is for immortality, which is itself perceived to be a good.

What good is in question here? Plato discerns a series of levels; each new one he considers higher than the previous one, in that it is more abstract. Hence, the object of love, for Plato, becomes more desirable as it becomes progressively abstract, less embodied. "The true order of going," he says, "is . . . to begin from the beauties of earth and mount upwards for the sake of that other beauty, *using these as steps only*" (Plato, 1953, p. 543, italics mine). The levels begin with the beauty of individual objects or persons and proceed thence to a perception and appreciation of physical beauty in general, thence to beauty of mind, of intellect as preferable to that of outward sensible appearance. The series continues with the stepping from the beauty of institutions and laws to the beauty of the sciences, thence to the science of beauty itself and finally to the apprehension of the nature of beauty itself. It is clear, then, that the object of Plato's Eros is to attain to the highest possible appreciation of abstraction, of beauty itself, and that these steps, each more abstract than the previous one, are considered higher precisely because they are more and more purified of earthly contact, free of the vulgar taint of the lower levels. It is also clear that, once having attained each higher level, one would not wish to return to the lower levels except to illuminate the inadequacy thereof and to teach and inspire longing for the higher levels.

Further, it is clear that in valuing the intellect as higher, in placing the intellectual nature or soul of man "above" his body, Plato has not here attained an integrated theory of human love. It is true that he speaks of human love together with the begetting of children, but the reason that he gives for their conception is the parents' desire for immortality, to see themselves continued in some way in their children. This is not *primarily* a human love of spouse or children, but an earthly reflection of the desire of the soul for immortality in its spiritual children—for example, in art, poetry, law. True love in its most complete form is not, for Plato, that of humans for each other, but is love of the purest abstractions, leaving human love far

below as a mere stepping-stone and poor reflection of the Ideal
or Form toward which the soul aspires.

Plato's concept of love or Eros, then, is a far more involved one than May has delineated. In his concern with the
thrust or dynamism of Plato's Eros, May has been so preoccupied with the direction of free aspiration toward union with the
beloved that he does not seem to have taken sufficient account
of the full implications of the concept, nor to have borne in
mind that in Plato's assertion of levels of abstraction and of the
ultimate aim as purest beauty there is implied the denigration of
embodied existence, which is seen as lower and as a mere mirror
of the real. However, it is the case that Plato's Eros is future
oriented and reaches for meaning and it is from this thrust of
Plato's concept that May draws a positive value.

Freud's and Plato's Eros Integrated: May

As cited earlier, May believes that "not only are the two
[*concepts* of love, Freud's and Plato's] *compatible*, but that
they represent two halves both of which, in a human being's
psychological development, are *required*" (*Love and Will*, p. 88,
italics mine). Now, we have examined Freud's and Plato's concepts of Eros both in their original form and in the forms as
understood by May. In both cases it was found that, as May had
indicated, neither concept alone could account for the whole
experience of human love. But it was also found that Freud saw
the loved one as object or means of outlet, while Plato saw the
loved one as mere reflection or stepping-stone to beauty itself.
In neither case is the loving relationship itself explored and
explicated or valued in all its overtones and meanings. Thus, the
two cannot simply be "added" together in order to achieve an
integrated appreciation of person and of the kinds of love. The
two concepts remain mutually exclusive, in fact, on the basis of
the metaphysical theory that subtends each separately, the
mechanistic and deterministic for Freud and the spiritual and
free for Plato. Even in the existential situation, as has already
been discussed in the first section of this chapter, the popular
expressions of the two conceptions have not been able to meet

and integrate. The two concepts, then, are not compatible, neither in theory nor in their popular understanding and expression.

Yet May holds that the two concepts are not only compatible but also represent two essential halves of normal development, aspects that must be integrated for normal existence. He proposes to illustrate their interrelationship with a case study of a patient caught in the contradiction between her strict, responsible, rigid upbringing and a wish for emotional freedom and spontaneity (*Love and Will,* pp. 89-94). It is at this point that May speaks of the "union of Eros" as the regressive and progressive aspects of emotions and correlates these with Freud (regressive) and Plato (progressive). And it is at this point, too, that it becomes clear that, in asserting the compatibility of Freud's and Plato's Eros, May is, unwittingly it seems, no longer considering each concept in its separate entirety with its own fundamental metaphysic but is concerned only with the thrust or direction of each one (*Love and Will,* p. 91). A lack of clarity in his use of the term *concept* seems to have led him in each case to identify the entire concept with its thrust. Although he began by considering each concept in greater detail and is clearly trying to encompass what he had already spoken of as the separation of sex from love in a reintegration of body and mind, by the time he comes to consider the two concepts together and to show their compatibility, he has retained only the notion of causality and thrust involved in each one. He has not, then, shown the concepts to be compatible and is illustrating rather his own integrated view of love, more basic than Freud's or Plato's thrusts, which at this point are but aspects of a single theory, rather than two theories "added" together.

In the whole structure of Eros, for May, Freud's or regressive (past, determining factors) aspect is correlated with efficient causality or "reason why," while Plato's or progressive (toward a goal) aspect, he says, is correlated with final causality or "purpose." Eros, as May envisages it, unites the two aspects of causality in a new, more basic structure in which both the causal factors of the past and instinctual urges are linked and channeled by future orientation toward a freely-chosen person or thing. The future assumes the decisive role, since the past would exercise only a deterministic power, while orientation to the present alone remains in the realm of whim. Future orientation, grounded in reflective choice for the creation of meaning, is the necessary basis for union of the two dynamisms, which would otherwise remain undifferentiated, a multiplicity of instinctual urges and a multiplicity of ideals or possibilities.

For May, then, Freud's preoccupation with the biological life of man is rejected, as is Plato's insistence on the higher worth of man's intellectual nature and the consequent devaluation of embodied existence. Now, grounding the two thrusts is the assertion of man as an embodied conscious being, as constituting meaning in his world, and as intersubjective in reciprocal relations freely chosen. Eros, for May, is not some instinctual emotion that wells up unasked and undirected. It is rather man's vitality in himself and toward others, instinctually generated and consciously or purposefully directed.

Whereas for Freud it was the attaching of libido to the object that made the object desirable, for Plato the desired qualities belonged properly to the beloved object in itself, which, by reflecting the archetype of beauty, arouses the desire of possession. The only "value" for Freud is the production and pleasurable elimination of tensions, whereas for Plato value is contingent both on the good intrinsically and on the conscious intentions that serve to disclose it. Even for Plato, then, the particular, finite good remains referential, although consciously intended. Emotions, for May, however, are neither merely an instinctual upsurge nor the attraction of some instance of beauty and goodness, but rather a *directed instinctual urge,* an impetus pointing toward "the way I *want* something to be" (*Love and Will,* p. 91). This is to unite both the surge of emotion and its arousal by and orientation to a *particular* person or thing. This is to integrate human biological urges and psychological orientation in a more basic appreciation of the specific humanity of intersubjective relationships, for example, and to understand man fundamentally as embodied consciousness.

It is entirely consistent that May decries what he sees as contemporary vagueness about feeling as whim or a chance state of the moment. For him, love is no mere haphazard instinctual urge, but a vital principle animated by the grasping of oneself as a self-identity. It is a means of communication, of consolidation in the interpersonal world or Mitwelt. It is, as he envisages it, a continuous replenishment of the self and a constant reaching out, both toward people and toward personal goals and ideals. Just as Freud realized that release of tension alone ultimately would serve the purposes not of the life instinct but of the death instinct, so also the Greek concept of Eros in its deterioration to the effete, mischief-making Cupid, asserts May, shows clearly, in symbolic form, the effect of the loss of vitality and passion on love. It is Eros, says May, "which impels people toward health in psychotherapy" (*Love and Will,* p. 78). Attainment of an integrated, creative life depends on vital regeneration, both instinctual and spiritual.

Toward an Ontology of Love

Bombarded with daily evidence of global inequity and apparent profiteering, sickened by the success of advertising, rebuffed at every turn by the ever-present computer numbers that touch every facet of his life, sensitive modern man has tried to be resilient, to develop a protective thick skin. In some cases, his very efforts have been all too successful. His nerve ends deadened by noise and hurry, his resilience may deteriorate into apathy, loss of feeling and care, and even a deadening of the ability to care. At the extreme level, he may go through the motions of living but without vitality, joy, or a sense of his own being.

Symptomatic of this lack of vital ontological awareness, or alive sense of his own being, is the grasping at straws or the desperate attempt of some twentieth-century individuals to allay their fear of loss or diminution of their being (anxiety), to escape from boredom and find meaning in a new center of interest, however fleeting, an attempt exemplified by incessant moving from one house to another or even from one place to another. This lack also produces symptoms such as the prevalent fear of silence as emptiness, and the characterizing of quiet introspection as morbid and even egotistical withdrawal. Sadly, preoccupation with novelty in place of commitment and lasting interest inevitably feeds the very anxiety that gave it birth, the anxiety of self-loss or self-dissipation.

Another sign of the lack of vital ontological awareness is a loss of courage, a neurotic determination on the part of the anxious person to anaesthetize himself, to preserve some inner center by shutting out the loneliness and turmoil of his world. Anxiety of self-loss or of spiritual diminution having become predominant in his sense of being, the person may cut himself adrift from his world for the sake of protecting his self. Yet self and world are correlates, in that a person cannot be in the fullest sense individual without participating in some way in a community from which he remains fully distinct. One is fully separate, distinct, and clearly individual only in fullest participation and communion with other completely separate and distinct individuals. Thus the decline of self must entail eventual decline of world and so, too, the person's shrinking or self-preservative reduction of the range of his possibilities must weaken and destroy his self in a gradual erosion of his ability to reach out, to care, to love.

Yet since self and world are interdependent, the person depressed by his diminished range may constructively attempt to overcome his isolation by seeking some reassurance and allaying his sense of detachment by attaching himself, in whatever manner and however fleetingly, to another person, thereby seeking to sense his own being by participating in some way in his world. However distorted or weak or even violent his action may seem, however inadequate his participation in the world of others, his attempt is basically characterized by the desire to know himself to be and to have some effect on others. This is a movement of his whole being toward another person or thing in order to overcome existential isolation and estrangement that are painfully expressed in his loss of a vital sense of self and the sense of his world as meaningful. This movement of separation or individuation and participation or longing to belong is the ontological nature of love. It encompasses both the volitional element, the will or desire for reunion, and the emotional element, which is experienced on different levels such as those of joy, pleasure, and contentment. The joy or pleasure, however, is not the motive force, for that equation would be to reduce love to only one of its subordinate, partial, and consequent elements. Such a reduction would envisage the loved one as only an object, a purveyor or means of pleasure or joy, in function of the Freudian pain-pleasure or reality-pleasure principle, for example. The fundamental, underlying, comprehensive, motive force of love remains the existential polarity or interdependence of self and world, of separate, distinct, centered, individual identity in participation or community or being-toward-others.

"Eros," asserts May, "is the drive toward union with what we belong to—union with our own possibilities, union with significant other persons in our world in relation to whom we discover our self-fulfillment" (*Love and Will*, p. 74). Here May is clearly identifying love as the ontological drive of the individual human self to affirm itself and to participate in community with others. Such envisioning grounds May's entire discussion of Eros. In his earliest work, prior to any exploration of love as such, prior to any explication of love as ontological, that is, a fundamental, defining, inalienable structure of human existence, May had, as has been seen, already defined personality as characterized by free individuality, social integration, and religious tension, and had also declared that the aim of therapy must be to help the patient toward creative, vital living. This living was envisaged as integration of mature, self-chosen goals, and the creative drive or instinctual urges of the "unconscious."

In two of his earliest books, *The Art of Counseling* (1939) and *Man's Search for Himself* (1953), as well as in his doctoral dissertation, published under the title of *The Meaning of Anxiety* (1950), May clearly placed great emphasis on what he was to consider later the centeredness or self-asserting identity of the person and on the tension between individuation or self-affirmation and participation or being-toward-others. In his preoccupation with the effect of that tension and its relation, more primarily, to the meaning of anxiety, however, he tended to circumscribe his treatment of love to the emotional orientation of person toward person, without apparent envisioning of it as ontological, and spoke separately of the creative drive as openness to possibility, as artistic sensitivity and instinctual vitality (*Man's Search,* pp. 120-122). The emotional element cannot, of course, be finally separated from love, whether of persons or of things, because without the emotional element love is merely a benevolent disposition. As yet, however, May's discussion of the emotion involved was more a psychological description of love as interpersonal and primarily heterosexual (in contrast with friendship or parental love, for example), and considered creativity as an entirely other force, than an explicit grounding of his description in its ontological structure. Yet his early description was not only of value but also prepared for the deepening of the concept in his later work.

The first brief treatment of love in May's work occurs late in *Man's Search for Himself,* where, having asserted that the real contemporary problem was to become *able* to love in an age increasingly conscious of anxiety and its social expression as loneliness, isolation, alienation, and so on, May went on to characterize the giving and receiving of mature love as based or grounded in the sense of self, or sense of one's essential being. Constantly recalling his conviction of the human being as free, May was, in *Man's Search for Himself,* already relating love to prior consciousness of one's self, although at this point he was more concerned with the *expression* of human love as interpersonal. This concern becomes clear on close examination of his definition of love as *"a delight in the presence of the other person and an affirming of his value and development as much as one's own"* (*Man's Search,* p. 206). May is quick to add that love presupposes freedom—this addition does not appear in his definition, already rendering it somewhat inadequate—since unfree persons could not love, but would be merely determined in a particular direction by their biological needs. Furthermore, the person who is "loved" because of biological need alone is reduced to an object from whom pleasure is sought and whose being (or person) is not essentially distinguishable from the next. In such a relationship, neither the lover nor the beloved are persons, but merely objects for which adequate substitutes could be found if necessary. We might here profitably remember that this reduction to object is exactly the case with the release of Freudian libido, which theory does not describe a personal relationship. One might also recall the Victorian use of the phrase "my person" in lieu of "my body," the latter phrase being thought to be too obvious and hence vulgar. The substitution of "person" for "body" speaks for itself in its alienation of the embodied dimension of human being.

Love further presupposes freedom in that it does not involve a demand for love in return. Such a demand would be to buy love that was *un*freely given and hence not love at all, but only conformity, compliance. Nor must love be confused with dependence. There are different kinds of dependence, from mutual aid to reciprocal satisfaction of desires or even as a pact against loneliness and isolation. None of these relationships is essentially more than a negative avoidance of real involvement and achieves its purpose only at the price of increased emptiness for those involved. For his part, May declares that one can love only in proportion to one's capacity for independence, that is, being a person in one's own right. Since, for May, mature love is primarily and essentially a matter of giving, one must clearly have a strong self from which to give if one is not to "empty" one's own being. Hence, love is not to be confused with weakness or need. Tenderness, May believes, is not weakness or clinging, but the gentleness of strength.

Love, although self-assertive and strong, must not be confused with aggression. In his definition, May has spoken not only of the "delight" of the lover, but also of his affirming the value and development of the other person *"as much as one's own."* To be thus loving is not to be possessively aggressive but to love the other for what he is and to want and further his individual freedom. Love does not seek to dominate, because domination reduces the other to an object. Nor does love seek to constrict the other, because constriction restricts his freedom, development, and hence capacity to love. In *The Meaning of Anxiety,* May characterizes the social manifestation of such as neurotic, as using collectivism as a shield against anxiety, and as a substitute for genuine community and caring.

By definition, love involves a "delight in the presence of

the other person." May explains what he means by "delight" as one's "joy and happiness" in the relation with the other. This explanation is not to characterize it as simple, sensuous pleasure, nor even as psychically appreciated, sensuous enjoyment, but rather as a fullness of being, a profound sense of fulfillment of one's being in a moment of being-together-with-another. This oneness is what May later recognizes and formulates as a momentary overcoming of our existential sense of aloneness and separation in a joyous union of two separate, fully centered beings, in a participation, a sharing that has meaning for both. Hence, we must assume that May does not mean "presence" in the literal, physical, spatial sense alone, but rather in its fullest connotation of encompassing the being of the other in an interdependence of two autonomous, loving selves. Nor can he mean an envisioning of the other as "object-out-there" but rather as the person in and through whom one's being-toward-others is most fully, freely, independently, and meaningfully realized. There are, necessarily, limiting, contracting configurations or features of intersubjectivity, that is to say, different levels of relationship. Of these, the most definitive is love, because in love one is most fully lost in the other and most fully oneself *simultaneously.*

Hence love, says May, requires the capacity to have "empathy" with the other person. Many years before he offered his definition of love in *Man's Search for Himself,* May had, in *The Art of Counseling,* offered the view that empathy was the fundamental process in love and had described it as the "feeling, or thinking, of one personality into another until some state of identification is achieved" (*Art of Counseling,* p. 77). Here May cannot merely mean the ordinary experience of "having a great deal in common," nor even a coincidence of outlook, but must necessarily be conceiving of something grounded in a more fundamental accord or harmony of identities or selves. Prior to the expression of love as such, verbally or physically, there is a process of coming together with something to which we already "belong," with which we are already "in tune." Although at this point May spoke of this basic accord as "empathy," one can perceive in this notion, as it has been more fully explicated here, a foreshadowing of the later broadening and deepening of the concept of love onto its ontological base.

Just as existence is never automatic but a ceaseless struggle to be, to realize oneself, so love is never automatic, never easy. Attraction is easy; love is not. Too often confused with dependence, weakness, need, desire, or attraction, love is not achieved once and for all in a happily-ever-after union, but is intimately related to maturity of self-feeling, of responsibility and freedom. Love, therefore, requires courage as a necessary corollary, the courage of continuing commitment. In May's words, *"it takes courage not only to assert one's self but to give one's self"* (*Man's Search,* p. 194). He means here the inner quality of the courage required to meet the anxiety generated by perception of potentialities and, more specifically, love as anxiety creating, exemplified in anxiety of the loss of the loved one, increased vulnerability of the self. Because, from his earliest writings, May held that personality was not static or vegetative, but dynamic, growing, and changing, it follows that he must and does envisage love as requiring courage to meet its continuous state of achieving and reaffirming the fulfillment of one's being.

Although May grounded his earliest definition of personality in "principles of creativity" (*Art of Counseling,* p. 45) and declared that the more sensitive the "balance" of tensions within the person, the greater his creativity, May does not identify love with creativity but contents himself with pointing out the relation they both bear to self-affirmation and self-realization. Love and creativity are both, for May, grounded in the ability of a strong self to affirm his own being and to reach out to participate in others, to produce or create something. And, just as love gives openly and freely, so creativity is an openness to possibility, a total absorption or merging of oneself in a moment of insight. The same paradox, then, says May, holds both for love and for "creative ecstasy," the paradox that the moment of fullest interdependence is grounded in fullest capacity "to be a person in one's own right." It must be borne in mind that May does not identify love and creativity, and that these points are made as analogies between the two. As yet, he is not explicitly treating of "creative drive," either, other than in a brief reference to "creative consciousness" or flow of "inner, instinctual urges," which he links more with a Freudian kind of "unconscious."

A curious point arises at the end of May's brief discussion of love in *Man's Search for Himself,* where, in a tortuous paragraph, he states that he does not in his discussion of love as shared ecstasy mean "to rule out or depreciate all of the other kinds of positive relationship" (p. 210). These he specifies as friendship, interchange of human warmth and understanding, sharing of sexual pleasure and passion, "and so on," and contrasts them explicitly with what he calls "love in its ideal sense." These statements would seem to indicate that May considers "love in its ideal sense" as completely other than friendship, warmth, passion, and so on, and yet there is offered no elucidation of a concept of ideal love. May neither qualifies nor modifies the phrase "love in its ideal sense," and therefore, because he differentiates it specifically from sexual pleasure and passion, shared human warmth, and from friendship, it is difficult to know precisely what he seeks to convey.

Love cannot be engaged in for its own sake, as though by "demand," for the sake of an "outside" ideal. For May, it is, rather, a matter of commitment of one individual to another. As Binswanger has shown, there is phenomenological ground for distinguishing between what he called "plural mode" or being together without true involvement and sharing, such as in functional relationships, and the "dual mode," which involves a reciprocity of caring. Without true commitment to the other, love as ideal to be attained must necessarily reify or reduce the beloved to an object through whom this ideal is to be realized. As such, "love in its ideal sense" has already been rejected in May's definition, wherein he firmly declared the element of valuing the being of the other as much as one's own. The phrase "love in its ideal sense" may perhaps refer to an uncritical, idealized conception of personal love and happiness as transcending "ordinary" human relations and as involving some "higher," romantic, spiritual communion. However, one may only surmise what is meant, because the separation of "love in its ideal sense" from "other positive relationships" as specified is not textually clarified and explicated, thus rendering difficult an understanding how it can be seen to accord with May's definition of love. Further, the interpretation surmised above is not easily harmonized with May's belief, repeatedly asserted, in the worth, dignity, and freedom of the individual human being as an embodied consciousness, nor with the recall of the sense of being on which May's theory and psychotherapy are grounded.

It was in *Existence,* in his second essay, "Contributions of Existential Psychotherapy," that May attempted to give his own formulation of the central insights of existential psychotherapy as he envisaged them (*Contributions,* pp. 37-91, especially pp. 64-65). Once again, as in *Man's Search for Himself,* May's mention of love is very brief, but its significance for his work is extensive. The three existential modes of being-in-the-world, Umwelt, Mitwelt, and Eigenwelt, as May envisages and describes them, together with what he considers the distinctive attitude of existential psychotherapy to time, he says, "give us a basis for the psychological understanding of love" (*Contributions,* p. 64).

In his discussion of the three modes of world, May distinguishes between the category of adjustment and adaptation in the Umwelt, or what he describes as the biological realm or "natural world," and the category of encounter and relation in the Mitwelt, or world of interpersonal awareness. In the Umwelt, one adjusts to cold or need for sleep or food, for example, whereas in the Mitwelt people encounter each other and are mutually affected by their awareness of each other. The third mode, Eigenwelt or "own-world," is the "mode of relationship to one's self" and is simultaneous with the other two modes of being-in-the-world. No one mode can be derived from or disclosed by the others. All three are involved in every moment of human existence. Hence, no one mode can be emphasized to the *exclusion* of the other two, the unifying, integrating principle being the sense of being or ontological awareness.

Although appreciative of the importance of understanding biological, instinctual and social aspects of love, May is of the opinion that without a proper concept of Eigenwelt, or "own-world," love cannot be fully understood. He believes that one must not ignore the question of the individual in relation to himself by overemphasizing the other two modes of world. Otherwise, as he sees it, the individual could be envisaged on the one hand as a weak ego buffeted by the id, or on the other hand as a reflector of or reactor to social pressures, for example. Any overemphasis of one mode of world can only distort the subsequent development of the whole theory. Love, May believes, is essentially related to all three modes of world, the vitality of Umwelt, social orientation of Mitwelt, and self-affirming power of Eigenwelt. May does not, however, go into detailed explication of the relation, but merely reiterates his conviction that love cannot be understood as purely biological but is also dependent on decision and commitment. Here the notion of will as structure, choice, decision, and enduringness has entered May's deliberations on love.

The "distinctive attitude" of existential therapists toward time as primarily future oriented is of importance in May's thought on love (*Contributions,* pp. 65-71). Whereas in *Man's Search for Himself* May stressed the necessity to grasp the immediate present in a vital way, to become aware of oneself as active, he now places that self-awareness on a deeper plane by his realization that one's grasping of the present is formed and molded by one's future, by what one wants or hopes to be or do, by one's aliveness and openness to possibility. Past causal factors in one's loving relationships are thus seen to be only one aspect of the whole and are also, in some sense, subordinate to the future orientation of the person's love. This orientation would include the attitude he has toward the future of the relationship, how he envisages its development and his own, and, as such, his orientation therefore plays a role in forming and guiding the relationship from the outset. The quality of the time or *duration* of love is dependent not on the measuring activity of the clock but on the significance of the loved ones for each other and for themselves, bringing us once again to the grounding leitmotiv, or recurrent theme, of ontological awareness or sense of being. Love's time, then, has to do with the *inner significance* of the events.

Again May draws a parallel between love and creative insight—in this instance the parallel is found in their sharing of time as qualitative, immediately experienced, and future projected, but never as merely measured. The significance of time for therapy, too, is clear, because the key to and quality of the patient's loving and creative relationships are revealed in his "experienced" time—for example, in the vividness of a chronologically brief memory compared with the dull lack of awareness that may obscure many years. The degree of one's loving cannot be measured by the number of years one has known the loved one nor can the quality of an insight, for example, be measured by the suddenness of its birth in time, but only by the heightening of awareness, the grasping of meaning or of a new possibility.

In his essay, "The Significance of Symbols" (pp. 27-29), May does not advance any new aspect of the subject of love, but reiterates that the symbols associated with love have become too closely identified with the need for security and hence relate more to dependence than to love. He also decries the identification of love with sexual technique and cites this as an example of the disintegration of the central symbol of love into satisfaction of need. He does not offer any interpretation or analysis of love nor explicit definition of this "central symbol," and concerns himself mainly with the quality of symbols in general as revelatory of meaning and orientation.

Again, in his first essay in *Existential Psychology,* May is concerned with love not in itself but as relationship within the therapeutic hour (*Emergence,* pp. 16-17). He speaks briefly of levels within the encounter of therapist and patient. These "levels" are the first evidence in May's work of a differentiation between "kinds" of love. He lists them as, first, response of one person to another, allaying physical loneliness; second, the level of friendly trust and concern; third, "erotic" or physical attraction, which, though remaining unexpressed, would, says May, constitute a dynamic resource for change; fourth, esteem or self-transcending concern for another. All of these, he says, constitute together in therapy a real relationship, a total encounter. (It might also have been fruitful to have integrated this discussion with that of empathy in *The Art of Counseling,* but May does not analyze in detail his proposed levels of encounter.)

He returns briefly, however, to the concept of esteem in "A Phenomenological Approach to Psychotherapy" (pp. 119-123), again with regard to encounter in therapy. An understanding of interpersonal relationship is essential for therapeutic encounter. Oversimplification of encounter in terms of erotic drives only, cannot, he holds, fully encompass the phenomenon of being-together, being concerned for the other, although erotic drives as a level of encounter can be a "dynamic resource for change." The patient has consulted the therapist, May believes, because he needs help to cope with difficult self-world relations and must, to maintain his centeredness, affirm his self and world. In the therapeutic encounter, no mere factual, scientific explanations or advice alone will reach such a person. In order to establish communication, a total relationship is required. This loving relationship is established at different levels of affirmation of the other, one level being esteem or self-transcending concern for the other or, as May now names it, *agape.*

Agape, says May, "is not a sublimation of eros, but a transcending of it in enduring tenderness, lasting concern for others" (*A Phenomenological Approach,* p. 119, see also p. 121). At this point, it must be recalled that, for May the term *erotic* is here understood to mean "having a general sexual tone," and eroticism is understood to be an influential but unexpressed aspect of therapeutic encounter—hence the necessity for an agapeic dimension of "enduring tenderness" or the less self-interested element in loving encounter, whether in therapy or elsewhere, rather than a mere "sublimation" of "erotic drives." Yet it is important to note that even when May adds the phrase "lasting concern for others," he has not explicitly differentiated agape from love or concern that begins in affinity. Thus the *ultimate* distinguishing characteristic of agape has not been *expressed* in this description, nor is it implied in the musical analogy of sympathetic resonance that was offered as an illustration of total encounter and agapeic concern.

An example of sympathetic resonance may help to make

this point clear. If two tuning forks *of the same pitch* be placed in proximity and the first one is struck to produce its note, the second will take up the vibrations sympathetically and sound its note, humming without having been struck. The first is called a *generator* and the second a *resonator*. The point of importance for this discussion is that, *prior to any* sounding, the two forks must already be *of the same pitch*. The analogy applied to therapy would require some affinity between the psychotherapist and the patient before true encounter would be possible, before any agapeic dimension of concern could develop.

If agape is grounded in sympathy or affinity (or, musically, the same tone), then there can be no possibility of "lasting concern for others," in this case, therapeutic concern, without prior liking or at least affinity on the part of the therapist and patient for each other. It is for this reason that the musical analogy is inappropriate to illustrate encounter and agape. Agape must transcend sympathy. Agape and therapeutic encounter must be a reaching out in concern independent of all contingent features, that is reaching out regardless of whether the other is attractive or not, regardless of pleasant or unpleasant qualities, and regardless of affinity or the lack thereof. This independence is the only genuine basis for lasting concern for others, and, as such, for therapy.

If the analogy of sympathetic resonance is applied to the *effect* of therapy rather than to the levels of encounter, however, it has some considerable illustrative value. If the aim of therapy is to aid the patient to deeper consciousness of himself and to a stronger sense and acceptance of his being, a corollary of ability to participate, to have empathy, and hence to love is also implied. The analogy of sympathetic resonance is then useful in a description of affinity or what is sometimes called "recognition of a kindred spirit," an element in loving relationships of friendship. This affinity might perhaps be *achieved* in therapy too, but cannot be indispensable to the levels of encounter nor assumed as a condition. Because the therapist inevitably meets a great many patients for whom he does not experience any liking or affinity, encounter, and agape in particular, must transcend mere empathy or sympathy.

Although May's understanding of agape is not without limitation, then, it is clear that his thought on love is beginning to open out to encompass more than a limited, personal connotation. Up to this point in his work—that is, prior to *Love and Will*—his writings on any aspect of love were somewhat sparse and brief. May had not yet undertaken a sustained examination of this topic but had referred to love only as it might throw light on the central theme of his discussion or as it might provide an example or analogy with which to further understanding of his position. For example, in *The Art of Counseling*, it was the consideration of empathy in counseling that occasioned a related mention of love, while in *The Meaning of Anxiety*, love was introduced only in its relation to anxiety, in that it increased vulnerability of the self, and so on. Again, in *Symbolism in Religion and Literature*, the subject of love is introduced only as it can illustrate the power of symbols or values to grasp the person, while in *Existential Psychology* and in *Psychology and the Human Dilemma*, love is discussed as of interest because of the concept of encounter in therapy, and again because of the relation of anxiety to love and values. In *Existence*, love was briefly referred to only in that the three modes of world and the concept of time seen as temporality would be important and valuable aids in the psychological understanding of love; while in *Man's Search for Himself*, May himself envisaged the whole project of the book as aiding people to a deeper sense of self, and he himself considered the book "a preface to love." In *Existential Psychotherapy*, one of his lectures or radio talks was devoted to creativity in its relation to the unconscious, while in *Dreams and Symbols*, May is concerned not with Susan's love relationships as such, but with the decisive attitude toward her own being and her world, which is at the root of her life, and therefore of those relationships as she sees them. In *Love and Will*, however, the discussion has love itself as one of its central themes. Here May concentrates explicitly on love although his inquiry will not become as coherent and integrated as was his study of anxiety.

"Every human experience of authentic love," says May, "is a blending in varying proportions, of these four [kinds of love] " (*Love and Will*, p. 38). These four kinds of love he names as *sex* or *libido*; *Eros*, or the drive to procreate or create; *philia*, that is, brotherly love and friendship; and *agape* or *caritas*, love devoted to the welfare of the other. If one were to expect a detailed and balanced analysis of each of the four kinds of love, one would be disappointed, because May's discussion does not evince a concern to the same extent with each of the four kinds, nor does he accord them all lengthy analysis. Perhaps because May's theoretical inquiries are undertaken basically for the purpose of returning to throw greater light on the concrete situation, in particular that of therapy, his principal focus is on the personal experience of love, especially as adult, mature, and heterosexual, while also seeking its base in an empirico-phenomenological understanding of creative vitality. However, in *Love and Will*, he moves beyond his earlier definition of love, to the naming of four kinds of love, and eventually to a comprehensive assertion of love (as Eros, or creative vitality) as ontological, as a fundamental, defining structure of human existence, inalienable in that Eros "constitutes man as man." Here May explicitly recognizes and describes the nature of love as the polar structure of reunion and separation, of participation and individual autonomy. He sees love, then, not as *a* source of happiness, but as *the* source of happiness, the dynamic of life itself, grounding both personal relationships and human creativity.

This ontological structure must now be seen to subtend all of the qualities associated with interpersonal loving and the levels of encounter. "Eros," says May, "is the longing to establish union, full relationship" (*Love and Will*, p. 75, see also pp. 113, 311). It is in function of this longing that love *becomes* personal. It is the ontological polarity of longing to overcome existential separation and yet maintain individual autonomy that channels love into an interpersonal relationship wherein each reaffirms the other's being while remaining fully centered and individual.

Existential anxiety, the anxiety of isolation, then, can be met only by courageous, balanced affirmation of self and world, by the creative participation toward which Eros aspires. Eros finds expression as the aspiration toward union with abstract forms, with esthetic or philosophical forms, with ethical forms, with other people. It is human vitality striving toward union with perceived possibilities. As such, in May's view, it is most obvious as the human longing for sexual union. Sexuality, however, is only one aspect or "kind" of love, albeit an important one that is grounded in the aspiration of the existentially isolated toward union with its own possibilities. The modern emphasis on sexuality, May says, required it to carry the weight of all our concern. This overemphasis has resulted in as many problems as repression of it caused in Freud's time, since it is an implicit attempt to reduce love to a technical mechanism, and recalls as such the earlier point about the consequent reduction of the other person to an object.

To reduce human sexuality to a biological need entails speaking of it in terms of tension requiring release rather than as an aspect of orientation toward self-fulfillment and fulfillment of the other in a union of beings. May is convinced that it is because of anxiety that the attempt is made to reduce love to a "technical preoccupation," to one of its aspects, to flee, as he puts it, to "the sensation of sex," for reassurance and comfort. He cites as root cause for this flight the anxiety of spiritual annihilation, that is, loss or diminution of one's being in surrender to and domination by the other. This, as has been seen in earlier discussion of May's definition of love, is not love at all.

Like Freud, May introduces the notion of love as Eros in order to broaden the notion of love from a purely self-defeating sexual base (*Love and Will,* pp. 86-87, 96-98). Unlike Freud, however, May's Eros is not merely a "producer of fresh tensions" on a physically vital level alone, but is the "whole reach of human imagination." Eros, then, is not limited to the biological realm but is the dynamic underlying all three simultaneous modes of man's being-in-the-world. Eros, as human vitality, then, is the center of creativity, the "heart and soul" of a culture, and, as such, the enemy of the "organization man," of technology that would reduce its dynamic to a mere process of continuation. The "enemies" of Eros are static, unyielding technique and soul-destroying apathy, both directly related to the refusal to live creatively, confronting anxiety. But Eros is not the enemy of discipline and form and must, says May, be seen in polar relation with them. It may be interesting to note that, in *The Art of Counseling,* May had already asserted the necessity for channeling or structuring human instinctual expression. He consistently stressed the necessity for purpose and structure in creative living, relating these to freedom and responsibility.

Because Eros is vital aspiration toward possibility and form, it stands in profound relation to anxiety and death. *"Love,"* says May, *"is not only enriched by our sense of mortality but constituted by it"* (*Love and Will,* p. 102). The negative aspect of opening one's being to another is that one risks loss or diminution of contentment, change or divergence of aspirations and even loss of the beloved. In opening oneself to new experiences, one risks disappointment, accident, imperfection, and disillusion. The experience of vulnerability and mortality bears more directly on one according as one's risks are greater (in parenthood, for example), says May. Love, then, sharpens our sense of our own mortality and that of the person loved, and introduces an element of protective urgency into our creative effort. Love's meaning and depth can thereby be increased in courageous affirmation or stifled in anxiety and loss of courage. For May, contemporary preoccupation with sexuality is grounded in this anxiety and in the desire to repress awareness of mortality.

It is at this point that May specifically uses the term *ontological* to describe the polarity of love as separation and reunion (*Love and Will,* pp. 111-113). Such description makes possible the perception of love as requiring a strong sense of being and as affecting intrinsically the character of "human" time. It is, perhaps, of importance to recall that it was also in existential consciousness of mortality that May's location of anxiety became ontological and his theory capable of becoming integrated. Because of the sense of mortality, love takes on immediacy and, for May, is not merely enriched but *constituted* by it.

Eros, as May sees it, is richly creative. Yet it also "destroys as it creates," he says, and characterizes it as "daimonic," the "antidaimon" being apathy (*Love and Will,* pp. 100,

122-123, 148, 123n). The spelling, *daimonic,* is, as May sees it, closer to the original Greek words *daimonikos* and *daimonion* and, for him, this spelling is "unambiguous" in including both positive and negative, the divine and the diabolical. In his earlier books, as indicated in the terminological appendix, May had occasionally used the adjectives "demonic" and "daemonic" with the general connotation of evil and destructive. In his opening section, "Defining the Daimonic," May introduces "the daimonic" as *"any natural function which has the power to take over the whole person,"* examples of which are "sex and eros, anger and rage, and the craving for power" (*Love and Will,* p. 123). It is perhaps noteworthy that this defining phrase, which opens the section, is the only one in this section to be italicized by May, suggesting thereby and by its prominence a possible preference on May's part for this formulation over the other nonitalicized connotations and further statements concerning his understanding of "the daimonic." He says that "the daimonic can be either creative or destructive and is normally both," having said earlier (p. 148) that Eros has to do with love and hate, with creativity and destruction, and he adds that "the daimonic is obviously not an entity but refers to a fundamental, archetypal function of human experience—an existential reality in modern man and, so far as we know, in all men" (*Love and Will,* p. 123).

May's use of the definite article ("*the* daimonic") does not help the reader to understand precisely what he means (it is not clear whether "daimonic" is an adjective or a noun) and at this point what seems to be emerging is a notion that may perhaps be stated as "that which is or can become daimonic, that is, creative or destructive or both." Also, May's conviction of human freedom would seem to harmonize more easily with a clearer reference in the initial definition of "the daimonic" to the personal responsibility of the individual seen as *choosing* to gratify without limit one drive or wish or urge, rather than with the phrase "which has the power to take over." It might also be noteworthy that both his italicized defining phrase and the examples following it have a negative import of imbalance or overemphasis, whereas following sentences and his footnote

indicate that he sees "the daimonic" as both positive and negative, constructive and destructive, holding that "all life is a flux
between these two aspects of the daimonic."

May goes on to say that "the daimonic is the urge in
every being to affirm itself, assert itself, perpetuate and increase
itself" (*Love and Will,* p. 123). "In its right proportion, the
daimonic is the urge to reach out toward others, to increase life
by way of sex, to create, to civilize" (p. 146). Eros also, for
May, "pushes toward self-fulfillment" (p. 80), and is associated
with reaching out, increasing life "by way of sex," with creativity and civilization. It becomes evil, he goes on, when it usurps
the total self without regard for the integration of that self or
that of others, appearing then, says May, as excessive aggression,
hostility, cruelty, and so on. These, he asserts, "are the reverse
side of the same assertion which empowers our creativity"
(*Love and Will,* p. 123), violence being, for May, "the daimonic
gone awry" (*Love and Will,* p. 130, italics mine). This he calls
"daimonic possession."

May also holds that "the *daimon* gives individual guidance in particular situations" (*Love and Will,* p. 125, italics
mine). It is not clear whether he means here an abstract noun
that might convey a conceptualizing *other* than Eros, or is referring perhaps to Eros, which was previously characterized as a
daimon. He goes on to mention the Latin conception of a
daemon (*genii*) as a tutelar spirit or presiding genius, and adds
that the daimonic is associated with creativity and leadership.
He describes it as "the unique pattern of sensibilities and
powers which constitutes the individual in relation to his
world" (*Love and Will,* p. 125), pointing to poets and philosophers who have written of "daemons" or "voices" that "offer
guidance." A pattern of coherence and integration, a guiding
voice within the self, "the daimonic" is not, says May, to be
confused or identified with conscience, which, he says here, is
"largely a social product" (*Love and Will,* p. 124). (In *The Art
of Counseling* [p. 60] and in *Man's Search for Himself* [p.
184], May subscribed to a very much more fundamental concept of conscience that itself was more consistent with his position on freedom and responsibility. He also rejected the concep-

tion of conscience as simply social, cultural, or parental influence.) The daimonic, he goes on, is "rooted in natural forces," arises rather "from the ground of being" than from "the self as such" and is "felt as the grasp of fate." "In the daimonic," asserts May, "lies our vitality, our capacity to open ourselves to the power of eros," concluding that modern man must not only "rediscover the daimonic" but must "recreate the reality of the daimonic" (*Love and Will*, p. 126). Later (p. 164), however, May states that the daimonic is "part of eros, and underlies both love and will."

"The daimonic needs to be directed and channeled" (*Love and Will*, p. 126) by human consciousness, because, says May, it is "initially experienced" as a "blind push," an "impersonal urge," "always having its biological base" (*Love and Will*, p. 126). It must, then, says May, be integrated by consciousness, being correlated with Eros rather than with sex or libido, and being "shown particularly in creativity." Thus, to *deny* the daimonic, May asserts, "*itself turns out to be daimonic, making us accomplices on the side of the destructive possession*" (*Love and Will*, p. 131).

It is not easy, then, to ascertain precisely what May intends to convey here nor what he seeks to add to the understanding of love or Eros by the introduction of the conception of the daimonic. Two chapters within the section on love are devoted to the conception, which, on examination, appears greatly to resemble Eros in that both are held to be creative-destructive, vital, self-assertive urges toward union and self-fulfillment. The daimonic is said to be *part of* Eros and to *underlie* love and will, while Eros is cited as an example of the daimonic, named as "a daimon," and identified with the daimonic at the outset of discussion. The daimonic is also spoken of as guiding the person and as needing guidance from the person, although it is not an entity but a function. That function is described as "fundamental, archetypal," but with the qualifying phrase that it is "an existential reality in modern man" and "*so far as we know, in all men.*" It is also somewhat difficult to see how a "blind push," needing to be directed and channeled by consciousness, can itself be an integrating principle or pattern of sensibilities constituting or guiding the individual. However, given the location of the discussion in the section on love, what does emerge strongly is that, for May, Eros and "the daimonic" are closely related and that irrational, spontaneous, strong, self-assertive, instinctual urges must not be discounted or glossed over in a comprehensive understanding of being human.

May concludes his section on love with a recapitulation of what he calls "stages of the daimonic" (*Love and Will,* p. 177), stating that it begins as an *impersonal* push by sexual appetite. The next stage is that of "mak[ing] my daimonic urges *personal*" by "transform[ing] this sexual appetite into the motivation to make love to, and be loved by, the woman I desire and choose" (*Love and Will,* p. 177). This seems analogous to the Freudian quantitative libido, which is *then* channeled toward a particular object and which would not easily harmonize with May's view of human freedom. The third or *transpersonal* stage of the daimonic consists of "a more sensitive understanding" of the meaning of human love. Thus, the daimonic pushes us "toward the logos" or universal structure of reality, in what May considers a coming-to-terms with our daimonic tendencies. This structure of daimonic stages, impersonal to personal to transpersonal, seems greatly repetitious of the concept of Eros as directed, channeled, vital striving for union with people, with ethical, philosophical, and esthetic forms, or as creative vitality and love in all its manifestations (*Love and Will,* pp. 74-75, 78-79, 91-94).

Despite his initial naming of four kinds of love, May's analysis of love ends without examination of philia or agape. In this book, May's treatment of philia and agape is confined to some brief paragraphs in the concluding chapter, long after the end of the sections separately devoted to elucidation of love and will. The brevity and location of the discussion of his third and fourth "kinds of love" would seem to suggest that, for May, neither of them warrants as extended or prominent an elucidation as do sex (libido) and Eros (*Love and Will,* pp. 317-319). It is only in the final chapter of his book, in the penultimate brief segment, that May states that just as Eros saved sex from self-destruction, so Eros "cannot live without philia, brotherly love and friendship" (*Love and Will,* p. 317). However, May's notion of philia seems to be confined to friendship as the moment of relaxation and rest from sexual love. Philia, he believes, gives Eros the necessary time to grow and develop. Although he refers to acceptance and relaxed liking of the other person, he appears to circumscribe its meaning, to relate philia basically to human love as sexual, rather than to friendship as such with no sexual overtones involved. This delimitation emerges more clearly still when he mentions early adolescent friendships between eight-to-twelve-year-olds of the same sex, seeing such a friendship as an important stage in development toward the possibility of mature, adult, heterosexual love. Philia, asserts May, is of great importance "in helping us *to find ourselves in the chum period and begin the development of identity*" (*Love and Will,* p. 319, italics mine). The import of the italicized phrase may suggest why philia was recalled so late in the discussion. It would seem that, for May, philia is basically a stage in development of identity and of mature heterosexuality.

As a further "confirmation" of the importance of philia, May cites the results of experiments carried out by H. Harlow with rhesus monkeys. Apparently, monkeys that were not allowed in their early years to have free, nonsexual play with other monkeys were later unable adequately to function sexually. "The period of play with peers is, in other words, an essential prerequisite to the learning of adequate sexual attraction and response to the opposite sex later," says May (*Love and Will,* pp. 318-319). It is clear that May, by analogy, considers early adolescent friendships between children of the same sex as a necessary stage in normal development toward adult sexuality. Further, it would seem to confirm the conclusion that philia, for May, is largely outgrown, since he understands it in this reduced way, that is, as a stage of growth, and it remains only as an element or relaxed moment in a relationship that is primarily sexual. This does not account satisfactorily for intersubjectivity as friendship in any context other than that of sexual development and relationship.

Philia, May goes on, needs agape. In two brief paragraphs, May describes agape as disinterested, selfless giving, the prototype of which is the love of God for man, and a biological analogy to which is parental love without self-interest. Even agapeic love, however, he says, is never totally disinterested, since there is always some element of self-fulfillment involved. In the same chapter, May had spoken of the importance, again in a sexual context, of ability to receive love in order to give love (*Love and Will,* p. 315). This polarity of giving and receiving was necessary, affirmed May, in order that the giving did not become "domination of the partner," and conversely, in a curiously physicalist analogy, because giving alone would empty one unless he were enriched by "active receiving" and absorption of the love of the other.

May concludes his thought on love with a declaration of its being related to will in that it requires form and discipline for its proper expression. Love and will, he holds, are united in that vitality, or creativity must not remain undifferentiated but must be channeled and structured. This structure he grounds in care or concern as the "necessary source" of all tenderness, liking, and creation, since he basically understands care to be the ontological principle that "things do matter" to the human being. Creativity, then, cannot remain undifferentiated, but requires form and structure for its fullest and finest expression, for the deepening of consciousness that, for May, is the aim of Eros.

Summary

Our examination of May's reflections on love has sought to witness the effort of a psychotherapist both to understand his own presuppositions and to integrate them into a comprehensive approach that may be brought to bear in the therapeutic hour. Therapist and patient do not meet on the level of mere naming of abstract psychotherapeutic or psychiatric categories or forms but in the dimension of encounter, of pretheoretical intersubjectivity.

The emphasis on encounter must not, however, be seen as a substitute for the disciplined application of accepted counseling techniques nor as rendering redundant established psychotherapeutic terminology and thorough clinical training. The emphasis on encounter serves rather to relocate the project of psychotherapy, to shift the emphasis from the narrower scope of "why" to the broader reach of "what" it is that underlies the "why." An understanding of past environment alone (family structure, for example) merely generates efficient explanations of what causal factors were involved in the patient's actions. A concentration on progressive aspects alone gives one some insight into the future hopes or orientation of the patient. This approach is another attempt at explanation. The relocation, however, of the whole project in terms of encounter attempts to subsume both of these aspects, to explore *with* the patient the "what" of his present, that is, to participate with the patient in the way in which he experiences, expresses, and works out in his everyday life both past factors and future orientation. This living relationship in therapy is constituted by a loving aliveness to the other, an empathy and comprehension of his standpoint and one's own. It would be likened perhaps to the analogy of making a word one's own. Intellectual knowledge of the dictionary definition or its etymology will not by themselves make an unfamiliar word mine; this is mere technical knowledge. The word becomes part of *my* vocabulary when I grasp not only its "meaning," but also its applications, connotations, overtones, and associations—when I appropriate its inner sense.

Now May, in relocating the concept of love onto its ontological base, that is, in recognizing it as a fundamental, inalienable, defining characteristic of human being, has tried not merely intellectually to understand its essential structure but also to grasp in an inner way the meaning of the emotional expression of love in all its forms, as relationship with people, forms, and ideas. His concern has been to ground his description of love as free, strong, tender, open, and so on in its ontological nature as inalienable being-in-the-world oriented toward others. Thence he seeks to return with greater understanding to love's expression in daily life. His main preoccupation remains a fuller explication of the "lived" meaning of love. He is primarily concerned with human existence as lived, as experienced, and his theoretical reflections on the structure of human existence are subservient to that basic concern.

From the earliest, he has stressed the importance, in particular for psychotherapy, of recalling the close relationship between love and a strong sense of self or firm, vital ontological awareness. This approach does not elevate individuality to greater importance than participation, for self and world are correlative and interdependent, as May sees it. Rather, it explicates a necessary element in loving encounter that must not be confused with clinging dependence nor with aggressive domination.

This analysis has sought to delineate the movement in May's thinking from separate envisioning of love as emotionally expressed between persons and of creative and artistic sensitivity. Even in *Existence,* however, although May spoke of a rapprochement between psychotherapy and ontology, he remained concerned with the psychological understanding of love in the concrete human situation, insofar as he mentioned love at all. He had by this time become convinced of the ontological nature of anxiety as an inalienable, defining element of human existence, giving meaning· to and throwing light on its psychological expression. In the case of love, however, although he linked love with the three existential modes of world, that is, the three fundamental, defining ways in which human being is in-the-world, May's consideration of love was not in terms of what it is in itself but of how it is expressed in the "lived," everyday, human situation. His concern remained with the concrete, practical situation, the fuller understanding of which would be of immediate therapeutic relevance. Love, for May, remained an emotion among emotions, to be understood in a psychological context.

Although he grounded his assertion that anxiety was ontological in that it strikes directly at the sense of being or ontological awareness, and had always understood love to require a strong sense of self, there is not expressed in *Existence* the corresponding realization of the fundamental inalienability of love as an ontological element in existence. The question of why it is that human beings do and *must* love was not yet a

consideration for May, who was merely concerned with asserting the way in which love must find expression in order that
that love be true and happy, that is, as free, individual, committed, valuing the other, and so forth.

His earlier envisioning has been shown to broaden and
deepen into a relocation of the shared source of interpersonal
love and creativity in the ontological nature of love or Eros. The
realization of the ontological nature of love has been the decisive moment in giving coherence and structure to May's psychological understanding of love as experienced, and in giving solid
ground to empirical, psychotherapeutic treatment. In broad
outline, May now envisages the expression of love not merely as
simple, adult relationship between persons, but as the whole
gamut of creative, vital orientation *toward,* the ontological
capacity to accept and affirm one's separation and one's individuality in simultaneous, joyous participation with others, that
is, with other people, with ideas and forms, and with one's own
potentialities.

May identified four kinds of love. These were sex or
libido, Eros, philia and agape. In our analysis of his work as a
whole, however, it was found that he generally emphasized love
as adult and heterosexual, particularly in his reflections in *Love
and Will.* The discussions of philia and agape were rather brief
and both concepts seemed to be discussed mainly as elements in
the experiencing of mature sexual love. It is May's continued
affirmation of human freedom and choice together with his
understanding of love or Eros as the desire for union, both with
people and with forms, that rescues his theoretical understanding from the danger of overconstriction and limitation. Love,
for May, is free, mature, active receiving and giving, oriented to
self-fulfillment by its nature, but not holding its own fulfillment
as its exclusive or even primary goal. For May, then, seen in its
fullest union, psychological as well as physical, sexual loving is
the closest analogy and best expression of the ontological
nature of love as union and separation, as fullest individuation
within closest participation.

It has emerged in our analysis that May's constant concern is with the concrete, everyday, "lived" human situation. As

a psychotherapist, May emphasizes the experience of love as it "should be," that is, as right, normal, bringing contentment and joy, fulfillment and growth, his concrete aim being to throw light on the basic structure not for itself but as it is best experienced. Thence, he hopes to enter into deeper comprehension together with the patient of what it is that has gone awry in his relationships with family and friends, his place in a social structure, his envisioning of himself or sense of his own being. But May does not explicate fully the necessity for human beings to love precisely because they are essentially coexistent beings. Although this is implied as the fundamental reason why love must be free, individual, committed, structured, and so on (all of which qualities May examines), he merely asserts the ontological or inalienable nature of love, seeing it as the rhythm of universal separation and return. The brevity of his remarks on philia and agape is perhaps indicative of his concrete preoccupation and psychotherapeutic orientation, in that people who are capable of experiencing close friendship and self-transcending concern are more likely to have a strong sense of their own being and less likely to need therapeutic counseling. Also, the vulnerability of the person with a weaker, less vital sense of his own being may well be soonest manifested in sexual problems, especially since the modern "freedom" of attitude has tended to overemphasize sexuality. In an era of changing values, such a person may feel bewildered, perhaps even disillusioned, about what it means to be adult, to be a man or woman, about how to reconcile this meaning and one's individuality. Some people, too, may experience anxiety about clashing values, in seeking to harmonize, without compromise, moral integrity with what is socially expected.

May's understanding, then, is intended to aid people, primarily his patients, to envisage more clearly their own situations and to identify and grasp why it is that they sense a problem with which they need help. He hopes, through clear-sighted yet concerned encounter, to help his patient to develop a sharper sense of his own being, his wishes and goals, in order to move beyond anxious, limited self-concern to structured, willed coexistence and some measure not merely of fleeting pleasure but of vital lasting joy.

I have been concerned in this chapter to elucidate and examine May's thought on love, to show how he moved from a psychological description of love at its best as an experienced, interpersonal relationship, to a deeper, ontological understanding of creative vitality in man as the basic, human urge of the separated, totally centered, individual self toward participation, reunion, and fulfillment in others, in persons, ideas, and forms. The predominant preoccupation, for May, however, remained the examination of interpersonal love, particularly sexual love, since, for him, it is in union with another person that anxious isolation is most effectively overcome and one's self most fulfilled. It has also been seen that, as May sees it, it is the failure of human beings to cope with such total relationships that is the main context of psychotherapy. Only in the close bond of self-commitment, of continued reinforcement of one's being as being-in-the-world, as May sees it, is affirmation of self and world possible in an integrated, joyous, courageous reliance on the love of the other.

To be a self and to have a world are at once the challenge of integrated existence. Hence, May's thought on love can be understood only in relation to integration and structure, to the quality of lasting concern that is grounded in care and channeled by creative decision. Love that is ephemeral is only anxious dependence and whim. Creative vitality or love should not be wasted and dissipated, uncontrolled, unguided, and undiscriminating. Love must endure in order to grow. In its ontological nature there is already a volitional element in the will to unite. Yet neither participation nor individuation is possible without the coinherence of structure, order, purpose, and resolution. The emotional element in love is not sufficient alone. For May, creative will as free, responsible choice is a necessary element in love. May has more than once stressed the necessity of enduringness in love, holding that only disorder and confusion can result from unstructured loving. Even in anxiety, the normal tendency is to focus on a specific problem and cope with that, rather than to lose oneself in vague apprehension. So, in love, the normal tendency is not to overflow with affection but rather to seek a particular person or discipline, to find affinity of interests and aims in order to feel "at home" or "to belong."

Authentic existence is neither automatic nor capricious, but an oriented becoming, an integration of freedom and destiny, a continuing effort to reconcile what we are with what we sense we could be, or would like to be, or should be. To give one's love is to open one's inner being to the other, to share one's world with him and grow together in that sharing. May's understanding of love, then, cannot be separated from his view of it as related to the sense of being, as the creative vitality that reaches toward possibilities, yet is constituted by mortality. Nor can his understanding of love be separated from it as purposeful and enduring, as interrelated with will and with the symbols by which man interprets the goals toward which he orients his existence.

FOUR

Significance of Will

It is in intentionality and will that the
human being experiences his identity.
"I" is the "I" of "I can."
Rollo May, *Love and Will*

In a century fraught with desperate decisions, many of them
born of our unparalleled technical power, contemporary man
finds himself in a dilemma. Amid the metallic gleam of ma-
chines that can compute answers faster than the human being
can ever hope to enunciate the questions, man stands bewildered as to what genuinely constitutes his happiness and what
questions he wishes to pose. He conducts endless surveys and
draws up a myriad of statistics, tries to improve socioeconomic
conditions, and wonders helplessly why this is not enough, why
the machine is unable to find for him simple answers to the

147

questions that sound the simplest and yet prove to be the most complex. Humanity is undoubtedly powerful, but individuals seem increasingly powerless. Humanity, as a species, is capable of tremendous achievement, but the human being, as individual, is left to wonder of what relevance such progress may be to him and what can it tell him of the significance of his existence.

Our age, says Rollo May, is one of crisis in human will, in the symbolic or integrating processes of wish and decision. Apathetic, unresponsive, frustrated, self-centered, and bored, modern man is bereft of the absolute belief in willpower that sustained, for example, the Victorian and Renaissance worlds. Frightened of the power of his own instinctual urges, he is afraid to "impose" discipline on himself, his children, and his world, for fear of the irreparable psychological damage and unjust encroachment on others' freedom of which contemporary society speaks so glibly. Yet he fears, too, the consequences of unrestrained yielding to instinctual wishes and desires. Recoiling from the burden of personal decision and responsibility, the individual has in many cases not only delegated management of his life to society and the "experts," but has also gradually ceded many rights and duties to the vast, impersonal bureaucracies, which can conveniently be blamed when results are not satisfactory. Thus, gradually, he has ceased to know what he, as a separated, centered individual wants or believes. He clamors for more and more social services and expensive facilities in the vain hope that these will alleviate his growing desire for unadulterated peace and happiness without guilt, tension, worry, or anxiety. This is, however, to abdicate his responsibility for himself and his world and carries its own burden of guilt, tension, worry, and anxiety.

Contemporary man, then, although seeming highly "active," busy, and constructive, is in many instances confused and torn between his doubts and fears, his wish to believe in human progress and not to be faced with human evildoing, his skeptical view of the "almighty will," his distrust of discipline, his longing for inner peace, and a simultaneous fear, sometimes neurotic, of his own wishes and urges. What he fears as egocentric irrational impulse and childish religious primitivism constantly war with his fundamental need and struggle to be at peace with himself, his world, and his fellow man.

At the level of popular experience and understanding, there are discernible two salient, exaggerated views on the controversial subjects of human will, decision, freedom, autonomy, and responsibility. One view, commonly associated with the name of Freud, is what might be characterized as a biological determinist conviction that, in this ordered, determined, systematic world, the human being is merely a more complicated, higher animal, a mass of confused complexes, childhood influences, moral inhibitions, rebellious reactions, whims, and wishes, some of which are more dominant than others in the search for continuous, sensuous, hedonistic satisfaction. An independent mind is only an illusion; instead, the sophisticated man is aware that the mind is really only akin to, even though more complex than, practical animal intelligence, tied to environmental (particularly parental) factors and influences and to inheritance, determined and completely predictable if only we "knew all the facts."

It remains true, however, that the deterministic self-understanding underlying such a view cannot theoretically encompass human freedom as experienced, cannot comprehend the creative response to contingency, to determined factors. Although one cannot ignore or minimize the insights of Freud and his successors concerning psychological processes and environmental influences, for example, it is nevertheless true that these insights are tied for the most part to a fundamental ideal of explanation at the source of which lies efficient, mechanical causality. Such an ideal cannot extend to encompass man's capacity to be creative and responsible in terms of the future. Paradoxically, then, there are those who seem to interpret freedom, will, and decision as the mere utilitarian accommodation of determined factors; yet the formulation of this accommodation in terms of the reality-pleasure principle does not alter the underlying, and, it seems, unwitting, assumption that one is free to make that very accommodation.

On the other hand, the second popular extreme view is characterized by a rationalistic belief that the development of human intelligence (and thus control of world and self) is what constitutes man's value and ideal. The body is but a servant, a means, an appendage, a useful harbor for the soaring mind or spirit that can delight in pure forms, in the clarity of ideas—in mathematical understanding, for example. In such a characterization of being human, it is the mind that is deemed to in*form* and create order out of the chaotically undifferentiated. All things are objects for the mind and are deemed susceptible of exact, precise, neat, and unequivocal formulation.

Exaggerated emphasis on the intellectual, rational, or volitional aspects of being human is not without its consequences for the embodied aspect of human being. Such exaggeration renders possible, and indeed facilitates, a radically dualistic understanding of the being of man, an understanding that alienates mind from body, "mental" or "spiritual" from "physical" or "natural," as this dualism is commonly expressed. Correspondingly, such a dualistic conception would militate against the reintegration of the corporeal and conscious aspects of human being.

At the precritical, pretheoretical level, one finds this instanced in the Victorian voluntarist repression of all "improper" emotions, impulses, and desires, and in the artificial imposition of a tightly disciplined order. This was, in essence, a system of external pressures that operated with the support of moral justification. It was essentially a system of social order maintained by a forced compliance known variously as *willpower, strength of character,* or even *moral rectitude.* In practice, such strength was often the negative strength of control or discipline for its own sake, or even an inability to exercise individual judgment and decision. The social order was quietly but firmly enforced by means of the threat of social condemnation or even total ostracism. The effect of such a punishment clearly would be to cut the person off from his world, to look on him as other, as alien and unacceptable, thus robbing him of his "place in the world." Such a punishment, which is, in essence, the core of all punishments, estranged the person from himself by denying him his world, thereby doing violence to his sense of his being, of his worth and value as an individual human being-in-the-world.

Yet by refusing to admit impulses, by categorizing virtually all spontaneity as unseemly, unthinking, and childish, the formality-conscious Victorians refused to acknowledge spontaneity as proper to human being and denied the role of wish as a creative exploration of one's own possibilities. By minimizing the role and importance of instinct and impulse, such a man delivered himself into the state of dilemma that still peculiarly colors the contemporary problem of will. Such a man, who might be characterized as a voluntarist, effectively denied himself any involvement in determining the content for decision and thereby implicitly disavowed the opportunity to use the disciplined, controlled, highly rational powers of judgment that he had been at such pains to develop and value. Instead, he forced himself into the straitjacket of externally imposed authority, the reasoning of which he, the supremely developed rationalist, did not allow himself to question, indeed, could not allow himself to question. Thus, thinking for oneself, making one's own decisions, forming one's own opinions—these were acceptable only when the result was in accord with the pre-ordained "rules." Hence, will and decision were for such a man only a futile exercise, a mere formality or face-saver, since the matter or content for decision was arbitrarily restricted and the so-called decision itself dictated and inexorably "guided" from without. Integrity in individuality, then, which the Victorians held in apparently high esteem, was thus curiously actually devalued in favor of the less dangerous integrity in conformity.

In our time, by contrast and perhaps in some measure because of reaction rather than genuine change, conformity has become, for many people, the ultimate social sin, in theory if not always in fact. In an oddly puritanical shudder at the "unnatural" external discipline of the Victorian world, contemporary society has avidly seized upon behavioristic and psychoanalytic terms such as *repression, neurosis, ego development,* and *self-expression,* and has haphazardly tried to legitimize immediate, spontaneous expression of all impulses. Lip service, in many cases, is paid to integrity and independence in an unquestioned and unreasoned allegiance to a vague belief in "authenticity" and the "freedom to be oneself, since one is in any case totally determined." Such belief, then, makes possible the legitimizing of doing as one pleases without responsibility or guilt. It makes possible, further, the envisioning of laws as mere pragmatic rules of order, aimed at allowing the greatest freedom for the greatest number of intelligent human animals to act according to their impulses. Good and evil cease to be acceptable categories. Conformity to old social customs, to more demanding conventions and values, is then easily rationalized as cowardly, inhibited, old-fashioned and dull, while, by some strange reasoning, to conform to the present-day ideal of change and "progress" is not seen as conformity at all, but as individuation, "being yourself."

The confusion of chaotic whim or license with freedom is apparently just as expedient as the confusion of externally imposed compliance with self-discipline. But either is a superficial approach to human existence. In both cases, man is unfree: On the one hand, he is ruled by impulse; on the other, by the absolutized demands of a man-made social system. In both cases, the cloth that is man has been ruthlessly cut and sewn to fit a preconceived pattern, and the process of will has been thrown out with the cuttings.

What is characteristic of these exaggerated modes of popular self-understanding, then—that of the "helpless," hedonistic determinist and that of the "controlled" rationalist—is their failure to come to terms with human being in all of its aspects. Such self-understanding on the subject of will is implicitly to separate the "finite spatio-temporal body" from the "free creative mind or spirit." At the direct, prereflective, experiential level, however, one does not encounter "body" nor "mind," but encounters individual persons who exist their being simultaneously bodily and mentally. Every thought, then, is made possible, however remotely, by sense experience, while human sense experience is located necessarily within a matrix of meaning. Such a conception of person, in that it is a reflective conception, is itself "removed" from the "lived" world, whose direct spontaneous action and reaction can never be perfectly mirrored and expressed; each person envisages the "lived" world through the maze of associations, overtones, personal experiences, moods, likes, dislikes, education, and environmental (including social) influences, which inhere at every moment in every act of perception. The self is in a continuous process of interaction with its world, constituting individual and participatory meaning at many levels.

The two popular extreme views, "determinist" and "rationalist," are too exclusive to be consistently livable and are theoretically possible only at the price of an artificial view of human living, that is, one reduced in perspective. Further, the "determinist" view, although denying the possibility of free, responsible human choice, has itself *chosen* to view human existence in this way. From his similarly arbitrarily reduced perspective, the "rationalist" tends to conceive of the body more as a hindrance to the realization of the meaning of being human. Neither view can encompass the totality of human experience in a meaningful way nor account for human freedom as it is experienced by the human being, an embodied conscious being, a meaning-disclosing, deciding, acting, responsible unity.

The strenuous efforts at forcible control that characterized the Victorian world, however, must not be minimized nor reduced in importance. Indeed, in their very insistence on the rationality of man, of his power to control himself and his world, the Victorians were bearing witness to the dignity of man, which is born in his ability to question and be responsible for his own being. Their failure, like that of other tightly ordered societies, lay in giving too much sovereignty to the social system that they themselves had built, such emphasis thereby undermining the exercise of free, human creativity and will. Yet this failure is understandable when it is seen to stem from the natural human desire to make or help to create something of lasting value that will continue to give guidance and service to future generations.

No detotalized view of human existence, however, can encompass the meaning of individual existence nor of individual will. Only by reaching out to comprehend the fundamental structures of human existence itself can one hope to throw light on these meanings. It is only when the human self is seen in dialectical relationship with the "world," when the self is seen in the perspective of a fundamental intentional orientation to the "world," that there arises the possibility of entering into the meaning of individual existence, the significance of individual will, and the perception of human freedom as experienced.

Will, then, cannot be adequately encompassed in either popular extreme view: the one amounting to a reduction of will to a useless battering against foreordained happenings or irresistible urges, and the other amounting to a blind belief in rational control or forced self-discipline. Will implies, rather, an integration of conscious and unconscious, of acceptance and moral autonomy, and a recognition of influences for what they are, whether they be cultural, environmental, familial, or biological. It implies, in the end, a responsible assertion of one's whole being-in-the-world, in mature dissent or agreement, in thoughtful choices and actions, together with the ability to shoulder the burden of human freedom, the burden of individual decision and responsibility. Every commitment, every decision, then, is seen to derive from an intentional orientation, an isolation of and attention to some factors, a rejection of others, a cutting off (de*cision*) or definition (limitation, clarification) of the area of concern, a conscious or unconscious attitude toward the whole as well as toward the components of the situation.

The problem of will for contemporary man, then, is the age-old struggle between what one is and what one senses one could or should be. It is the conflict of self and world, the difficulty of coming to terms with the complex human situation or condition, with one's world in all its aspects. Man's attempts to reduce the significance of human will to a matter of forcible rational "control" or instrument of "repression," or to an illusion of human vanity in a wholly determined world, have made it difficult for him to integrate the notion of will with the existential situation in which he finds himself. Nor can he understand why he experiences pain, anxiety, guilt, or even dulling apathy, since he has shifted the fundamental responsibility for himself and his fellowman to society, to groups, to organizations, associations, and companies, to governments and their agencies. He should be joyously free and happy, but instead he feels chained, hemmed in, and restless. The acceptance of either of the popular misunderstandings of will implies a refusal to accept full individual responsibility and commitment and carries with it the possibility of feeling ultimately that one has become somehow diminished and thereby correspondingly less able effectively to shoulder that responsibility.

For his part, from the outset of his writings, Rollo May has clearly stated his opposition to both of these popular, detotalized misunderstandings of human will and decision and declares them to be diminished, narrow, and therefore inadequate. He has always been as much opposed to what he calls "surface willing" as he is against chaotic whim. He regards a belief in total determinism as irresponsible, childish desire to shift the burden of freedom to someone else, while forcible, driving voluntarism is, he asserts, a deliberate ignoring of the richness of human nature, a self-imposed, narrow rigidity for fear of the power of instinctual urges.

The significance of will, May believes, is coextensive with being human, with all of the aspects of being-in-the-world and with man's capacity to symbolize, that is, integratedly to envision, examine, and grasp his being and his world. As May envisages the whole question, man becomes truly and fully human only in thoughtful decision, when he shoulders his responsibility for himself and his world, when he symbolizes this in commitment to structured, coherent coexistence and individual autonomy.

The "I," for May, remains vague and unreal until the person deliberates, chooses, commits, and acts, bringing into reality the identity, the being, that was sensed as a dream, a wish, a possibility. Further, May believes that since the human being is a conscious being and cannot *not* question his own existence, his very orientation to existence itself begins as a choice, a commitment, a "decision," or a "cutting off" of some possibilities, a definition of others as desirable. Will, then, is not a question merely of choice between alternative courses of action and their implications, but rather is a question of the very orientation or primary commitment to existence that guides and directs the person's whole existence as an individual being-in-the-world. It is ultimately, for May, a question of the most fundamental relatedness of the person to existence.

May's reflections on will begin from his early consideration of will as decisive, conscious action, and of values as the goals in function of which one shapes such actions. Later he reaches out to a deeper, integrated, comprehensive envisioning of will as the basic intentionality of human existence, as explicitly ontological, as the fundamental, structured recognition by the separated, totally centered, individual, valuing-knowing-striving self of its complex symbolic relationship to its world. There are no definitions of will in May's early work, but there is evident concern not merely with self-expression or spontaneous vitality but with *responsible* freedom and *structured* self-expression as being more effective in the healthy development of creative personality. Later, however, May moves to the deeper question of the ground (and basis of that greater effectiveness) of that structure in his consideration of the fundamental orientedness of the human self toward symbolic meaning with its necessary implications for choice and commitment.

The task of will as May sees it, as the ontological intentionality or fundamental orientedness of human existence, is to mold and form self and world, to give order and coherence to the creative vitality of love that is, to accept one's relatedness to oneself, to one's fellow man and one's world, to reach out for the possibilities sensed in anxiety, to shoulder the guilt and responsibility of human imperfection and striving, and continuously to affirm the everchanging, symbolic, situational relatedness of self and world in greater strength and freedom.

The next section explicates and examines the earliest moments of May's understanding of will and critically witnesses how already they foreshadow his mature view of will as the fundamental process of orientedness, of molding, forming, and reforming one's whole existence, as always going *toward* something. May's mature envisioning of man as beginning in decisive orientation, in primary commitment, as sensing and deciding his being in terms of symbols or symbolizing his being in decisive manner, is shown to grow and develop from his early consideration of the aim of therapy as helping the patient to grow toward integrated, courageous, structured living.

Toward Structured Self-Expression

"Every act of consciousness," asserts May in *Love and Will,* "*tends toward* something . . . and has within it, no matter how latent, some push toward a direction for action" (*Love and Will,* p. 230). In other words, the structure of human consciousness is fundamentally intentional, in the broadest sense of the word, that is, it includes both reflective *intentions* or chosen purposes, and the wishes, instincts, needs, drives, potentialities, and tendencies of which the person may be least aware. Now, in his discussion of the six ontological characteristics, May offers the view that self-consciousness in man changes the whole Gestalt, that centeredness, self-affirmation, participation, and awareness in man can be understood only in terms of the change wrought by the emergence of self-consciousness. Also, having held throughout his work, and particularly in *Existence* (*Contributions,* p. 90-91), that he could not accept the "blank check" or "cellar" notion of the unconscious, May maintained that "unconscious" must not be understood literally as "not-in-consciousness," nor as a "place"; that consciousness is not merely a matter of what is present to attention or of what is reflected on, but colors and tempers all human awareness, experience, and potentialities. The term *unconscious,* for May, must be understood to refer to conscious material denied, repressed, or forgotten; potentialities experienced or sensed, underlying "irrational" impulse and "spontaneous" urge, "the potentialities for awareness, knowing and feeling which we cannot yet actualize" (*Existential Psychotherapy,* p. 46). "We observe when these insights occur that the breakthrough never comes 'hit and miss,' but in accordance with a pattern one essential element of which is our own commitment" (*Dreams and Symbols,* pp. 6-8). For example, at a given moment I may suddenly become conscious of having very strongly disliked for some time someone whom I had consciously thought I liked; although on some level I knew my true feelings about the person, I "refused" to admit to myself or to become explicitly conscious of my real dislike, because of the pressure of a strong motive—perhaps that of social conformity and acceptance—that is now overcome by a stronger wish—perhaps that of continuing to see myself as honest and straightforward, both desires being important in that they related closely to my sense of being. "The person is engaged with his world not only on levels that include consciousness and fantasy but on other levels that are often lumped together in many gradations of 'pre-' or 'sub-' or 'un'-consciousness . . . unconscious life is also *intentional*. It is oriented in some direction: the dream or fantasy is saying, this is the way I see the world, and this is the way I see myself in it" (*Dreams and Symbols*, p. 8). Thus, particularly for the patient in therapy who first seeks to know and understand himself and his world and their interrelationship, the importance of such a conception of "unconscious" is that it confronts him squarely with his share of responsibility for the fundamental quality of that self-world relationship. May calls this stage in therapy *the transmuting of awareness into consciousness* (*Love and Will*, pp. 266-267) and my analysis returns specifically to this point in the fourth section of this chapter.

It is, then, asserts May, in intentionality and will, in the broad reach of human orientation toward meaning, decision, and act, in the weighing, deciding, and acting on possibilities sensed, that the individual·person experiences his identity, exercises his freedom, and senses his being. Already, in his earliest work, May offers as his fundamental conviction the view that the self is that which the person is always in process of becoming. This becoming, this dynamic emerging, although limited and contingent, is free. It is not automatic nor is it wholly determined. It is rather the constant achievement and attainment of possibility, grounded in consciousness or the human capacity to be aware of self and world, of the passage of time and of its meaning in duration, of human situatedness or everchanging relatedness. This becoming is a symbolic process, that is, a creative attention to and grasping of possibilities, their meaning for the individual's whole existence, and the constant, increasingly reflective deliberation and decision as to which goals or values will predominate in the constitution of his being. Hence, it is quite consistent that May would assert that the important thing in therapy is that the person discover his being, that he take his existence seriously. The patient must develop the "orientation of commitment," for he cannot permit himself to understand and confront the problems underlying his symptoms until he makes, with his whole being, the primary decision truthfully and courageously to accept and explore his existence, his total intentionality (*Contributions,* pp. 87-88). In *Love and Will* (p. 138), May indicates that his use of the term *symbolic* is correlated with his understanding of its Greek etymology in *"sym-bollein,"* a verb meaning "to throw or put together," to unite and integrate, contrasting with *"dia-bollein,"* to tear apart.

Thirty years before his thought on the intentionality of human existence was to be explicitly articulated with particular emphasis on the importance of understanding intentionality in therapy, May was already holding that, since personality is never static, but always emerging, becoming, the element of choice was crucial to what he then called *personality health.* In *The Art of Counseling,* May had already offered the observation that mental health was directly correlated with the patient's ability creatively to accept and mold the materials of his own life, to appropriate his potentiality of freedom (*Art of Counseling,* pp. 51-53, 213). Correspondingly, May held that neurosis was caused by the patient's inability to will constructively, to affirm himself, his situation with his fellow men, and life as a whole, to respond actively and joyously to his own possibilities.

Such affirmation, however, such *individuation* and *social integration,* to use May's early terms, could be successful and constructive only if it was integrated, guided, and structured. Unrestricted and unguided self-expression, or the satisfaction of all impulses without discrimination, would lead to destruction and must be seen to provide only the content of living. Such ungoverned expression of vitality would not suffice for the achievement of integrated existence. What is needed, says May, is cooperation between instinctual impulses or vital urges and conscious aims or purposes, not merely a surface cooperation or superficial "wrestling match" resulting in a forced compliance, but more deeply a "becoming resolved" that involves the whole person. This cooperation in terms of "the necessary structure" of moral living is, as May sees it, basic to personality health, or integrated existence, as it is only when they are based in such a "becoming resolved" that decisions can be powerful and effective.

To find this "necessary structure," May looks first to what he calls the *norms of social living* (*Art of Counseling,* p. 195). Here he finds that only with unselfishness and cooperation is social living possible and that the individual, highly dependent on his fellow man for survival, must learn to control his impulses and have consideration for the well-being of the group. But any cultural structure, however highly developed, is, as May sees it, a partial answer only, because one cannot prescribe or explain unselfishness and cooperation in terms solely of adjustment to changing conventions or social conditions. The individual can still decide to be egocentric and ignore the well-being of the group.

May might have added, by way of further explication, that one cannot explain cooperation in terms of adjustment alone because human freedom liberates man to involve himself in a continuing reflective effort to know and understand of what his happiness consists. Each individual is directly and unequivocally concerned in seeking his own happiness and fulfillment. Correspondingly, then, with regard to social provisions for his conduct, man always wants to know *why* he must act in a certain way, what it will do for him, how it will benefit him. He is all the more concerned to know *why* and will accept only what seems to him a basically worthwhile reason comporting *some* element of personal benefit, however remote, especially if the particular act or restraint happens to inconvenience him. Thus, involuntarily, he makes an initial act of faith or trust in the overall intelligibility and worth of human existence together with a fundamental assertive recognition of his own worth as an autonomous, existing, thinking, responsible human being, while also acknowledging that he is already situated in coexistence with other human beings. Even the most dictatorial regimes, sensing that pragmatic regulation of society must be seen to have some good purpose other than itself, seek to convince their citizens that such regulation is intended to bring about change for the better in their society and therefore in each individual life, and that without such regulation, their economy and their state would crumble in anarchic decay, ruining all of their individual lives. Even if a given individual should decide that existence itself is absurd, his very decision bears witness to his original belief in and search for meaning in existence. Further, even in his considered declaration of the absurdity of existence, he is positing the paradoxical conclusion that the meaning of existence is "un-meaning." In other words, he is still trying to understand and encompass the reason why existence is as it is, why things are so; he is still attempting to do what he declares cannot be done, to render existence understandable, if only by exposing what he believes to be its central lack of intelligibility.

At this early point in his work, however, Rollo May does not proceed to such further considerations, but states only briefly, and in a very general way, that the individual "learns by painful experience" (*Art of Counseling*, p. 195) that he must direct his self-expression in accord with the norms of social living, for otherwise he is lost outside the group and can only be readmitted when he "renounces egocentricity" in favor of working for general well-being. This somewhat negative approach (which is reminiscent of Freud's reality-pleasure principle) is not easily reconciled with May's earlier insistence on the necessity of balance of individuation and social integration. Perhaps realizing this, May hastens to assert that, however helpful social norms may be to understanding social existence as lived, the norms of social living can be viewed only as a partial answer in his search for the necessary structure that must underlie such healthy self-expression or achievement of integrated existence.

Again, May might have added a further point of explication. Although human existence is lived in and through coexistence, an envisioning of human existence as a kind of undifferentiated collectivity does violence to that essential structure. Human being, then, is known properly not as a collectivity but as individual-in-society, individual-in-participation. It is not merely negatively, or as May put it, through "painful experience," that the individual learns of the human "web of interdependence" to which May briefly refers (*Art of Counseling,*

pp. 195, 62-63). The individual also learns, in family, in friendship, and in all the gamut of loving relationships, his need and
wish to love and be loved, to deal well with his fellow men in
order that they may complement and aid each other's growth
and fulfillment in the human search for peace and happiness.
But however great one individual's insight into the lives and purposes of others, there remains always an impenetrable barrier
between one individual and another. This barrier is their very
individuality. No total merging or complete understanding of
any other is possible for human beings who, by their consciousness of themselves, are aware that each is totally centered and
separated, and therefore all the more an individual-in-participation. Without such awareness of individuality, there could be no
human social integration nor individual presence, but only a
kind of instinctual mass existence.

Now it is clear, overall, that May's early work is deeply
concerned with balance of individuation and social integration
and that May envisages neurosis as failure to integrate the two
or the failure to affirm such balance. Hence, his phrase "to renounce egocentricity" in favor of greater social concern is
obviously not to be understood to mean a denial of self or sub-
merging of individual existence in favor of group conformism or
exaggerated social orientation. The phrase must instead be
understood to mean a renunciation of the *negative* self-concern
or self-preoccupation that could, in May's view, dangerously
reduce social integration and that carries the risk of social rejection and neurosis. Yet even this interpretation of May's meaning, although in accord with his overall thinking, does little
more than restate his earlier negative assertion that the individual learns by painful experience that he must coordinate his
self-expression with the norms of social living. Thus, May has
not really explicated why it is that these norms are only a partial answer to his search for "the necessary structure."

Earlier in *The Art of Counseling,* May had stated that he
considers social *adjustment* alone inadequate for social integration and he now reiterates this, stating simply that the norms of
social living are to be seen as only "one aspect of something
much deeper and broader" (*Art of Counseling,* p. 196). What

May does not explicate is that the norms of social living are inadequate as a structure for the achievement of integrated existence, not only because such norms do not take full account of individuation, but also because, even with regard to social living, such norms are, at their very best, only a flexible *frame* or code of behavior. The norms of social living, more concerned with human *conduct* than with the *meaning* of human being as individual-in-participation or individual-in-community, are, then, changing conventions, restrictions, and restraints that are intended to provide only a frame of good order for well-regulated daily living, in which individuals may safely, without undue obstruction or interference from others, seek to build their lives. Further, these norms, concerned directly, in a *practical* manner, with concrete day-to-day living, are largely negative and *thus* only a partial reflection of something beyond themselves, namely; the *meaning* or *understanding* of existence that gave them birth. Taken in isolation from that meaning or understanding, therefore, the norms of social living, in their tenuous and changing nature, can provide a partial answer only.

In his search, then, for the necessary structure that, May is convinced, can alone enable a man to attain moral autonomy and responsibility, that is, to meet the challenge of integrated existence, May offers "a more profound approach to a moral structure" (*Art of Counseling,* p. 196, see also pp. 57-61, 232, n. 18). He proceeds to consider what he calls "moral archetypes . . . 'inborn morality' . . . moral patterns which we have because we are born as men . . . humanity's psychic depository of morality" (*Art of Counseling,* p. 196). May posits levels of unconscious and patterns or "ways of thought which a man possesses simply because he is a man" (*Art of Counseling,* p. 59). These are, says May, deep, universal principles or eternal patterns arising out of the very structure of existence, in the very roots of man's being, whose faint outline may be found in one's own depths, patterns or principles that are passed on from age to age through the collective unconscious of humanity. This, asserts May, is an "inner approach" to moral structure; these patterns or principles or archetypes are on a deeper level than "specific morals," he says, and have therefore a "claim to universality." He cites "similar moral ideas" in unconnected races and cultures as expressions or examples of these universal moral archetypes, as fundamental human intuitions of moral structure, or of how human beings envisage their conduct "at the deepest level"; these examples are prohibition of murder, incest, and rape, and "the demand for justice" or balancing of human relationships. These, says May, are expressions of universally felt moral archetypes, and "crop up" in every culture.

What May would seem to be positing here is a collective unconscious awareness of a dimly perceived moral structure and he frankly admits the difficulty of trying to explain and render more distinct such a fleeting perception. He speaks of penetrating through one's own unconsciousness to the collective unconscious of mankind in order to "tap the universal archetypes" (*Art of Counseling,* p. 197). "The great artist," he said earlier, "serves as an artesian well through which eternal patterns spring into expression" (*Art of Counseling,* p. 60). May seems to envisage this operation analogically, rather as one might draw water from a well or bore through many strata of rock to reach a known valuable stratum. This would seem to imply that, as May sees them, these archetypes are somehow independent, stored up by past generations in a kind of centuries-old deposit of proven, veteran wisdom and understanding of human existence, to be rediscovered and reformulated by "the great geniuses of goodness" (*Art of Counseling,* p. 197). Yet May holds that even such archetypes do not offer a complete structure that could underlie and guide the person toward integrated, healthy self-expression. Such a structure, he goes on, would be only partial and incomplete if based only on the archetypes since, in practice, races and nations have been known to grow powerful and strong from their collective unconscious of racial and national hatred and destructiveness and have succeeded in channeling and using such collective unconscious force very effectively *against* others.

Now May might profitably have remembered that many of the prohibitions of murder, incest, and rape, which he gave as examples of universal moral archetypes, have been quite unknown in some cultures. Infanticide, particularly of unwanted female or sickly male babies, was, for some cultures, an accepted means of controlling and safeguarding healthy race growth, for example, in ancient Rome, as late as the second century A.D., legal exposure of newborn infants. Some of the Pharaohs of Egypt married their sisters for the multiple purpose of protecting the state against internecine wars of succession, in order to limit and cement claims to the throne and even to keep the royal bloodline intact. Euthanasia has also been known as a means of protecting the mobility and/or food-supply, and hence survival, of the race, particularly of nomadic tribes contending against overwhelmingly difficult climatic conditions. Prohibition of rape, in some cultural manifestations, was more to protect a valuable family asset, that is, the possibility of power, position, or wealth through the woman making a "good" marriage or reaching high priestly office. This may explain why the victim of rape, blameless as she might be, was deemed to have been dishonored and therefore somehow "guilty," the depth of her "shame" being in direct proportion to her family's social eminence and aspirations. These, then, are not necessarily *moral* archetypes nor even *universally* felt in the sense of ethical intuitions, but can indeed be seen as cultural expressions of an economic or political understanding of human existence in terms of assets and liabilities.

May's other example, that of the "demand for justice" or for "balancing of human relations," is indeed more basic than the cited prohibitions. This demand, says May, "crops up in every culture (*Art of Counseling*, p. 196). Yet this example is too vague and means little in itself and of itself as the living proof from human experience that May intended it to be. In the existential human situation, in many rigidly class- or caste-structured societies, some human beings, known variously as *villeins, serfs,* or *slaves,* were regarded as less than human and incapable of appreciating or of having any rights. In a word, to be human was not enough in order to be treated as such. In such a situation, a man's *humanity* had little or nothing to do with the life he lived or with the demands made on him to serve as an object or as a work unit, and he could be put to death for any attempt to escape servitude. It would seem, then, that May, in seeing a demand for "justice" or balance in human relations as "cropping up in every culture," and therefore as archetypal, is, in fact, confusing or even equating justice with the concrete manifestations of social order and pragmatic utilitarian balance. For example, one slaveowner or landlord or naval captain might be deemed by his peers to be harsh or less kindly than other men in adhering rigidly to the legal prescription of flogging or other severe punishment for offences on the part of slaves or villeins or conscripts, but he would not be deemed *unjust*. Clearly, such pragmatic balance is not *necessarily* grounded in a conception of justice based on equity and responsibility of all men in their common humanity, taking into account their rights, opportunities, circumstances, and duties as members of a particular society. The maintenance, for example, of the rights of a powerful few at the expense of other human beings may preserve some order and regulation in society, and has indeed been typical or at least widespread in many cultures, even some based originally on a deeper concept of love and justice toward men, but it is not of itself expressive of a universal, deeply felt, archetypal demand for justice.

May's "demand for justice," like his other archetypes and "the norms of social living," is not sufficient in and of itself, then, but points beyond itself to a greater value that gives it significance and ground. It is not complete in itself, but is only the very general and elusive reflection of the greater value as it is interpreted and expressed in existence, such as the worth of individual existence, the necessity of racial survival or of ordered coexistence. This May intuits—but does not explicate—since he expresses the view (*Art of Counseling,* p. 198) that his "moral archetypes" cannot provide a total or complete answer, that is, cannot be relied on to give the "necessary moral structure" to instinctual urges or self-expression. Although, as May sees it, one's moral "code," or "conscience," is more than parental or social influence alone and is based in awareness, more or less clear, of a morality guided by what he sees as universal, moral, archetypal patterns, he is still not satisfied that such awareness, however clear, is adequate as an "ultimate structure" for moral living.

However, as in the case of the norms of social living, May does not seem to have realized that the inadequacy of his moral archetype is not that they do not always prevail, nor that man can err, but simply and properly that they are only parts of a frame, only partial expressions of cultural understanding of something beyond themselves. They are largely a negative code of rules, again not *directly* related to affirmation of meaning, a variable system of *conduct,* not concerned essentially with individual happiness and fulfillment within society, but only with prevention of *un*happiness and with the provision of good order and a well-regulated society in which the individual may seek to build his life. Yet May did realize that one must seek further the positive value or meaning on which such provisions and prohibitions can properly be grounded and for that from which positive, structured, instinctual self-expression can spring.

To achieve integrated existence or, in May's earlier terminology, to guide instinctual impulses in healthy self-expression, no simple structure of moral archetypes or changing social norms is enough. It is not easy to reach out for and maintain ever-greater freedom, to control and guide impulses, to deliberate and decide between various urges rather than to deny them in *un*-freedom and fear. With conviction but little specific explication, May declares that the only structure adequate for decisive moral living is "that based upon the ultimate meaning of life" (*Art of Counseling,* p. 200), and that each person must decide on the "most adequate concept" of this meaning on which to base his morality or self-expression. Only in function of an ultimate meaning, says May, can the person's self-expression be healthy, that is, spontaneous, genuine, and original, from the depths of his self, in harmony with himself and his world. Such a meaning will include and transcend all partial and specific meanings. It will be universal and objective, possessing ultimate value not only within the individual but also outside him. Belief in such meaning, in "the reasonable, meaningful structure of life," "logos," or "God," asserts May, is not only imperative for personality health, but is, in fact, the ground of all meaning and purpose, the wellspring of human vitality and striving to know, the source of man's desire to understand and

govern his existence, to give coherence and order to his instinctual expression (*Art of Counseling,* p. 200).

The "principles" of that meaningful structure are, asserts
May, "the principles which underlie life from the beginning of
creation to the end," "the nature of God," "the principles of
God" (*Art of Counseling,* p. 201), transcending and including
all partial structures. Conscience, he goes on, is our perception
of the structure, our dim awareness of our original, essentially
good nature, in accord with ourselves, prior to the conflicts of
self-knowledge and moral consciousness, at peace with self,
world, and life as a whole. This dim awareness of goodness, of
wholeness and peace, struggles with our present, imperfect,
finite, erring condition, in which our egocentric inclinations are
strong and in which our estrangement from what we ought to
be is a constant irritant and pain. May recalls briefly the story
of Adam, "the classical attempt at explanation" (*Art of Counseling,* p. 202), and states that man, after the fall or the development of moral consciousness, retains an awareness of the essential aspect of his nature, or of his original "good" nature from
which he has fallen. This fall, May continues, is not to be seen
as a historical or chronological matter; the fall was not a once-
and-for-all matter. Adam, or fallen man's egocentric will, and
Christ, or essential "good" nature or God's will or image, "hold
a tension within every individual in every decision" (*Art of
Counseling,* p. 202). Thus, asserts May, the "logos," or the
meaningful structure of life, is a living part of every man; it is
his "essential nature," and it is this, adds May, that makes it
possible for a man to recognize spontaneously the perfect form
of love in Christ's law of love as a love that reaches out to all
men. "The contradiction within man *thus* is between his essential nature, his 'God-basis,' and his present state of egocentricity" (*Art of Counseling,* p. 202, italics mine).

Thus, asserts May, the great moral imperative comes in
some form to all men, and man knows what he ought to be. Yet
he is not forced to live according to the structure, in a straitjacket or according to a rigidly defined or determined pattern,
but can deliberate and decide freely to follow his egocentric
whims or to act unselfishly for the general well-being. Man,

then, is caught in the contradiction between his willing to be in accord with the structure as "it makes itself felt within the individual" (*Art of Counseling,* p. 203) (or God's will or "mind," as May also chooses to term it) and his "fallen," egocentric willing to do otherwise, to put himself at the center of things, to satisfy his more immediate, spontaneously self-centered desires without any regard for any ultimate structure, substituting his own purposes, choosing "to set up [his] own structures" (*Art of Counseling,* p. 204). But the individual who "realizes his relation to the ultimate structure" (*Art of Counseling,* p. 204) can overcome, to the extent of living with, the contradiction between his essential nature and his existential "fallen" state, and is thereby enabled to attain courageous and healthy self-expression. Such a creative, moral response differs specifically in each individual, says May, since only the individual can realize his own relation to the structure and forge his own creative solutions.

Now, out of these assertions of May's arise many problems, not the least of which is that although May has said a little about the characteristics of the ultimate structure (it is universal, objective, the logos, and so on) and a great deal about what it is supposed to do within the individual, he has been rather vague as to what this ultimate structure is. He has stated it to be the "reasonable, meaningful structure of life," the "logos," the "mind of God," the "principles of God," the "principles which underlie life," and so forth, but what those principles are, and how they are translated or interpreted in such depth and detail as to create specific ethical awareness within the individual, May has not explored and perhaps has overlooked altogether. A further difficulty arises in that May seems to envisage this ultimate structure as somehow separate from the individual, who, through his awareness of his essential nature, arrives at a series of precepts for action in his existential striving, yet which striving is also guided by the "ultimate structure." Further, May has, from the beginning of this section of *The Art of Counseling,* implicitly presupposed for self-expression the necessity not merely of structure but of an ultimate structure, and has virtually derived it from his own assumption of the need for it and

from what he regards as corroborating proof from living experience of this need for it, that is, a consciousness within man of a
contradiction arising from awareness of an essential "good"
nature over *against* or vying with existential propensities for
destructive self-concern. His method of presenting this conviction—namely, to assert the "contradiction," to recall as an
explanation the story of Adam and thence to consider that this
formulation of man's existential state is now *proven* and can be
the base for further deliberations—this method is questionable
from both the logical and scientific points of view, that is, "scientific" in the sense of *scientia* or closely coordinated body of
knowledge. May himself stipulates that the "ultimate structure"
must be *universal* and *objective* (*Art of Counseling,* pp. 198,
200).

In a book whose purpose is the examination of the art of
counseling *as such,* to introduce suddenly and arbitrarily the
Judeo-Christian account of human genesis as furnishing an explanation and therefore proof of May's conviction that man is
pulling in one direction while God or the universe seeks to pull
him in another, scarcely satisfies May's own stipulation of universality and objectivity and would certainly restrict the appli-
cability of his psychotherapy. The problem is that May does not
first explore the theoretical ground for his assertion of a contradiction within man, but simply assumes it. Then he assumes
that this contradiction is between an essential good nature and
existential "fallen" egocentric nature and, having briefly referred to the story of Adam, seems to assume that there is no
further need of qualification of his positing of this essential
good nature. That May originally delivered the contents of this
book as lectures to a denominational Christian group does not
legitimize the use he has made of a specifically Judeo-Christian
story to give weight to his version of his "contradiction," seen
as *fact* while simultaneously stated to be the "classical attempt
at *explanation*" (*Art of Counseling,* p. 202, italics mine).

It is not any particular story or attempt at explanation,
illustration or understanding of man's origin and his human condition that grounds the individual's grasp of contingency, but
the reverse. That is, it is the existential grasp of contingency

that grounds the early stories and myths by which man tried to account for himself and his world and to symbolize his situation within being as a whole. This is not, of course, to impugn the inspiration, divine or otherwise, of such accounts or interpretations.

Once again, it is clear that May does not seek to pursue and explicate his inquiry at the absolutely theoretical level, particularly at this early stage in his thinking, and that he cannot quite envisage and express with clarity the ontological grounds and implications of his assertions. Yet it is also very clear that his psychological understanding of the necessity for structure in self-expression rings true, and that his continuing preoccupation with returning to the concrete therapeutic aid of troubled people can only be enriched by his undoubted understanding of the problem of existential living as fraught with inalienable conflict, as striving toward consistency and clarification of ethical awareness, and as the attempt to come to terms with oneself, one's possibilities and limitations, one's gifts and failings.

Further, May's own insistence on the balance of individuation and social integration carries within it the seeds of the answer to his problem in elucidating (as contrasted with asserting) a "necessary structure." The necessary structure of human ethical awareness and decision that May seeks is born in the self-world polarity, in the polar structure of individuation and participation that, in the final analysis, characterizes all things. Every thing is necessarily separate and centered, self-affirming, and inalienably individual, yet simultaneously part of the whole, already in participation or relatedness with every other totally centered, separate thing. Every individual human being, like all existing things, is necessarily situated in coexistence, and is centered and self-affirming. Encounter with other things or persons in the already going concern of coexistence requires the unconditional recognition of the other as individual, separate, and totally centered. It is this unconditional recognition in human awareness that is the wellspring in human consciousness of ethical choice, decision, and commitment. To say so is not to posit an essential nature pulling or striving against existential living, but rather to posit a free and conscious sensitivity to the possibilities of consistent existential self-realization in participation, of the intelligibility and value of what is done, of harmony in the self-world polarity as each one of us changes and develops it. Without this consciousness of himself and his world, of individuality in coexistence, without his striving toward consistency between his knowing and his doing, toward self-realization-in-participation, there would remain only determined instincts or chaotic whim, and there would be no possibility for the individual of understanding of what is to be done nor of the recognition of unconditional love of one's fellow man as the highest and most *unself*ish form of coexistence.

May, however, spoke of the individual realizing or denying his "relation to the structure," thereby separating man (subject) and universe (object), as though the relation did not exist until the individual recognized it. May even spoke of the individual "setting up his own structures," and did not make it clear that "the structure" is, for him, the ultimate, fundamental structure, while those set up by the individual could be only partial, specific, and hence finally inadequate. Further, May said at the outset of his positing of an "ultimate meaning" that each person must decide on the most adequate concept of this meaning on which he could then base his structured self-expression. This is again an unfortunate example of terminological confusion and difficulty of meaning resulting in a lack of theoretical clarity and perhaps even preventing May from ascertaining what his ultimate structure is.

Indeed, before his ethical capacity, his decisive willing, can *develop and become effective* within him, the individual must become conscious of and sensitive to, must relate to, his human condition, his finiteness and vulnerability, his individuality and situatedness with his fellow men and with his world as a whole. Yet he preexists this realization in that he is an essential, inalienable constituent in that relationship. The relationship is given; what he creates, in a reflective way, is its meaning, purpose, worth, and value. He is not merely an existent, but a striving existent, an existent of ever-greater meaning and breadth, self-knowing and strongly self-affirming. Thus, the individual does not set up his own structures instead of the ultimate structure, as though he were opting out of the ultimate structure. He cannot *not* be an individual in participation, but he can choose to center his affirmation on himself while actively willing or merely weakly allowing the deterioration of fellow man and world. That this is a denial of the right of his fellow man to affirm fully his centeredness and his world in participation is clear.

It is this, the source of human ethical awareness and decision, that May has tried to elucidate and has not quite yet clarified theoretically, because he unintentionally prejudiced his deliberations by the arbitrary and somewhat hasty introduction of a specifically Judeo-Christian account and by his positing of the individual as somehow capable of putting himself outside the ultimate structure by means of denying it. It is to the polar structure of individuation and social integration, however, that May's later deliberations return again and again, each time with greater understanding in his reflections on the significance of human will and ethical choice and their interrelation with a structure of meaning.

For the moment, in *The Art of Counseling,* May is satisfied that he has found the universal structure that will complete his view of personality health and ill health or neurosis. It is this ultimate, universal structure, he says, that is at the root of social living, of social conventions in which only a partial structure could be found. It is at the root, too, of the moral archetypes through which, says May, the universal structure, which is God, makes itself felt (*Art of Counseling,* p. 203). It follows, then, that man's willing and decision can be truly fulfilling, as well as purposeful and effective, only when it is a question of instinctual expression guided by universal structure. But May does not intend, he says, to propose a specific or particular "moral system," because only the individual can realize his own relation to the structure and this relation is a dynamic process, constantly changing and growing. Instead, May states, his considerations have been intended to arrive at a "basic frame of reference" (*Art of Counseling,* p. 205), wherein each person, in particular those seeking such counsel, can be helped to find his own creative morality, to elucidate his own individual relation to the "meaningful structure of life," in order that he may learn to judge and accept his potentialities and limitations, to decide between the various courses open in any situation, and to reach out for and further his own development and "insight into the universal structure of goodness" (*Art of Counseling,* p. 206). Realizing his minuteness and insignificance in the universe, he simultaneously comes to know his own individual worth through the realization that "he participates in the divine logos of meaning" (*Art of Counseling,* p. 220). He becomes "clarified," asserts May; he becomes more sensitive to his imperfect condition, better able to accept and bear the limitations and tensions of his personality and the anxious insecurity of existence. He becomes willing to "affirm truth and goodness" (*Art of Counseling,* p. 223) and, having accepted responsibility for himself and his world, to strive for and affirm ever-greater freedom and unselfishness. "He can be to some extent the channel of meaning of the universe . . . he can become 'clarified' " (*Art of Counseling,* p. 220).

It is the lack of such affirmation of meaning that is precisely the problem of the neurotic, asserts May (*Art of Counseling,* pp. 213-218). "The individual must have some belief in purpose in his life, however fragmentary, if he is to achieve personality health. Without purpose there cannot be meaning; and without meaning one cannot, in the end, live" (*Art of Counseling,* p. 216). His inability to affirm himself and his world stems directly from his lack of belief in himself and his world. His instinctual striving is therefore purposeless and chaotic. Now, May holds that true or healthy religion is the basic attitude of belief in purpose and meaning in existence, as opposed to what he calls "neurotic religion" or a seeking in religion for a hiding place or dogmatic authority that will relieve one of the burden of freedom and decision. Hence, he holds that the neurotic's inability to affirm is at base a religious problem, since it stems directly from his loss of meaning. Personality health, says May, is grounded in the individual's belief not only in himself but in his fellow men, his world, "in some purpose in the total life-process" (*Art of Counseling,* p. 217). Individual creation of meaning would be neither possible nor sustainable within a meaningless universe; religion, holds May, is the affirmation of that fundamental meaning, individual and universal in harmony, as man confronts his existence, and is the indispensable undergirding of personality health or structured self-expression.

Thus, May's basic position on will in *The Art of Counseling* is that personality health is not compatible with surface willpower, chaotic whim, or rigid determinism. Rather, personality health, for May, is a matter of creative will, of structured vital expression springing from fundamental acceptance of self, of one's situation with one's fellow men, not regarding them with the destructive suspicion and hostility of the neurotic, not regarding them with fear and distrust, but with acceptance and unconditional acknowledgment of them as persons. This springs too from acceptance of life as a whole, of its freedoms and limitations, its marvellous minute detail and its overall magnificence, its joys and sorrows. Acceptance gives birth to and is further reinforced by affirmation, which brings with it the joys and achievements of human freedom in action, as well as the humbling but spurring sorrows of failure, imperfection and error. Neurotic withdrawal brings only an insecurity deepened by further sense of guilt and betrayal of one's potentialities and responsibilities, making decisive choice and action ever more difficult and hope ever more distant. Affirmation of individual and social purpose, however, although continuing to remind one of existential vulnerability and insecurity, will also bring development of ability and new possibilities, together with greater joy, fulfillment, the happiness of decisive effort from one's whole being, and the hope of occasional success in some endeavors, however limited.

The individual, then, says May, creates his own personality by his creative willing, his decisive response, not by a "surface willing" but by a deep "reorganization of his whole self." He grows in freedom as he reaches out for greater harmony of individual development within social integration, as he continually "molds the materials of heredity and environment into his own unique pattern" (*Art of Counseling*, p. 52). The human being is not rigidly determined nor bound to an environment, but can weigh different impulses in the balance, can evaluate different ways of life, before deciding which one to follow. This he does by assessing not merely which course of action will be least likely to bring him into painful collision with his world (as in the case of the reality-pleasure principle) but which course will matter more to him and be preeminent or prevail in value over the others. For such a process, he must develop a criterion or structure of value in order to decide which impulse or course of action *ought* to predominate, which one is in greater harmony with his self and his world. Hence his need to affirm an overall structure, a reasonable, meaningful structure of life.

The psychotherapist, then, seeks to help the person to know and accept himself, to achieve and affirm a balanced self-world relationship, to take responsibility for himself and know his purposes, to affirm and participate in life as a whole, and to assess and direct his own life; in short, in May's later terminology, the psychotherapist seeks to help the patient to experience and sense strongly and affirmatively his own being-in-the-world.

Toward an Ontology of Will

In *The Meaning of Anxiety* (1950), May explains his conviction that anxiety is experienced as the threat of loss or annihilation of those values (or symbols) that the individual holds to be essential to his existence as a person (*Meaning of Anxiety*, pp. 40-41, 45, 99, 105, 190-234). The measure of man's potentiality for anxiety, however, is also the measure of his freedom, for the two are interdependent. The more sense of one's being, the more sensitivity to oneself and one's world, the greater also, then, the range of possibilities and the greater the individual's freedom. Anxiety, viewed positively as the measure of the individual's grasp and confrontation of his "finite freedom" is, for May, correlated with the individual's capacity for creative, decisive exploration of his own possibilities. If not confronted with the vital courage to affirm existence, to deliberate, decide, and act, anxiety stifles and destroys the individual's free, moral, autonomous self-realization. Inability to will constructively is not only at base related to loss of meaning, and therefore to threatened loss of purpose and even of existence itself, but it is also characterized by stultifying anxiety.

It is consistent, then, that in *Man's Search for Himself* (1953), May begins from a moving restatement of anxiety in contemporary life and from the expression of anxiety in alienation, boredom, loneliness, loss of purpose, and coherence, and that he then proceeds to the consideration of what it is to cope with these expressions, to grow in freedom in spite of anxiety, and to develop a strong, vital and decisive sense of self. May is deeply concerned with the study of integration, or what he formerly called "healthy, balanced self-expression," which he envisages as essentially and inalienably related to the maturing of the human capacity for ethical judgment, decision, and action. In this book, May explicates his conviction that man's capacity for ethical judgment or integrated, conscious choice and affirmation of goals (values, symbols) in which he can believe, through which he can strive to make something of his existence, is born in the consciousness of himself (*Man's Search*, pp. 138-142). Man's sense of freedom is born and grows with his sense of identity, with his emerging awareness of himself and his world (*Man's Search*, pp. 74-77, 138-142). As his consciousness of self grows, his range of freedom, of possible choices, increases too.

Freedom, as May has so often asserted, is not automatic. It must be constantly achieved in choice and affirmation. It is, however, cumulative, asserts May; that is, each choice made with an element of freedom makes possible greater freedom in the next choice. This element of freedom, he says, is the capacity to pause and deliberate, to be aware of oneself in a situation, to assess the alternative possibilities, to take a hand in one's development, and to direct one's own life. This statement does not imply that there are no determining influences in one's life, but rather to hold that one's range of freedom and strength are shown precisely in how one reacts to these determining influences, how aware of them and ready to accept their existence one is, how ready or willing to recognize them and govern their effect on one's choices as an individual. Freedom, then, for May, ultimately means a recognition and acceptance of contingency, and the development of the power not merely to say yes or no in a specific situation, but also of the underlying capacity to mold and create one's self, to say yes or no as a function of an integrated, clear-sighted awareness of what that yes or no means for one's being-in-the-world.

It must be noted at this point that although May is deeply concerned with the theoretical explication of human freedom, his main and overall practical purpose is and has been to convince people, notably his counselees and patients, that they are free and therefore responsible, that they can and must direct their own lives through conscious choice and affirmation. In other words, he is concerned mainly with will in action, with the concrete implications for human living, not merely with the grounding of therapy in the aim of having the patient sense his own being in a free, responsible way, but with the ultimate goal of having the patient develop a strong enough sense of being for decisive, responsible, autonomous action as an individual-in-participation-with-his-world.

Once again, May moves to the consideration of freedom and structure for he has always maintained that freedom and choice in the human world of interpersonal relationships and individual integrity must be characterized by responsibility. The individual must make his own decisions, and his existence as a person depends on his choices, as an individual and "in continual interaction with the other significant persons in his world" (*Man's Search,* p. 142). Further, the individual constantly assumes some structure or other in his self-world relationship, that is, his acts are a function of *some* assumptions, conscious or unconscious, reflective or automatic (for example, habitual, through family influences). As May sees it, it is more consistent to examine and know consciously what structure or set of assumptions is involved in one's decisions if one is to achieve inward freedom (*Man's Search,* pp. 133-138, 144-149).

To achieve inward freedom is to affirm responsibility for one's own life, one's self, one's whole existence, not merely to be carried along in unquestioning routine or simple conformity. Inward freedom is openness, not planlessness; flexibility, not anarchic chaos. It is the recognition of one's given existence, acceptance of responsibility for this given existence and for its possibilities and destiny, and it implies disciplined acceptance of the necessity of making one's own basic choices as to what one wants to do with one's life, and toward what goals or values (symbols of worth and good) one wishes to orient one's self-realization.

Not only *can* the human being make such choices of values and goals, but he *must* do so, says May, if he is to attain integration, to use May's earlier terminology, if the individual is to balance individuation and social integration in healthy self-expression (*Man's Search,* pp. 150-155; *Freedom and Responsibility Reexamined,* pp. 168-181; *Anxiety and Values,* pp. 72-83). His consciousness of himself, his ability to envision and grasp his being and his world, to remember past acts and to imagine future consequences, and to put himself figuratively in someone else's place or to see himself "from the outside," as it were—this is the beginning of his capacity to be aware of the effects of his choices on others, and of theirs on him, of the given interrelationships of his human condition. Knowing what he wants is the beginning of his capacity to grow in freedom, understanding, and integration, to choose among the things he wants those that will carry greater weight in his decisions because their realization or attainment is more important to him than that of other things. Maturity, for May, then, is the increasing ability to choose and creatively affirm those values that will strengthen one's psychological core (or, as he says later, that will affirm one's centeredness and strengthen his sense of being) while also affirming his fellow man and his world. This formulation restates in greater depth May's continuing belief in man's capacity to "mold the materials of heredity and environment" (*Art of Counseling,* p. 52), or ability to choose not merely what to do, but what ought to be done, that is to say, the ability to achieve ethical awareness in the creative exercise of his freedom.

Yet this ethical awareness is never easy (*Man's Search,* pp. 155-166). Like freedom and consciousness of self out of which it is born, ethical awareness is accompanied by inner conflict and anxiety that are not eased by a flight to authority or to tradition for their own sake alone. May cites the myths of Adam and Prometheus as man's early or primitive attempts to understand, enter into, and grasp the difficult notion of the development of self-consciousness and ethical insight. It would be inaccurate to see both merely as examples of rebellion punished, says May. For him, the story of Adam clearly represents the development of self-consciousness with its corresponding longing for peace without conflict, for rest without work or anxiety. Prometheus, for May, is the symbol of human creativity, the inner anxiety, toil, pain, and yet necessity of striving onward from the known. Neither myth, then, can be dismissed as representing solely man's struggle against the limitations of his finite condition; both must also be seen as attempts to understand the fundamental import of that struggle. This fundamental import May understands to be the problem of personal responsibility in conflict with authority, or the courageous, creative confrontation of the possibilities inherent in self-consciousness, and the necessity of individual decision and choice for individual self-realization.

The emergence of new values, of new life, the courage to be, develop and grow in ethical freedom, *will* and *must clash* with the entrenched ideas and authority, asserts May. The anxiety of leaving the old, the habit of obedience, and the tendency toward conformity as the easier, less painful way, all combine to "resist new creativity" (*Man's Search,* p. 161). Although May is careful to say that no society could survive for long without both old forms and new vitality, without the interplay of change and stability, and has always deprecated directionless vital expression, he does nevertheless exhibit a tendency to identify the stable, conservative element in ethical matters with a static, unyielding, fundamentalist approach; that is to say, May seems unwittingly to confuse authority with authoritarianism. Now, psychologically it is quite accurate to say that the development of ethical awareness and insight, personal growth in free, creative, decisive responsibility, will always tend to involve at least some difficulty and perhaps conflict. Whether this conflict takes the form of external difficulty with other people or internal difficulty and struggle with one's old familiar way and habit, it is quite clear that change must involve decisions and choice, and therefore not merely a reaching for the new, but a rejection of whatever the new way must exclude. May, however, goes further and states somewhat gratuitously that new ethical insights and ethical leaders are always in tension with and even at outright war with existing religious and social institutions. Although ethical leaders are born and nourished in the religious tradition, "a bitter warfare exists," he says, "between ethically sensitive people and religious institutions" (*Man's Search,* p. 164). May speaks of this as the "same double relation" (between ethics and religion) as that between parent and child, the double relation of dependence and conflict, of nourishment and domination as *opposed* to independence and freedom. He posits an *inevitable conflict* between ethics and religion, and compares their relationship to the double relationship between child and parent, between the spirit and letter of the law, between individual ethics and organized, static religious or social systems.

As May has always opposed directionless vital expression just as strongly as he opposes authoritarianism, which he calls "the neurotic form of authority" (*Man's Search,* p. 176), it is not to be concluded lightly that he intends, in fact, to emphasize the value of change for its own sake. Yet he does give evidence of a definite tendency toward emphasizing "individuation-*in-spite-of*" (exemplified by having to overcome conflict with or repression by parents, authority, established ideas, and determining factors), all the while underplaying—or even, at times, ignoring altogether—"individuation-as-nourished-and-supported-by" (for example, as given impetus toward a strong sense of being and decisive freedom by the loving encouragement of parents, educators, and religious and social leaders). May's tendency to view individuation (or freedom exercised, or affirmation of self, or even centeredness affirmed) mostly, if not exclusively, in terms of the difficulties and conflicts to be overcome results in a virtual categorizing of parents, society, organized religions, and so on as overwhelmingly and inexorably conservative. This is particularly true of his view of mothers, who, as May sees them, seem to be characterized as the fundamental sheltering, preservative, protective, dominating, primitive, mythical Earth Mother type, symbolized by the womb, and reinforced by the physical closeness of the pre- and postnatal period (*Man's Search,* pp. 103-122; *Love and Will,* pp. 111-117, 134; *Significance of Symbols,* pp. 27, 38-39; *Dreams and Symbols,* pp. 84-86, 114-118). From these associations he then reaches the conclusion that, conservative as they are, established authorities cannot *not* be in conflict with—and must necessarily seek to repress—children, change, new ideas, that is, to hold back the thrust of creative vitality. For May, the child, the ethical leader, and the new idea, are all free, vital, and creative, and must, for their growth and development, push against, conflict with, and overcome the necessarily repressive-protective dominance by the stable, the unchanging, the old, and therefore the out-of-date and intransigent, as represented by parents, institutions, and established ways.

What seemed, then, to be a tendency on May's part toward overemphasis of traditional associations and overtones has now been revealed to be at base a more serious tendency toward a reductive view of individuation, participation, and integration, of vitality and change construed as separate from and *opposed* to stability and form. This tendency implicitly separates and reifies both individuation and participation and is not consistent with May's positing of polar relation or balance or correlation of individuation and participation (or the self-world polarity), a polar relation that May has always proposed as necessary for personality health or integrated existence. Again, one might also recall that in his positing of six ontological processes or characteristics, May had some analogous difficulty with the concept of centeredness (essence, unity, identity, and/or individuality), not wishing it to seem static and unyielding, yet confusing the notion somewhat by his examples because of an apparent inability to envisage centeredness as distinct but not separate from self-affirmation. The same tendency to reify, as separate rather than distinct, the notions of centeredness and affirmation, of individuation and participation, of essence and existence, recurs in May's work, not being confined to his early work (*Jean-Paul Sartre and Psychoanalysis,* pp.

140-141; *Context,* pp. 94-95). Further, he then spoke of "self-affirmation *and* participation"; it was pointed out in discussion of *this* separation that his earlier term "individuation" was more felicitous, and that the import of the polar relation that May wished to convey would have been considerably more clearly expressed had he spoken of "centeredness" and "self-affirmation as individuating and participatory," or had he merely retained his original, more simple terminology. Here, in *Man's Search for Himself,* when speaking of the development of decisive free responsibility in individuation (*in spite of* participation, as it were), he has overemphasized the difficulties, problems, and conflicts that he sees as inhering in individuation, at the expense of virtually ignoring the supporting, encouraging, loving aspects of healthy individuation-in-participation. This formulation separates unduly individuation and participation, is even reminiscent of the willpower notion that May has always decried, and is perhaps caused by a misunderstanding on May's part of what it means to posit a polar relation or balance between individuation and participation.

The further point also arises that institutions, whether religious or social, have their existence solely through the individual members who form them, and cannot therefore be dismissed as represented exclusively by their conservative elements. Indeed, although they may, and usually do, number some authoritarian conservatives among their members, particularly at higher levels, it is not the case that new ideas, reforms, or insights are always repugnant. In effect, it is the inalienable function of politics, literature, and journalism, as well as that of the executive councils, conferences, and synods of world churches, universities, and national and local governments, constantly and carefully to reevaluate their society, their achievements, their central aims and beliefs, to listen to new interpretations and form policy in a thoughtful, decisive manner. One must therefore be careful not to confuse deliberation and caution with fear and rejection, nor invariably to equate preservation with repression, change with progress, popularity with quality.

This brings one to the questions that arise out of May's

interpretation of the Orestes and Oedipus myths as presenting
the struggle for self-knowledge, the conflicts of individuation
(again particularly with the protective-repressive mother) and
the development of a strong sense of self. May does not in
Man's Search for Himself present any real definition or even
description of what he understands "myth" and "symbol" to
be, but in his article in *Symbolism in Religion and Literature* he
states that he understands symbols to be flexible, versatile,
powerful confrontations and penetrations of the fundamental,
vital meaning of one's being-in-the-world (*Significance of
Symbols,* pp. 14-22). Conceived and molded by conscious and
unconscious, symbols are, for May, the very language of the
totality of inner experience as relating to the outer world; they
are the quintessential expression of man's understanding and
entering into the meaning of his self-world relationship. Myths,
holds May, develop and elaborate that understanding by means
of a story that grasps in a "total figure" the "vital meaning" of
this experience (*Man's Search,* pp. 108-122, 212-216, 234; *Significance of Symbols,* pp. 11-23, 34, 36n.; *Existential Psychotherapy,* pp. 11-20; *Love and Will,* p. 20).

We may, however, note a tendency on May's part to confuse the issue by mixing myth and drama, although he claims
that this is to be more faithful to the "meaning and inner consistency" of the *myth* itself. It is not, however, the *myths* of
Oedipus and Orestes on which May bases his reflections but the
highly charged, compressed, dramatic-poetic productions of
Sophocles and Aeschylus. These are not myths but conscious
and detailed works of psychological drama carrying a *wholly
intended* power and intensity. In the original myth fragments,
not only are the thoughts and words of the protagonists missing
entirely, not to mention the lack of psychological character and
development—and it is these in the *dramas* that May uses to support and illustrate his point—but also the "facts," actions, and
even identities are confused and doubtful, varying from one
version to another, of uncertain historical veracity and motivation, and not at all concerned with the psychological conflicts
so convincingly and subtly introduced by the dramatists. May
is, then, using not the "facts" of the myths, but the keen

psychological insight, technical and linguistic power of individual playwrights and poets to illustrate his thesis concerning the inalienable fundamentality of conflict in individuation. It is, then, the inserted meaning and intense consistency of situation, charged with the clash of cultural values and ethical judgment, rather than the "primitive" and "universally immediate" myth, that May finds so strikingly illustrative of the struggle to become a person, that is, a meaning-disclosing, experiencing, responsible being, free of domination by others. While the Adam and Prometheus myths can be said to be direct attempts to understand the human condition, the Oedipus and Orestes myths cannot be said to be (in their original form) any more than fragments of early history or story telling, and they remain no more until a symbolic meaning is inserted and explicated. May himself seems to sense this when he admits that Clytemnaestra, the mother of Orestes, cannot of course be taken to be symbolic of all mothers, though she can be envisaged as symbolic of destructive matriarchal domination.

Because of his emphasis on conflict in individuation to the detriment of the supporting, loving aspects of individuation-in-participation, with particular regard to parents, May would appear to be convinced that the child-parent relationship is characterized more by conflict and difficulty-to-be-overcome than by love and encouragement. That is to say, May seems to propose that individuation "takes place" in spite of parents, particularly the mother, who, by implication, would unconsciously seek to frustrate and repress the child's growing independence and freedom. The child's relationship with its parents, then, is a *problem* to be overcome and solved before the child can gain his right to exist as an individual. Although in experience—and certainly in the cases that May cites, culminating in the Orestes drama—such may sometimes be the case, it is not thereby an inalienable, predominating feature of all child-parent relationships. It would seem that May does not give sufficient weight to the theoretical possibility of parents finding great joy and happiness—not merely pride or reflected glory—in their children's achievement of greater independence. Parental caring is not necessarily stifling nor dominating nor exploitative, though

in a given parent it may be overwhelmingly characterized by
any or all of these tendencies. Further, in the human situation,
the parent-child relationship is not "outgrown"; it is, rather, a
"given" bond of blood or of adoption that remains, even when
the "child" reaches maturity and even old age, no matter what
changes or developments have superseded one another in the
state of that relationship, and no matter what strength and individual "independence" of each other the parent and child may
have attained. It is, then, theoretically inappropriate to use
the Orestes drama as myth-and-therefore-characteristic—though
extreme—of the problem of individuation, or of becoming a person with a strong sense of being. Too many other aspects of
integrated individuation, such as developing a strong center at
first supported and dependent and later self-reliant and loving,
would thereby unwarrantably and perhaps simplistically be
omitted from consideration.

Now, May has affirmed that freedom is cumulative, that
each exercise of creative will extends further the person's freedom or capacity to mold his own life, to reach for greater self-
expression. He has also affirmed that, since the self is born and
grows in interpersonal relationships in the world, the individual
is not free as though in a vacuum or on a desert island; as a
person, he is born and grows among other persons, in a world of
contingency, of limitation, of natural desires, joys, and dis-
appointments. To know what he wants, or what he would like
to be, is thus an inalienable necessity for creative choice on the
part of the individual, that is, to know how he would wish to
form his life as a responsible being-in-the-world. This knowing,
or experiencing what one wants or toward what he is going,
asserts May, involves fighting against and overcoming whatever
would prevent one from feeling and wanting, from disclosing
the meaning of one's individual existence, from setting up one's
goals and ideas, and from beginning the dynamic personal development that integration and balance really mean. It involves,
says May, a continuous effort to change the current situation,
to reach out and go beyond in what May calls "the continuum
of differentiation from the 'mass' toward freedom as an individual" (*Man's Search,* p. 103, see also pp. 234-235). It is a con-

tinual struggle to reduce one's dependence, to open one's horizons and extend one's power by developing one's capabilities, to become not merely a physical or biological individual but a psychological and ethical individual, capable of greater self-affirmation and responsibility. May is opposed to obedience or conformity for its own sake alone and states that he sees nothing particularly ethical in blind conformity to unquestioned regulation. Correspondingly, he affirms that *ethical* decisions are those made in terms not only of authority, but in terms of an inner assent expressed in action. Inner assent alone, May believes, will not make a value or goal or symbol worthy in itself nor does unthinking obedience without prior reflective commitment confer any virtue or demonstrate any ethical quality. The individual's power to make ethical, responsible decisions, for example, to decide to be obedient or to seek change, must, however, be rooted in inner conviction of the worth of what is to be done, in order to remain effective and consistent.

At the point of choice and decision, says May, the person choosing in self-awareness is "placing himself on the line"; that is to say, his choice is "an expression of his inward motives and attitudes" (*Man's Search*, p. 188). Hence the necessity for inner conviction and consistency before his choices can have real effectiveness. The decision is more than a mere product of the confluences of determining forces, and involves a commitment, greater or lesser according to the circumstances. His act of choosing, May goes on, brings a new element, however slight, into the picture. This, says May, is the "creative and the dynamic element in decision" (*Man's Search*, p. 188). Further, it is not often realized, asserts May, that this element is creative not merely because it "changes the configuration," but because conscious decisions, carefully and thoughtfully made, "can change the direction in which unconscious forces push" (*Man's Search*, p. 188; *Contributions*, pp. 88-89; *Existential Psychotherapy*, pp. 41-50). May speaks of the individual struggling for a long time in anxious waking hours and conflicting dreams to make a serious decision, and states that, in his therapeutic experience, a careful final decision is usually paralleled, as it were, by reinforcing dreams, as though the thoughtful final decision released the tensions within the person and he could now allow himself to explore positively the implications of his decision in constructive dreams.

This insight, on May's part, though incomplete as yet, clearly shows the direction in which May's thought on will is moving, and is perhaps the iceberg tip of his mature view of the intentionality of human consciousness. As yet, however, May remains basically concerned with will in action, with decisive choice and integrated action and, at the conclusion of *Man's Search for Himself*, he asserts that the ultimate criteria of integrated existence are honesty, integrity, love, and courage (*Man's Search*, pp. 234-236; *Existential Psychotherapy*, p. 62). The task of the human being, says May, is to grow in freedom and responsibility, in ever-widening consciousness of himself, in progressive differentiation, in creative work and integration with others in freely chosen love and consciously affirmed meaning. The significance of will, as May sees it, is commitment, not merely advisable but essential for whole, fulfilling, ethical existence.

It follows that, in *Existence* (1958), having spoken of the chief goal of therapy as the patient's discovery of his being, his Dasein, May would again emphasize commitment and decision (*Contributions*, pp. 87-89; *Existential Therapy*, pp. 134-135). Since knowledge is quite clearly a necessary condition for thoughtful, effective, integrated choice, it had, says May, been assumed in psychotherapy that knowledge precedes decision: As the patient learns to know himself better, he will be better able to make decisions and to take hold of his own life. Yet, says May, in an insight that proves to be crucial for his whole theory of will and for the understanding of dreams in relation to decision, what was *not* realized was that this is only a half-truth. The other half, he goes on, is that the patient cannot *permit* himself to know himself, to grasp, understand and accept himself decisively, until he makes the preliminary decisive commitment, the primary willing orientation, that is, until he takes up a prior original orientation toward existence, a primary choice of becoming attentive to and honest with himself in the seeking of his real being, as he is, as he might be, and as he would like to be. In this sense, then, says May, "knowledge and insight follow decision" (*Contributions*, p. 88; *Existential Therapy*, p. 134; *Existential Psychotherapy*, pp. 8-9, 36). That is, it is a fundamental, primary decision or choice of moving toward integration and greater freedom, no matter what he must face about himself, that frees the patient to recall memories and explore his thoughts, motives, goals and actions honestly and fruitfully. Memory, says May, works on the basis of what was significant in the past and has to do with the *meaning* rather than the *passage* of time, with present orientation to existence and the way in which one relates to one's future. In other words, pleasant or unpleasant memories that are most vivid are those that have greatest significance with regard to the sense of one's being and are vividly impressed on one because of great joy in one's being or because one's sense of being was deeply ·violated, whether by one's action or that of another person. Only when the self-aware being decides primarily to take his existence seriously, to explore and take issue with his own motives and goals, only then will he be *able* to gain knowledge of and insight into the meaning of his memories, his dreams, and his present and future. Only by a primary decision to face himself, holds May, will he be *capable* of learning about himself and of attempting to develop a coherent, integrated, open, and flexible sense of his being.

This formulation on May's part is clearly a crucial development in his reflections on the significance of will, opening up as it does the relation of will not only to freedom exercised in action and the development of ethical judgment, but also the relation of will to memories and dreams, wishes and goals, spontaneous likes and aversions, insight and direction of thought, work, and values as symbolic and quintessentially interpretive of the meaningful tenor of one's whole existence. From this point on, May's thought on will reaches out to the broader concept of human intentionality as primary orientation to existence, encompassing each and every "choice" inherent in one's least act of perception and decisively constituting one's very approach to every instant of existence. For May, man is a meaning-disclosing existent, whose knowledge and willing are interdependent in his concerned presence to the world.

In his article in *Symbolism in Religion and Literature*,

"The Significance of Symbols" (pp. 15-20, 46-47), May returns to the question of primary orientation preceding knowledge, of decision preceding insight. Following his formulation of the significance of symbols as the language of self-consciousness, as man's grasping of his being and his world, May gives a highly illustrative example from his own therapeutic experience. It is that of a dream reported by a young man, a lawyer who at first sight seemed very successful in the world, but who despite his socioeconomic position, education, and ability, was deeply troubled and anxious. His dream, of standing in a cave with one of his feet caught in quicksand in the middle of the cave floor and his other foot on solid ground, while he experienced both terror and fascination, brought the young man to realize more powerfully and immediately than by any technical explanation alone just how strongly he longed for and simultaneously feared both protective sheltering (or mothering) and decisive, active individual independence. The dream symbol, says May, represents a bringing together of the unconscious (involuntary) wishes and conscious (voluntary, attentive, reflective) struggles of this apparently highly successful young man (objectively seen), who had been perplexed and frustrated by his own anxiety because he had not previously understood properly how *un*sure he really was about his being and his world. The symbol, then, is remarkable for the uncompromising clarity with which it expresses his primary decision to face, grasp, and understand himself.

It may be appropriate to recall that by "unconscious" May means forgotten memories and knowledge, potentialities that the person cannot or will not yet actualize or admit to or face, or merely that are not centrally present to attention (*Significance of Symbols,* pp. 45-48; *Existential Psychotherapy,* p. 46). Grasping of one's total being involves a clear entering into what one is or how one is situated and how or what one would genuinely like to be. What May identifies as the regressive function of the dream symbol, such as the cave of the example given, is precisely to bring into awareness the repressed or inadvertent or resolutely ignored reactions, longings and dreams, while the progressive function, says May, is the revelation of goals, of new ethical insights and understanding (*Significance of Symbols,* p. 45; *Dreams and Symbols,* pp. 13-14, 9). Such a clear grasp, once brought into full consciousness, attention, and acceptance, alone can enable the individual to make truly effective decisions that belie neither his reflective convictions and aims nor his spontaneous, affective reactions or primary orientation, but, rather, integrate both his experience and his future aims.

The dream symbol of the cave, then, must not, states May firmly, be oversimplified into a conflict between infantile and adult wishes, but is a clear confrontation on the part of the young man of the aspects of his own struggle toward integrating his existence. Further, he could not, says May, *have let himself* create such a powerful and demanding dream until he was "ready in some way to confront the decision posed in the symbol" (*Significance of Symbols,* p. 17). Willing, as May sees it, does not merely follow wishing, but also gives rise to it, that is, it is an overall willingness or decisive orientation toward existence that allows the self to see and disclose meaning through wish. That is, *what* one wishes is already influenced and guided by one's primary decisions or orientation, by what May later calls one's *intentionality.*

We recall now May's early formulation of the self as that which the person is always in process of becoming and can now see that indeed his later view of the significance of will as creative intentionality was contained implicitly therein, although May does not make this point. "Man," holds May, "understands himself as he is projected toward something" (*Existential Psychotherapy,* p. 8). The person (in the case of therapy, the patient) is already orienting himself in some way to himself as he sees himself, to his life, his existence in general, and his problems are, in fact, symptomatic of his way of relating to his existence. Neurosis, then, is no longer, for May, a *lack* of adjustment (balance) of tensions, as he spoke of it in his earlier work. It is not a lack of choice, of commitment, of balance, nor even an *ad hoc* or spontaneous particular adjustment to an experienced difficulty or pain. Neurosis is, as May sees it, symptomatic rather of a primary orientation, a way of constituting existence and its meaning, an orientation characterized by increasingly negative, intense self-restriction of the demands, the meaning, and broad significance of the person's whole existence. The mature or integrated person, the individual with a strong sense of his being-in-the-world, of his worth and value as a striving existent in coexistence, and of the overall value of his aims and purposes, will be able to cope courageously with new situations and new problems. He will be able to make adjustments and to alter his actions without detriment to his being, without inconsistency in his self-realization, since he is already decisively oriented toward openness, ever-wider freedom, and self-consciousness, having willingly accepted the possibility of error, limitation, contingency, and imperfection.

The significance of will, then, for May, is coextensive with being human, or as he puts it, "self-consciousness . . . brings in inseparably the element of decision at every moment"; to be self-conscious is to have the capacity to be fully aware "that the vast, complex, protean flow of experience is (one's own) experience" (*Existential Psychotherapy*, p. 36; *Love and Will*, p. 204). It is this capacity, asserts May, that enables man to experience himself both as subject and as object, to "objectify" himself and his world, to "stand back from" and transcend the immediate situation, to remember his past and envisage his future, to "try on" in imagination the various possibilities for action that seem discernible in his immediate or remote future (*Introduction: What is the Human Dilemma*, pp. 6-24; *Questions*, pp. 194-195; *Love and Will*, pp. 223-225; *Dreams and Symbols*, pp. 5-6). This "dilemma" or "polarity"—May uses both descriptive terms—that is, the "dilemma" of experiencing himself "both as subject and as object," is not an opposition, but a process of oscillation, out of which, as May sees it, arises man's capacity to symbolize his world, that is, to grasp it and to express that grasp in concepts, to isolate and name what he experiences in his world, that experience being in turn mediated and colored or given perspective and context at least partially by the concepts in which he expresses it. Man is conscious of himself, and therefore his becoming is a conscious becoming, a series of choices (even if only negative exclusions) made at every instant (*Contributions*, p. 42; *Love and Will*, p.

204). Thus, much more is involved in the realm of will and decision than the mere "surface" choice or rejection of a course of action. In *Existential Psychotherapy* (pp. 31-50) and throughout *Love and Will* May presents and explores this formulation.

In the task of understanding in human existence the fundamental import and significance of will and decision, May asserts that one must first turn to the question of the interrelationship of wish and will, and then to intentionality as underlying the entire process. Wish, says May, is never merely spontaneous need or drive; because of human self-consciousness and ability to sense one's being, human needs and drives are located within a matrix of meaning. A human being's needs and wishes are experienced and known by him, says May, in symbolic meanings: His wishing is not merely a drive for satisfaction, not a purely "economic" need, but is experienced selectively as an element of molding his existence, of remembering past and forming future. Human wishing is an expression of the symbolic meaning, overtones, and associations that the particular need or wish has for the particular individual. In other words, the individual's needs and wishes, however purely bodily they may appear to the detached, objective, scientific observer, are located within a meaningful context or matrix or configuration and are, in some way, personal, individual and selective. Thus May calls wishing a "symbolic process," "a molding by a symbolic process that includes both memory and fantasy.... The wish is the beginning of orienting ourselves to the future, an admission that we want the future to be such and such" (*Love and Will,* p. 211).

Wishing, then, for May, includes a dimension of meaning and can take place only in terms of one's primary orientation or willingness or intentional orientation to existence. That is to say, what one is at any given moment *attentive to* does not exhaust the whole range of wishing; rather, wishing is related to the way in which one senses one's being or to the decisive (predominant) orientation to existence that characterizes that sense of one's being. "In the revealing and exploring of the deterministic forces in his life, the patient is already orienting himself in some particular way to the data and thus is engaged in some choice, no matter how seemingly insignificant" (*Existential Psychotherapy,* p. 35). Wishing does not occur in a vacuum, but is located in the context of the possible meaning encompassed by one's whole existence and delimited by the determining factors of that existence.

Thus, according to May, there is "no will without prior wish" (*Love and Will,* p. 211, see also p. 222). Centering on what he sees as the interrelation of wish and will, May is concerned with exploring the two both separately and in the whole process of orientation to existence. He is concerned with explicating wishing and willing: wishing as the autonomous, creative, spontaneous elements and willing as the necessity of deciding, of being for or against and of making conscious, reflective, effortful choices (*Love and Will,* pp. 215-218; *Existential Psychotherapy,* pp. 36-39; *Dreams and Symbols,* pp. 6-9). Wish, as May sees it, is "the imaginative playing with the possibility of some state or act occurring" while will "is the capacity to organize one's self . . . toward a certain goal" (*Love and Will,* p. 218). It is noteworthy at this point that May has now begun, without explicitly stating any such intention or even awareness of it, to use the term *will* in a second and more restricted sense than the comprehensive way in which up to now he has used it. That is, will, for May, now means both the organizing capacity, as distinct from wish as creative, vital, spontaneous exploring of possibilities; and also the whole process of free structuring of existence, subsuming orientation, wish, decision, and responsibility. For the second, broader conception May will shortly employ the term *intentionality* as the more encompassing, more expressive concept.

Will as organizing capacity (as distinct from wish) requires *self*-consciousness, says May: It has to do, he continues, with the realization that "*I*-am-the-one-who-has-these-wishes" (*Love and Will,* pp. 266-267). This, he explains, incorporates wish on "a higher level of consciousness," or of explicit self-relatedness. For example, asserts May, on the level of awareness (wish), one experiences the beauty of blue sky behind golden forsythia blooms; the element of will enters with the realization that "I am the one who is experiencing, and so forth, and would like to continue, affirm, and perhaps even share and communicate this experience." To explicate this further—May, however, does not offer further explication—the level of will as organizing capacity, for May, has to do with the implications of wishes and their relationship to the sense of one's being and the possibility of making choices, the implications of choosing "for" in awareness both of what that "for" is and what it excludes, of choosing "against" in active conviction that one must do so to be consistent and integral in one's being and values. Such will, or capacity to organize, depends for its content on spontaneous, rich, free wishing and openness to the possibilities of one's existence if will is not to be restricted, that is, to be only negative exclusion and withdrawal. Will, then, is interdependent with wish in the process of integrating existence. Wish without will remains in the realm of chaotic whim and disintegrative impulse with only fleeting, superficial attraction in place of guiding purpose and fulfillment. Will without wish, as May sees it, is dry, arid organization for no end but iself, lacking in fullness, ignoring at least some aspects of living, reducing and depreciating the scope and meaning of existence.

Central, asserts May, to the process of willing is attention. Whereas wish is spontaneous, vital orientation to existence, the free, responsible exercise of choice and decision or organization or priority is interdependent with the effort involved in the attention or focus of the person on specific wishes and their realization or attainment. The *intention* of the individual, too, says May, is greatly involved in his reflective ability to *attend* to, to focus on, and to isolate the matter for decision. Once again, one is reminded of May's formulation of the original decision (predominant) orientation to existence that characterizes the person's sense of his being.

It is, then, says May, no mere conscious (or surface) analysis alone of one's wishes and motives nor a mere push of instincts alone that brings the individual to a decision. This is accomplished rather by an interplay of conscious intentions and the underlying orientation of one's whole existence as expressed in the wishes and tendencies of which one may, at a given moment, be least aware. Intentionality, says May, is the "dimension which cuts across and includes both conscious and unconscious, both cognition and conation" (*Love and Will,* p. 222). As has already been indicated and explicated, May uses the term *unconscious* to signify the individual's potentialities for knowing, feeling, and wanting that he has not yet actualized, whether because he cannot yet focus clearly on them or because he refuses to try to envisage them clearly. For May, intentionality is orientation to existence, the fundamental meaning-disclosing relatedness of the individual to his world. As such, it underlies wish, will, and decision; it is the structure that makes possible the disclosure of meaning and it underlies the capacity to shape and mold one's existence, to become reflectively aware of affinities and aversions, of wishes and their implications; to experience oneself as "subject" and "object"; to constitute one's world as "object"; to transcend the immediate present; and to anticipate the future.

To be human, then, is to be intentional, to be oriented toward oneself and one's world, toward responsible assertion of one's being-in-the-world as individual, centered and participatory. "Intentionality," asserts May, "carries the meaning of reality as we know it" (*Love and Will,* p. 224). It is our given relatedness to existence, our "way of knowing reality," of knowing and understanding self and world in polarity. For May, intentionality is not to be identified with intentions, but it does include them. Because it is the structure underlying meaningful contents of consciousness, as May defines it, intentionality is what enables several human beings to view one object from many perspectives of emotions, hopes, fears, associations, and even training. As the capacity to disclose meaning, it underlies the human being's capacity, and indeed desire, to question, care for, and form his own existence; to constitute, have concern for (to *tend,* at*tend* to, in*tend*) and participate in his world.

In order to illustrate what the term *intentionality* means, May speaks of looking at a house in the mountains (*Love and Will,* p. 224) from the point of view of (1) a prospective tenant; (2) a real-estate speculator; (3) being there as the welcome guest of a good friend; (4) a social acquaintance on somewhat acrimonious terms with the owner; and (5) an artist wishing to sketch the house. May says:

> *We shall define it [intentionality] in two
> stages; the preliminary stage is the fact that our in-
> tentions are decisive with respect to how we per-
> ceive the world . . . in each [instance], it is the
> same house that provides the stimulus and I am the
> same man responding to it. But in each case, the
> house and experience have an entirely different
> meaning . . . . But this is only one side of intention-
> ality. The other side is that it also* does *come from
> the object. Intentionality is the bridge between
> these. It is the structure of meaning which makes it
> possible for us, subjects that we are, to see and
> understand the outside world, objective as it is. In
> intentionality, the dichotomy between subject and
> object is partially overcome* [Love and Will, *pp.*
> *224-225].*

The particular mentality or role through which May looks
at the house is in each case greatly involved in the way in which
he judges the house to be attractive or not, desirable or undesir-
able, having an enviable or unenviable aspect or situation, or
whether he sees it primarily in terms of line, features, artistic
possibilities. Our intentions, says May, are decisive with respect
to how we perceive the world; yet it is in each case the same
house and he is the same person responding to it in various
ways. It is, for May, then, not the reality of the house that
changes, but the meaning ascribed to it by the individual looking at it. Clearly, here, May is concerned with illustrating his
notion of intentionality by showing how fundamental the perspective or frame of reference of the subject is in the way he
constitutes the meaning-for-him of what he encounters.

It might be useful to recall that in *Existence,* May had
briefly mentioned Binswanger's "discussion of von Uexküll's
metaphor of the contrasting environments of the tree in the
forest" and the various meanings the tree held for the woods-
man, the romantic girl, and so forth (*Contributions,* p. 76;
Binswanger, 1967, pp. 194-199). May's concern, when he cited
this discussion, was to illustrate the close relationship between
psychological health and "freedom in designing world" or the

capacity to envisage oneself in many different situations and roles, and to contrast the *un*-freedom and constricted intensity of neurotic anxiety with the free, varied, changing and growing "world" born of a strong sense of being.

May is not naturally a subjectivist, however, and in *Love and Will,* following his example of the possibility of one person responding in many ways to the house in the mountains, he declares that this response is only one "side" of intentionality. "The other side," he says, "is that it also *does* come from the object" (*Love and Will,* p. 225), and he speaks of intentionality as a "bridge" between subject and object. At this point, May gives no evidence of considering a need for further and more detailed explication of these statements. Later (p. 324), he terms himself an "inbred realist" who, on the basis of his "assumptions," assumes that the world exists. In view of his overall position of what one might call practical realism, one can only assume that he means that the object (in this case the house) exists in space and time independently of the subject or observer and that it itself is not changed by the various frames of reference through which the person sees it or encounters it, that it presents itself as it is with a given shape, size, color, condition, and, independently of the particular observer, that it is already constituted as a house, sharing all the essential features of "house," already carrying the human meaning inserted into it by the intention of its builder and by the collective recognition of, assent to, and experience of what it is that we call "house." In the relationship constituted by my observation of the house, I am the subject observing, while the house is the object observed. A crucial difference in relationship exists, however, when the two poles of the relationship are two human beings, in which case they are both simultaneously subjects and objects both for themselves and for each other, and the quality of the relationship is essentially *inter*subjective. This question and its importance for psychotherapeutic encounter in particular have already been dealt with at some length in discussion of Mitwelt and of love in the earlier chapters of this book.

At this point, in his discussion of intentionality, May does not go into any such explication, but merely adds that, as he sees it, "in intentionality, the dichotomy between subject and object is partially overcome" (*Love and Will*, p. 225). Here, however, one might recall the first chapter in *Psychology and the Human Dilemma* (pp. 3-22), wherein he characterizes the "human dilemma" as the subject-object polarity, or man's capacity to envisage himself as subject and object, and again, man's capacity to envisage himself and his world as subject and object, and yet again, man's capacity to be "subjective" or involved, or "objective" and scientifically disinterested, detached, and impersonal. Yet, in *Existence,* May speaks of existentialism as "the endeavor to understand man by cutting below the cleavage between subject and object which has bedevilled Western thought" (*Origins,* p. 11; see also *Contributions,* p. 46). These various statements, many variations of which can be found in his work, make it difficult to be quite sure with which meaning May is using the terms *subject* and *object* at a given time. Only careful and repeated contextual examination together with constant recall of May's practical "realism" and psychotherapeutic orientation help one come to an understanding whether in a given instance he means (1) man envisaging himself as subject and as object; (2) man as subject constituting "the world" as object; (3) patient seen both as subject and object of psychotherapy; or (4) *subjective* as philosophically meaning "relating to subject" or colloquially meaning "involved" and perhaps "prejudiced"; *objective* as philosophically meaning "relating to object" or colloquially meaning "with scientific detachment," "unprejudiced," or perhaps even, "tending toward *un*concern about the individual person as a person."

Further, the statement that "in intentionality, the dichotomy between subject and object is partially overcome" is a very confusing one indeed, since it is suddenly not at all clear whether May is speaking in a technical sense (of the philosophical notion of dichotomy) or in a colloquial sense (wherein *dichotomy* is generally inaccurately and vaguely understood as "separate" without clarifying the meaning any further). Now May has, in the context of the cited statement, been speaking of the person (subject) looking at the house (object). Throughout his work, however, he continually refers to the Cartesian body-mind split as "the dichotomy" and cites it as one of the root causes of scientism, of compartmentalization, of "methodolatry," of unreflective, irresponsible, deterministic sloughing off of existence, and of the reduction of "person" to "object of study," "instance of something," or "object among objects." However, in his discussion of intentionality and his example of the house in the mountains, he has been speaking from his practical "realist" standpoint of the person responding, albeit in different ways, to the stimulus provided by the house. He has not hitherto in this context indicated any difficulty with any dichotomy, nor has he even mentioned any dichotomy; yet he seems to regard it as necessary to say that "the dichotomy" has been "partially overcome," as though the dichotomy is there, a separate reality, an inalienable, independent fact, or an obstacle or practical problem to be overcome or solved. It does, then, remain uncertain whether May realizes what the force and emphasis of the philosophical notion of dichotomy are, as opposed to the casual, colloquial associations of the word.

Moreover, the *philosophical* notion of "dichotomy," like the notion of intentionality, is itself a conceptualization, not a "fact" but an *interpretation,* a hermeneutic of human existence, a reflective grasping in a particular way, a specific formulation of what it is to be a conscious individual-in-participation, a self confronting his world. Now, *colloquially* the word *dichotomy* may loosely express May's "realist" view of the independent existence of person and house in this instance; as *hermeneutic* or reflective interpretation, however, "the dichotomy" does not have an inalienable, independent existence of its own and cannot offer resistance or difficulty-to-be-overcome before intentionality, itself also a hermeneutic of human existence, can be deemed to enclose, encompass, and sustain simultaneously the relatedness and separatedness of individuals-in-participation. In other words, subject and object are *distinct but not dichotomized* in the technical sense. They are mutually constitutive; that is, the subject is subject in relation to object, and the reverse; neither can be deemed subject or object without the other to which to be related in this manner. Further, in a discussion of intentionality, to introduce a "dichotomy" of subject and object tends fundamentally to oppose and confuse the primacy of the polarity of relatedness and separatedness, of individuation and participation, already established as fundamental in May's work as a whole. Such an introduction only obscures his view of human being as intentional, of man as a meaning-disclosing existent oriented to self and world. The use of the term *dichotomy* in this context, together with the unexplained sense of the modifying adverb *partially,* can only serve to confuse since May does not state what he means by "overcome," nor whether he intends the word *dichotomy* to be understood in a vague, colloquial sense of "separate" or "different from" or some other sense, as compared with his more usual use of the term within the context and implication of the Cartesian conception.

One may perhaps surmise that having spoken loosely, or at most metaphorically, of intentionality as a "bridge," May unwittingly carries on the metaphor, assuming then that there must be something-needing-to-be-bridged, an imaginary divide or gap yawning between subject and object, and that without this bridge, subject and object would remain totally separated, divided, unlinked in any way. In other words, it would seem that despite May's apparently realistic acceptance of person and house (the subject and object in this instance) as real, separated, and yet linked by the person's observation of the stimulus house (already constituted as a house, preexisting the observation), his terminological and conceptual imprecisions do little to remove the impression that "subject" and "object" have somehow been reified or given separate, independent, "factual" existence, without the relatedness that constitutes or brings into being their "subjectness" and "objectness" for each other. In view of the lack of explication, however, it remains unclear as to whether May is aware of the possibility of any confusion or imprecision of expression. The reader is, then, left to fall back on May's vague statements that intentionality "comes from" both the subject and the object and that it "carries the meaning of reality as we know it."

However, despite such inexactness of conceptual expression and the demonstrated incompleteness of explication as compared with brief illustrations or examples, May's overall meaning and concrete purpose are clear enough, and the conceptual deficiencies can be, and have been here, clarified and rectified without doing violence to the tenor of May's work as a whole. For May, it is in intentionality (will); in the broad reach of human orientation toward meaning, decision and act; in the weighing, deciding, and acting on sensed possibilities; in the consistency of wishes, affinities, and aversions, which may be least in awareness, with responsible assertion of one's individuality-in-participation—that is, it is in wholeness, integration, and consistency of wish, will, decision, and responsibility that the person experiences his being and senses and decides his identity. Intentionality, as May envisages it, underlies the spontaneity of wish, the conscious attention and isolation of will, the direction of decision, and the degree of responsibility for one's actions. We know our world, says May, by virtue of its intent for us, that is to say, through our concerns, our attention, our disclosure of its meaning for us (*Love and Will,* pp. 229-230, 236). We know our world, May continues, through our primary willing of it; we will (that is, desire, decide, and shape) our world through knowing it. Man is constantly forming and being formed by both his knowing and his willing of reality, while reality is constantly changing and being changed by this interrelationship. Language, for May, is the symbolizing, the naming, isolating, conceptualizing, deliberating, meaning-disclosing process by which we grasp our world, by which we *per*ceive it, express that perception, conceptualize it, decide and shape our world, and give structured expression to the creative vitality of existence. Consciousness, for May, "creates" its world in the sense that it perceives its world, having shaped and expressed its perception in concepts or symbols. The individual's experiencing of his world, then, is a continuous, reciprocal, responsive relationship, as much constituted by the world-as-encountered as the world is constituted by the encountering individual.

The significance of will, as May sees it, is the broad reach of intentionality, of human existence as embodied consciousness creating, disclosing, and shaping meaning through wish, will, decision, action, and responsible assertion of individuality-in-participation. The individual's will is not a floating spirit nor a vague illusion, but an embodied, structured response related in space and time to his particular world, biologically, culturally, and ethically. It is, holds May, in that embodied structuring of his creative vitality, of his possibilities in the world, that the person experiences his fundamental individual relatedness-in-meaning and his strength and happiness in thoughtful loving and enduring commitment. It is in the decisive grasping of his own existence and of his world that the individual senses his identity, his whole being. Potentialities are experienced not as something "outside" or separate, but on one's own pulse as one's *own* possibilities, one's own inner response to existence; then, as May sees it, "I" becomes truly and effectively the "I" of "I can." This, for May, is the deep significance of will, interrelated as it is with the sense of being, the anxiety of potentiality, and the vitality of love.

The importance of such a conception of existence for the concrete practice of psychotherapy is obvious. The quality and degree of the patient's intentional orientation to existence is clearly fundamentally related to his willingness and capacity to enter into (participate, take part in, be part of, and cooperate) and be actively and vitally concerned (caring, serious, and involved) in the psychotherapeutic task of exploring, understanding, and recreating, which task faces psychotherapist and patient together. The focus of the next section, then, will be the consideration of intentionality in therapy as May sees it, and the integrated understanding of wish, will, and decision, as viewed by May, as representing stages in therapy. With regard to May's conception of the interrelationship of will-as-intentionality and the patient's sense of being, two of May's case histories (that of Preston in *Love and Will* and that of Susan, the sole subject of *Dreams and Symbols*) will be briefly examined.

Intentionality in Therapy: Wish, Will, and Decision

The significance of will as intentionality, then, for May, is, in terms of concrete and practical considerations, the patient's capacity to remain at and persevere with the therapeutic

task of self-understanding, elucidating, ameliorating, and perhaps evaluating his own decisive or predominant orientation to
existence (*Love and Will,* pp. 246-272; *Existential Psychotherapy,* pp. 31-40; *A Phenomenological Approach,* pp. 123-127;
Dreams and Symbols, pp. 8, 21). The task of the therapist,
asserts May, is "to be conscious . . . of what the intentionality
of the patient is in a particular session" (*Love and Will,* p. 247).
He must, continues May, seek to understand and clarify this
intentionality and must try to bring the patient to consciousness of it and responsibility for it.

It is to be observed here that, without warning or re-
definition, and perhaps even unwittingly, May is now using the
term *intentionality* in a second sense, with a different import
from that which it had earlier. Whereas he had been up to this
juncture speaking of human intentionality *as such,* or that
orientedness or relatedness that is inalienable from and characteristic of human existence, and hence ontological in it, he is
now speaking of "the patient's intentionality" or *orientation* in
a particular therapeutic session. That is, May is now speaking of
the particular modification or expression of the patient in therapy at a specific time, and by implication only, of the predominant orientation of the patient to his existence as a whole.
Thus, May is no longer speaking of the *orientedness* or intentionality of human existence as such (the ontological characteristic of human being as such), but rather of the predominant
expression of that characteristic orientedness or the *particular
orientation* of a particular patient in a particular session of
therapy.

Although one may cavil at the ambiguity of using the
term *intentionality* with a second and unindicated connotation,
it must be borne in mind that as always May is concerned with
theoretical deliberations not for their own sake but for the sake
of the light they can bring to psychotherapeutic practice. It is
not, however, conducive to clarity of meaning to have thus
changed without explicit statement the import of the term
intentionality and one may further wonder whether May was
aware of this imprecision. He does not explicate his notion of
intentionality in therapy any further but again moves to illustra-

tion-by-example of his notion of intentionality in a particular session of therapy.

In "The Case of Preston," May presents, with lengthy quotations from the verbatim record, a session that he holds to be illustrative of his view of the significance of intentionality in therapy (*Love and Will,* pp. 248-262, 304). Preston, says May, is a creative writer of middle years, faced with a recurring "writing block" with painful tension, anxiety, depression, and sexual problems. After five years of analysis with another therapist, he has, at the time of the cited session, been under May's therapeutic guidance for seven months. In this particular session, Preston's declared, consciously affirmed purpose (or to use May's words, his "conscious *intention*") is, because he has been experiencing severe inability to cope with his writing block despite familiarity with his material, "to get Dr. May *to do something* about this" (*Love and Will,* p. 258, italics mine). The patient's attitude in the therapeutic hour, as cited by May, is not a straightforward appeal for help, however, but ranges from apathy, seeming despair, anger, fear, cynicism, and self-revulsion to momentary earnestness. In speech, he repeatedly attempts to analyze and summarize himself, his worth as a person, and his dreams and thoughts, and yet just as constantly surrenders himself into depressed frustration. In the patient's manner, however —clenched teeth, tense body attitudes, for example—May notes suppressed rage and resentment to which, says the therapist, Preston is apparently not attentive, and of which he only gradually becomes explicitly conscious.

In his discussion of this session, May quotes verbatim from the tapescript what he considers and indicates as key exchanges. Further, he singles out some of Preston's remarks as particularly significant or revelatory of the patient's "whole intentionality," that is, not merely as explanatory of his stated difficulties, but as indications of his inclusive, more fundamental orientation toward the therapist, toward his need for therapy, as indications of "his way of relating to [May] on the whole" (*Love and Will,* p. 258), although at first this is present on the level of awareness only. In one of the cited exchanges, Preston speaks of thinking that if he sits at his typewriter long enough, something will "happen," the "magic will come," "somehow it will write itself." Yet he adds later that no matter what he experiences, there is such a "weight of habit" behind his depression and incapacity that the effect on him of any experience is as fleeting as "a pin-prick in those self-seal tires" (p. 250). He wants May to decide the course and content of the conversation and resents the therapist's expressed preference for having Preston decide the topic. Yet he remarks that he is "so used to [him] self as a stage-manager around here" (p. 250). Later, he says that he has no will to put himself "inside" his work, that nothing is "happening," that consciously he wants to work well, but that "will is all unconscious anyway" (p. 252). Again and again he remarks that, in spite of efforts to work, he "can't" help himself, "can't work"; yet his description of his efforts reveals that he has not really tried, but has constantly interrupted himself with the most trivial excuses (p. 252). May recalls also in his commentary that earlier treatment under drugs had been attended by some difficulty and that Preston had expressed the fear that "what would come out [that is, what he would say] would not be what they wanted to hear" (p. 250).

A clear contradiction, asserts May, exists between Preston's lackadaisical, apathetic speech and his obvious, real suffering and upset; between his attempts to cooperate and describe his condition and his real, underlying anger and resentment. This rage, says May, is an understandable accompaniment of the conflict between the patient's declared, simple purpose of getting May to help him with his writing block, and his "overall intentionality" or "way of relating to May as a whole" with the complication of "intrapsychic conflicts" (pp. 258, 253). His *overall intentionality* is much more complex than his stated purpose or *intention*, since the former encompasses the simple, conscious desire for help and yet reduces it to a half-hearted, lackadaisical, depressed statement of inability.

In an examination of the patient's *intentionality* (*Love and Will*, pp. 253-260), May recalls Preston's references to himself as a "self-seal tire" and as a "stage-manager," together with the suppressed anger revealed in his physical attitudes and only

later surfacing in his speech, at May's instigation. While profess-
ing to be asking for help and unwittingly resenting having to do
so, Preston is, in reality, says May, trying aggressively to force
the therapist to assume responsibility for him, to be sorry for
him, to "find" a solution or "magic cure" for his condition.
Further, with his constant interruptions of "attempts" to work,
Preston reveals that he does not wish to work. The phrase "will
is all unconscious anyway," May is convinced, reveals that on
some level Preston is aware of what he is doing, although he has
refused to face it consciously in the full light of attention. Only
when the patient has been faced with the fact of his own anger
and resentment and with the "*I won't*" that really underlies the
stated "*I can't* work," only then, says May, can Preston begin to
explore the reasons, both remote and proximate, for his present
difficulties. Only when Preston becomes attentive to and admits
responsibility for what he is really doing (that is, trying to push
his problem away from himself onto his therapist from whom
he is demanding "magical" intervention and the "conferring" of
great writing), only then does Preston have, as May sees it, some
genuine possibility of connecting the "what" with the "whys"
and the "wherefores," and some future possibility of assuming
responsibility for what he would really like to do with his life.
In other words (although May does not express it in this manner), the goal of therapy in Preston's case is, as always, to aid
the patient to sense (and decide) his being, through the aided
exploration and clarification of his "intentionality" in particular sessions and of his predominant orientation or intentionality
toward his whole existence, to come to a point wherein the
patient can experience what his particular existence is, how he
has been expressing or negating it, toward what he wishes to
proceed or orient himself, how he would like to envision his
existence in the future.

"To live in a polarity of intent and act," says May,
"means to live with one's anxiety" (*Love and Will*, pp.
260-261). Preston, like other patients, and indeed like all human beings, must learn to experience honestly and acknowledge
responsibility for both his intentions and his actions, without
self-deception as to his real motives, his real acts, and their

effects and implications. And he must learn to accept the attendant anxiety and doubt. Only then can he begin to make constructive decisions as a relative unity, in place of sloughing off his existence in a destructive self-contradiction and inconsistency. May emphasizes that mere "acting out in therapy" of what the patient thinks he wants to do does not confront him with the *meaning* of the act. He must experience not merely the emotion involved but must experience and become conscious of the meaning of that emotion in his own life, of its overtones and implications, and of its consequences and effects. He must learn whether that emotion or desire is self-destructive or constructive. He must confront it not merely for the purpose of simply expressing it or of gaining some relief or release at most temporary (as though "lancing an abscess"), but in order to gain understanding of it as a signpost to the true state of the whole relationship that gave rise to it, that is, understanding of his own whole intentionality or particular orientation to existence (and thence, May might have added, understanding of his fundamental sense of being). A patient must not, says May, be allowed to escape into thought alone of the desired act, but rather must be aided to gain understanding of the full implications, social and personal, of his intention. A patient who "intellectualizes" his difficulties by using psychological terminology, adds May, "is precisely taking the *intentionality* out of the experience" (*Love and Will*, p. 260).

However one may admire the apparent simplicity and common sense of May's psychotherapeutic objectives, this latest phrase on his part ("taking the *intentionality* out") presents difficulties. In view of the fact that, as has already been pointed out, May neither redefined the term *intentionality* for this discussion of its place in therapy, nor gave any indication that he understood its import to have changed, it now becomes questionable whether May genuinely understands what it is to have offered the view that to be human is to be intentional, or that intentionality is ontological in human existence. This ambiguity may be traced to May's somewhat less than precise terminological usages, as, for instance, when he described intentionality as "the structure that gives meaning to experience" and "man's capacity to have intentions" (*Love and Will*, pp. 223-224). Intentionality as such cannot be "taken out of" human experience. Although the individual may change, alter, modify, repress consciousness of, or merely deny his *intention*, he cannot cease to be *intentional*, that is, oriented toward meaning, nor can he render his action unconnected to any intention. If the term *intentionality* is understood to have changed in import and scope as explored earlier in this section, the person can then be said to "take *the* intentionality out," meaning that he is "taking out" the specific, particular orientation or intention out of the act by convincing himself that he does it for some other substitute intention. This distinction concerning the changing import, scope, and meaning of the term *intentionality* has not, however, been made or in any way acknowledged by May himself.

The process of therapy with individual patients, says May, is an integrating process, "bringing together the three dimensions of wish, will and decision" (*Love and Will*, p. 262; *Existential Psychotherapy*, pp. 35-40, 45). Each dimension represents a stage in therapy; a stage is transcended, retained, and incorporated, but not superseded by the next. "Intentionality," says May, "is present on all three dimensions" (*Love and Will*, p. 262).

Once again the term *intentionality* has become ambiguous and may refer to any one or more than one or even all of the following *four* senses of the term, implied as they are both by the context and by May's overall notion of primary intentionality, and given that one must be careful to bear in mind the tenor of concrete, practical realism of all May's work. These four senses (which May does not clarify and of which he is perhaps quite unaware) are: (1) human orientedness toward meaning, that is, the ontological characteristic of orientedness, relatedness; (2) the particular self-appropriated orientation toward meaning that characterizes a particular person's (in this context, patient's) way of relating to himself, to his therapist, or to existence as a whole; (3) the particular orientation (or expression thereof) exhibited by a particular patient in a particular session of therapy; and (4) an effective, integrating, "curing" intentionality or orientation toward positive reconstitution of one's self-world relationship. This last import is a new one, implied in May's declaration that the process of therapy is an integrating one, a process that newly relates and joins the three stages of wish, will, and decision in an increasingly developing, opening, broadening, freeing self-world relationship.

This implied conception of an integrating intentionality evokes again (although May does not say so) his notion (as it was expressed in *Existence* but disclosed and explored in this book as already underlying his thought in *The Art of Counseling*) that decision is at the basis of all knowledge, and that a primary positive choice in the direction of integrated existence (as exemplified by the girl who arrived at the "I-am" experience, explored in Chapter One, Section Three of this book) must underlie any real progress, change, or conversion, and hence therapy. May has never believed therapy to be the prescription and application of an "automatic cure," nor the conditioning of the patient to "feel cured" or "adjusted" merely because he accepts apathetically his existence and "feels less." As May presents it, therapy is a long, slow, at times painful process, undertaken in loving encounter between the troubled patient and the concerned, yet disciplined and trained, therapist-friend-observer; a process of examination, clarification, and search for meaning, with a primary decision to accept whatever "growing-pains" and tribulations may be ahead during that process and after it. Hence, May names the stages in that process the stages of *wish, will,* and *decision,* which, as he sees them, are dimensions all underlain by a primary intentionality, a curing orientation toward meaningful, positive self-reconstitution.

The first stage, wish, is correlated for May with awareness (*Love and Will,* pp. 262-266; *Existential Psychotherapy,* pp. 38-39). It supplies the content for will and decision. It is particularly important in a period when sophistication tends to be confused with cynical noninvolvement, boredom, and lack of spontaneous wishes, and when adult freedom, construed as license to do as one pleases, often ends in overindulgence and disillusion. This, as May has frequently pointed out in his writings, is most often accompanied by and arises out of an anxious apprehension of vulnerability, and, he might have added, an undeveloped sense of being, a lack of direction and integrated, reflective purpose. Yet to be alive to one's own possibilities is necessarily correlated with one's aliveness to one's whole self, world, situatedness, and relatedness. Heightened sensitivity to one's wishes carries with it the possibility of increased anxiety of vulnerability, but it also makes possible increased hope of joy and happiness, even of simple enjoyment and appreciation. To reduce awareness of sights, sounds, to repress or deny wish for fear of hurt or disappointment is, then, simultaneously to reduce the possibility of creative living. The goal of this stage in therapy, as May sees it, then, is to have the patient experience his wishes, to bring him to the realization that he *wants* something. One might here recall (although May does not do so) that Preston had first to realize that he did *want something* before any isolation - and recognition of *what* that was could be attained.

The second stage, will, is what May calls "the transmuting of awareness into self-consciousness" or into what he calls "self-conscious intentions" (*Love and Will*, pp. 266-267; *Existential Psychotherapy*, pp. 39-40). This stage he describes as the acceptance of oneself as the person who has these wishes, or desires, as the one who has this world and who can do something about himself and his world, can communicate something of what he feels, thinks, sees, and hears. Again, May might well, for purposes of illustration, have related this stage of therapy to the case of Preston, who had to reach the point of clearly seeing and recognizing himself as the one who had the wish to work or not to work, who would have to accept responsibility for and confront honestly himself and his world, no longer trying to put "it" outside of himself, as it were, no longer asking why "*it* wouldn't work," but seeing clearly his own inability, his anger, his *un*willingness, and his rejection of himself as impotent and angry.

In speaking of the three dimensions, May had named the third stage simply the dimension of decision. However, when he comes to discuss the third stage he now speaks of it as that of decision and responsibility (*Love and Will*, pp. 267-268; *Exis-*

tential Psychotherapy, p. 40). This is noteworthy (although May does not make this point), since it changes the aim of therapy from the mere goal (implied in the term *decision*) of the patient's self-assertion or decisiveness to the goal of his *responsible* self-assertion. Responsible self-assertion has, of course, always been one of May's most strongly held convictions in his early "picture of personality" and later, in his elucidation of what it is to be human. For May, the human being who is "moving toward self-realization, integration, maturity" is characterized not merely by decisiveness, nor only by his decisive, predominant orientation to existence, but also by responsibility (*Love and Will,* p. 267; *Man's Search,* p. 235; *Existential Psychotherapy,* p. 40). Decision, for May, incorporates and transcends the stages of wish and will and creates out of them a pattern of living and acting. Responsibility, for May, is the double dimension of being *responsive to* and *responsible for* what he calls "significant other-persons," toward the realization of "long-term goals." The third stage of therapy, decision and responsibility, is reached when the patient begins to be decisively responsible for and responsive to the wishes, intentions, actions, and implications of his self-world relationship, that is to say, having regard and concern not merely for himself nor merely for others but for both in their inalienable relatedness and separatedness. In this capacity of the human being to transcend or go beyond the merely self-oriented wish or intention, to have a care for other persons as well as honest regard for himself, to posit long-term goals with other people in mind, to find joy and contentment in seeking as much as in attaining those goals, in this capacity May sees the beginning of ethics.

It follows, then, that May would consider as a hopeful indication any sign on the part of the patient that he is, however momentarily, considering any person other than himself. Later, when speaking of care as a relationship of concern (*Love and Will,* pp. 303-304). May recalls again his taped interview with Preston. He cites a moment wherein Preston expresses sympathy for any therapist's constant problem of whether to speak or not to speak. In particular, Preston expresses some concern for May as a person. May affirms that "this upsurgence of a genuine human feeling of sympathy" (*Love and Will*, p. 304), however simple and momentary, is a critical moment in psychotherapy, in that it points to the possibilities for the patient of eventually breaking out of his apathy, self-concern, and restricting self-preoccupation. In the cited instance, the moment is a very fleeting moment indeed, since Preston links it immediately with his own difficulties, but it does, however, illustrate the point May wished to make, that greater awareness of the actual situation leads to greater awareness of and even concern for self and others, and is necessary for clarifying the real intentionality or particular orientation of the patient.

Since he holds that the patient's overall intentionality is far more complex than his mere stated purposes or "conscious intentions," it follows that May would wish to envisage a patient's dreams, not in terms of static concepts or abstract formulations or interpretations, but in terms of the deeper, more direct, overall way in which the dreaming person is experiencing his being and his world. Concerning Susan in *Dreams and Symbols*, May asks the following questions: How is she seeing, changing, molding, and remolding herself and her world? What latent problems or decisions are being proposed and perhaps even explored and answered, however partially or confusedly, in her dreams? And those symbols or quintessential conceptions, those meaningful, gripping preoccupations that recur in her dreams, particularly at critical points—what do they tell one of the living totality and basic intentionality of Susan herself (*Dreams and Symbols*, pp. 20-22, 23)?

Subtitled *Man's Unconscious Language*, this psychological study, centering on one woman in therapy—the patient identified as "Susan"—is divided into two parts, the first of which (*Dreams and Symbols*, pp. 3-128) was written by May after Susan's psychotherapeutic treatment with Caligor had come to an end. To sum up, May seeks, in effect, to explore Susan's whole intentionality in therapy, with particular emphasis on what he sees as the meaning and scope as well as the healing and revelatory power of symbols in therapy; in this instance, the symbols in question are the most recurrent ones in the series of dreams Susan reported in therapy. Caligor asked May to analyze and comment on the dream series only, without initial reference to Caligor's notes or judgments. The second section of the book (*The Case of Susan,* pp. 131-300) consists of Caligor's full record of the case.

After considerable discussion of the series of dreams, each one separately as well as all taken together, and of the most basic, recurring symbols and their latent meanings (hair, mirror, triangle, and pregnancy-as-cancer, for example) and the ever-shifting pattern of complex interpersonal encounters in her dreams, May arrives at the conclusion that his initial impression of Susan's inability and yet fearful longing to sense her own being was borne out in the growing revelation of her self-world relationship. He sees this most clearly in the panic-stricken anxiety and arresting detail of those dreams that, even while she is consciously recalling them for the therapist, disturb and involve her the most, often to the extent of trying to "explain" them away (*Dreams and Symbols,* pp. 10-11, 125-128). May notes with great emphasis that whenever Susan tries to "rationalize" or "intellectualize" her dreams or has a simplistic dream about "everything coming out right," the genuine dream symbols that are really, fundamentally joining the issue return in a more involving, clearly more disturbing, and hence more basic way that promises the possibility of genuine self-understanding and eventual integration.

From the dream series, May deduces that Susan longs to know and be herself, to be feminine and mature, and yet fears that feminine maturity in her will be like that of her aggressive mother. She is doubly afraid of this tendency in herself since she envisages men as like her father making little real impact or impression except as demanding sexual satisfaction from women, but otherwise ineffectual, weak, and susceptible of manipulation, thus reinforcing her own aggressive tendencies. Susan is also worried about how she herself appears to others, and reveals in her "mirror" dreams, among others, that she knows neither what others really think of her, nor what she thinks of herself, and that she is trying to be like her mother and yet is also rejecting that effort. Hence, the pregnancy-as-cancer motif is understandable in that she is afraid of what she may become, what she is "inside," and even what sort of monstrous "infant" (or future Susan) she may be "carrying." Further, her mother has taught her to look on men as predators and on bodily functions as disgusting, and thus sexual intimacy, instead of promising peace, contentedness, joy, and togetherness in a union of two whole lives, is, for Susan, an ambivalent promise of "animal" pleasure, physical pain, and "mental" revulsion. Her constant preoccupation with "hair" reveals her fears about her real nature, about her desperate hope for renewal and happiness, about the changes wrought in her by her therapy, and her distrust of her own judgment and fear of influences. Later in therapy, she does briefly dream of pregnancy as a happy possibility, of a less frenetic relationship with a quiet, strong man, and of waiting rather than running away. She even begins to have some self-assertive dreams, wherein reality presents a quieter, more controlled, happier aspect, rather than merely appearing as quick opportunities for pleasure. Susan's eventual decision to end therapy is based on her better understanding of the continuing problems and anxieties in her life and on her resolve and greater success in trying to cope with life without the ever-present aid of her therapist. It is, at the very least, a step in the direction not merely of self-understanding and assertion but of responsible self-assertion and acceptance of her being.

In his discussion of the case, May has quite clearly reached beyond the stated aims and conscious intentions of the patient, beyond the obvious, retrospective meanings (or "explanations") of Susan's dreams to the latent intentionality or basic orientation (quest for direction and decisiveness, answers to problems that are all fundamentally offshoots of the basic problem) that gave rise to them. Susan's most basic problem is that of identity, says May (*Dreams and Symbols*, pp. 6-7, 124-125). As always, his concern is that the patient be enabled to experience his existence as real, as worthwhile, as individual, complex, interesting, although having inevitable anxiety, and that the patient be enabled to know, accept and cope with his being and his world. "We can often get a more accurate and meaningful picture of the significant changes in the patient's life from the symbols and myths he creates and then molds and recreates in his dream existence than we can from what he says" (*Dreams and Symbols,* p. 3).

Again, although May does not do so, one might well here recall the "I-am" experience referred to in Chapter One, Section Three, of this book, wherein a similarly troubled patient set herself to "stripping away" the nonessential (to her being) facts about her existence, such as being unwanted and illegitimate, and found that she could now see, with a great surge or sensing of her *own* being, that what she was might no longer be circumscribed and dominated by these facts. She realized that her being was *the* fact, that the bearing and direction of her life were, to the greatest extent, contingent on and supported by her own decision, her assertion, and her commitment and responsibility to herself and her world. "Susan's difficult bind is that, to establish an identity of her own, she must revolt against the very one who has given her her sense of significance to start with. And ersatz though this identity was, it was about all she had" (*Dreams and Symbols,* p. 125). Susan has not given any evidence of strong, clear-sighted self-appraisal and redirection as the woman of "I am," yet she is prepared courageously to strike out and try on her own to come to terms with existence, to broaden and deepen her personal and social base. Susan both longs for and dreads full, mature existence. She cannot yet fully sense her own being as a totally separated, centered, independent individual-in-participation, since she fears what she knows of individuality-in-participation, and fears what she may become.

Susan's dreams show her seeing herself mirrored, distorted, and manipulated by others who express their will about her. Yet while Susan herself has chosen to view herself as used and manipulated, it is noteworthy that she, like Preston, tries both consciously and in dreaming (in the dreams and in her conscious recall of and comments upon them) to manipulate everyone else to fulfill her wishes without her having to admit responsibility for those wishes nor consequently to put herself in the position of having to acknowledge what those wishes mean in terms of her sense of her own being.

With or without the aid of a trained psychotherapist-counselor, Susan needs to learn to know and accept herself honestly; to recognize her world and the tone of her relationship with the people closest to her; to be constructively decisive, however small the decision; and to love with honesty and commitment herself, her world, and the future possibilities of that self-world relationship. Her later development and growth toward joyous, integrated existence will clearly depend upon the new sensing of her being that balance of anxiety with possibility in love and clear-sighted, decisive responsibility will engender.

Summary

The purpose of this chapter has been to disclose, articulate and examine the development of May's mature view of will as fundamental, inalienable orientedness toward meaning, as primary orientation, as response and decision inseparable from the very structure of human existence. The practical, concrete concern of psychotherapy, in May's view, is the aiding of the patient to sense his own being-in-and-toward-the-world in a decisive self-appropriation, in intentional responsibility.

I examined briefly, at the level of popular experience and understanding, two salient, exaggerated, contemporary views on the controversial subjects of will, wish, decision, autonomy, freedom, and responsibility. I then noted how May envisages both forcible willpower and irresponsible, deterministic whim as inadequate and misleading, and how he conceives of human existence as free, as individual-in-participation and oriented toward peace and fulfillment in structured meaning and purpose.

I analyzed May's early view of freedom and structure in existence, and noted his definition of creative personality as free, individual, social, and possessing religious tension. May believes that freedom in moral living, of human vital expression or affirmation, needs guidance and control, and thus necessitates structure, then necessitates or necessarily points to the existence of an ultimate structure. Altogether, May's attempts to find such a structure posit an ultimate being or God as disclosed by consciousness of one's own liability to failure, imperfection, and error, or, as otherwise also expressed by May, by man's consciousness of his existential state of imperfection in contrast to his dim awareness of the possibility of doing better, of reaching out to an archetypal good consciousness or to an essential good nature or his "better self." Yet, the real solution to May's search for a structure of morality lay not in mythical or archetypal awareness, but in the self-world polarity that he had always said must be balanced and integrated.

Constantly underlying May's position of regarding authentic freedom as understandable and attainable only within acceptance of structure and control, there remained clearly observable his practical, concrete, therapeutic concern. This emerged in a continuing preoccupation with man's attempt to cope with guilt and anxiety; to attain some coherence, consistency, and fulfillment in his living; to accept responsibility for himself and his world even in the face of contemporary determinist, post-Freudian disillusion and despair and the resulting, dispiriting tendency to dismiss freedom as an illusion and human dignity as absurd. May was, even in his first book, already showing a considerable grasp and understanding, at the concrete and practical level in particular, of the fundamental orientedness toward meaning and purpose that characterizes human existence.

Thus, his patients' efforts to cope with existence, whether those efforts were distorted and confused by neurotic withdrawal or by frenetic overreaction to social demands and influences, remained for May a problem of meaning, a problem of freedom denied or frustrated, an unbalanced, overintensified, reductive or *un*-integrating, and hence ultimately *dis*-integrating, response to the challenge of existence. The earliest moments of May's understanding of will foreshadowed and prepared his mature view of will as the fundamental process of molding, forming, and reforming one's existence, as always "going toward something."

May's work at this point also shows a growing, more explicit conviction that man begins in decisive orientation, in primary commitment; that he senses and decides his being in terms of symbols, in terms of commitment to what he holds as worthwhile or important values; and that indeed man cannot *not* answer the challenge of existence, however confused or inarticulate that primary decisive response may be. Indeed, for May, man symbolizes or envisions and grasps his being-in-the-world in decisive manner, and greater maturity depends on greater clarity and reflective understanding of that envisioning. This view grew and developed from his early consideration of the overall aim of psychotherapy as helping the patient to grow toward integrated, constructive living. In other words, May's later view of the significance of will, effectively and practically speaking—although not always with the desired clarity of theoretical exposition—is that will is coextensive with being human, that the structure of human existence is fundamentally intentional, basically oriented toward meaningful and purposeful knowing and doing, not an "addition" of consciousness to characteristics shared with other organisms, but a fundamental changing of the whole Gestalt so that human existence cannot truly be understood or grasped in terms of "biological-plus-mental." Not only can the human being consciously (in the sense here of *reflectively*) make choices of intentions, purposes, and goals, but he cannot *not* at every moment question and decide, or respond to, his being-in-the-world, in a situation, however unreflective or imprecise that response may be. Very simply, for the human being, response to being-in-the-world is inalienable from a context of human meaning, whether he is at a given time responding fully attentively or on the level of nonreflective awareness.

Thus, says May, the "unconscious" life of the human being is also intentional. His wishes, needs, dreams, and drives; "spontaneous" aversions and likes; conscious material denied, ignored, repressed, or forgotten; potentialities sensed but not yet in the full light of attention or in some instances not yet fully acknowledged or assented to; tendencies of which the person may at a given moment be least aware—all such "unconscious" life is, as May sees it, intentional. In other words, it is oriented, having meaning and purpose and interrelated with the overall intentionality or orientation of the person's existence, interrelated also, then, with the sense of his being, as he is, as he might be and as he would like to be, or thinks he ought to be.

I have also considered the question of intentionality as emerging in therapy, and May's theory that, together, psychotherapist and patient, meeting in real encounter, must seek to elucidate the patient's intentionality or orientation. As was pointed out, nowhere does May indicate any awareness of using the term *intentionality* with several meanings; however, these implicit, but never stated or noted, senses of the term were carefully isolated and explicated, together with further examination of their overtones and imports, in the abstract as well as in relation to the case studies that were under discussion. The various senses of the term were, then, seen to offer, once the necessary clarity and definition had been supplied, the possibility of constructive, coherent, theoretical restatement of the significance in psychotherapy as May sees it of the concept of will as intentionality.

In the progressive elucidation of his intentionality or orientation in therapy, the patient moves through the stages of wish, will, and decision. This process is a complex unravelling of his orientation to himself, to his world, to existence as a whole, to psychotherapy, to the specific session of therapy and to the psychotherapist, in general and at specific times. This progressive elucidation was seen to mean, for May, an integrating or curing process of disclosure and exploration of the patient's predominant values, aims, and symbols, as these are evidenced, for example, in dreams with their overtones, powerful associations, and latent meanings, or in family relationships with their power to grasp, influence, disturb, and even repel. The psychotherapeutic process, as May sees it, is, then, a series of encounters wherein the patient learns to know, come to grips with, accept, understand, and then perhaps even reconstitute or reorient his whole existence.

This integrating process thus implies a view of intentionality in therapy not only as basic orientedness as characteristic of human existence; not solely as particular orientation or the predominant modes of the patient's existence; but cumulatively, both of these together with intentionality as integrating or "curing" intentionality. That is to say, although May does not explicate or give any evidence of being aware of this import in his rather brief theoretical exposition, intentionality in therapy ultimately must attain development of a positive thrust (or, develop explicitly a strong, "curing" intention) toward grasping and reconstituting the patient's self-world relationship, together with continuing concern for meaning, purpose, and fulfillment in existence.

From his earliest work, as has been shown, May has always seen human maturity as ordered freedom, as oriented becoming, as free, responsible individuation-in-social-integration. To grow in freedom toward mature or creative, integrated, responsive, and responsible existence is to be progressively aware of, and decisively to accept, the limitations and influences, the heredity and environment, the real possibilities, that are the materials of one's existence. It is in the decisive grasping of his own existence that the human being senses his identity, his whole being, and learns to know, create, and continually recreate himself and his world. For May, then, the "I," at its greatest point of achievement of integration, is the "I" of "I *can*." Potentially experienced as one's own possibilities, as one's own inner perspective on and response to existence and one's choice within the finite freedom of being-in-the-world as an already going concern—this, for May, is the deepest significance of will, primarily concerned as he is with the practical centrality and concrete, fundamental inalienability of individual choice and responsibility in the search for happiness and integration in human existence.

FIVE

Challenge of Integrated Existence

My primary commitment is to existence, not to a theory about existence, even an existential theory.

Adrian van Kaam,
The Art of Existential Counseling

As a therapist whose theoretical and methodological orientation is at once existential and phenomenological, Rollo May (1) does not accept a deterministic or behavioristic position; (2) refuses to reduce human relatedness to "fixed" need for release of tension and attainment of satisfaction, with socially permitted outlets replacing the primarily desired objects; and (3) cannot conceive of existence as truly human other than in terms of finite freedom and responsibility. However, May does not wish to reject established counseling techniques nor generally accepted psychotherapeutic terminology and aspectual understanding, but seeks rather to relocate their meaning and significance within the context of man understood as man, that is, of man understood existentially as an embodied conscious being-in-the-world.

The verb *to exist* (from the Latin words *exsistere, exstare,* "to stand out from") means more than merely being actual, more than merely sharing those characteristics without which man would not be man. As May sees it, then, it means to take up an attitude toward being, toward being in the world and of it, toward being influenced and molded by it, and yet not of it, fully centered and self-aware, molding and forming oneself and one's world by one's own creative response or decisive self-world relationship. May's emphasis as a therapist, then, falls not so much on trained, clinical observation (which role must yet remain of importance), but on "encounter," on grasping and being grasped by the being, the actual existence, of the patient. May's aim is a perceptive exploring-together with the patient of the patient's whole self-world relationship or "world-design," his sense of his own being and fundamental orientation. May's basic psychotherapeutic disposition, supported by an ontological understanding of man, is to seek to understand the patient as he is becoming, as he is projecting himself toward the future. This disposition is thus preferred to one drawing its inspiration from a deterministic conception of man, preferred to one that is oriented to removing obstacles to the patient's healthy self expression by means of a purgative exploration of his past. May, therefore, cannot accept the reductivistic location of the human self within the idiomatic and conceptual framework of deterministic psychic mechanisms with circumscribed or assigned meanings, such as the Oedipus complex or castration complex, for example. Clarification of the patient's past is, for May, only a part of the process of therapy, albeit an important part in reaching for understanding of the patient's world and his response to and role in it.

The fundamental contribution of existential psychotherapy, as May sees it, is its understanding of man as being, as existing, as "always going toward something." The "sense of being" is the unifying, grounding principle in May's own understanding of man as Dasein, as being-in-the-world, and in his view of psychotherapy as seeking to clarify and strengthen the patient's grasp of his own existence as an embodied-conscious-existent-in-the-world. To understand and elucidate the specific, distinguishing characteristics of the human being, and to grasp what it is to achieve courageous, decisive, integrated response to the challenge inherent in existence, have been shown to be a continuing preoccupation in May's writings.

In his earliest work, May explicitly *presupposed* human personality to be free, individual, social, and possessing religious tension. He later reconstituted that understanding with a more fundamental approach, now speaking of the ontological characteristics of human being as centeredness, self-affirmation or individuation, participation, awareness, and consciousness. Further, he spoke of world as world experienced in a threefold manner, as Umwelt, Mitwelt, and Eigenwelt, distinguishable but not separable from each other, inextricably interrelated and mutually influential. These characteristics of human existence May posited as a structural base for psychotherapy. Such a structural base, May is convinced, offers the following advantages: (1) it facilitates better understanding of the process of psychotherapy; (2) it offers greater possibility of genuine explication and clarification within encounter; (3) it renders possible a scientific study of the patient in therapy without doing violence to his humanity; and (4) it offers the possibility of a scientific study of the structures of human existence through empirico-phenomenological inquiry.

These advantages, supported by the desire "to study man scientifically and still see him whole," can, May believes, be attained (1) when in psychotherapy there is utmost faithfulness to the "lived" world as known by patient and therapist; (2) when the patient is envisioned primarily as a person (and not as an instance of a particular psychotherapeutic or psychoanalytic category); (3) when the *meaning* of the patient's existence is of primary concern in the elucidation of his orientation or intentionality, that is to say, when the focus of psychotherapeutic inquiry is to ascertain how the patient affirms himself and his world, what he constitutes as important to him, as desirable, as worthwhile; (4) when an experientially grounded inquiry is undertaken into the understanding and clarification of the specific, distinguishing characteristics of man.

This, says May, is *not* "to analyze being," but to analyze "ontology"; for even if you could analyze being, says May, it would be a "harmful" thing to do (*Danger,* pp. 156-157; *Contributions,* pp. 40-41; *Love and Will,* pp. 19-20). To understand the specific, distinguishing characteristics of man, to bring to psychotherapy an ontological approach to man is *not,* holds May, to approach the patient with a theory of human being to which he must be made to conform (for this would be to subordinate the person to techniques) but is rather *to assume his being* and to analyze the manner in which he realizes those "fundamental qualities which constitute him as a human being" (*Danger,* p. 157).

In this examination of May's philosophic reflections on the being of man, particularly as May encounters man in psychotherapy, there has been disclosed in May's work an understanding of the person as meaning oriented, embodied-conscious-existent, self-conscious, and therefore free, however limited and finite that freedom. It was seen, too, that, for May, time is less a chronological question and more a matter of duration as related intrinsically to the significance of events experienced. The human self knows that his time will end. Each of us, says May, is more or less conscious of death; we do not know *when* we shall die, but we do know *that* we will die, that we are at any given moment vulnerable; and the uncertainty of when renders vulnerability personal and ever-present, although perhaps not often in reflective attention. The tonality of this realization is anxiety or dread, the inalienable awareness of finitude as our own finitude, of limit, of imperfection, of error, of potentiality, of desire to make something of one's existence, and of longing to achieve something, to matter somehow to ourselves and to others.

The individual knows *that* he will die; he does not know *when* he will die. For May, the normal individual, the man characterized by fundamental acceptance of self and world and an average degree of courage in response to the demands of exis-

tence, accepts this common foreknowledge of death, albeit
generally without refining too clearly that it is, for him, question ultimately not merely of human existence as finite, but of
his *own* death. Thus, the normal individual acts on the assumption that he has a future, however brief it may prove to be. He
is constantly considering possibilities, projecting his changing
idea of himself, his loved ones, his work, and so on, into future
situations; he makes his plans in the reasonable hope that he
will have the time to carry them out and makes alternative plans
that will meet his responsibilities when his personal time runs
out. He is convinced that, given good health and opportunity,
he can realize his plans if they have been well made and sensible, and are not outside his scope or reach. When unforeseen
developments disturb or delay or even upset his projects, he
accepts this with more or less ultimate equanimity and resigna-
tion, after the initial annoyance or anger. Then he turns his
attention to revision of his situation, and the state of his plans,
and estimates how he may cope with the problems, or "get
around" the difficulty, or change entirely his project in order to
encompass the new situation. He does not ignore the problems,
but faces them, seeks to grasp and solve them; if they are
insoluble, he admits and accepts this, reexamines his projects
and develops new ones or new approaches to them. This examination has shown that this attitude is, in the concrete human
situation, what May means by constructive, courageous confrontation of anxiety. Such courageous confrontation of one's
own finitude, of one's individuality-in-participation, of the
limits and imperfections of one's existence, is only possible
within a structure of decisive acceptance of existence as being-
in-and-toward-the-world in a limited and contingent manner.

For May, the occasions of anxiety are numerous and ever-
present; reminders of imperfection and vulnerability are every-
where. Occasions are proximate expressions, social, individual,
and cultural, of anxiety as ontological; as such, occasions of
anxiety must be distinguished from the capacity to be anxious
that is born in man's ability to know and reflect on his own
being as limited and contingent but that is yet no mere aggrega-
tion of successive moments.

Faced with the same certainty of his own death, and with the uncertainty of when, the neurotic, May believes, is "fixated" by both. Reducing and constricting his range of freedom in order to cope with existence, he maintains a precarious balance. Discontinuity, suddenness, and unfamiliarity upset that precarious balance and loosen his grip on himself and his world, requiring an adjustment that he is not capable of making quickly nor even of making after an initial period of anger, shock, or hurt. In a world reduced by the predominance of anxiety and by the fear of contingency and vulnerability, he reduces further the normal range of interests in awareness in order to reduce the sense of threat that is his primordial response to the challenge of existence. He may become concerned, as did Ellen West in the case explored by Ludwig Binswanger (*Existence*, pp. 237-364), with keeping at bay the dread abyss of nothingness and oblivion by compulsive attention to detail, that is, by circumscribing the range of his concentration to matters of succession or of exactitude, as though to retain thus his grip on existence, his grasp of "world."

Although it may take many forms, neurotic anxiety is distinguished not only as disproportionately responsive to threat, but also as reductive, intensive, and constrictive of "world" and hence, correlatively, of "self." Neurotic anxiety is not merely anxiety about contingency, about potentiality, but is also anxiety *about anxiety*. The individual whose self-world relationship is predominantly characterized by anxiety is also anxious lest an occasion of anxiety should recur, lest new occasions should occur, lest the pain and apprehension return. Thus, his anxiety, in a sense, feeds on itself, in a gradual diminution of his ability to "stand back" from himself, to see himself in the world as an acting, experiencing subject, reflectively to disclose meaning and thoughtfully to choose purposes, goals, and values. This decreasing capacity, this reduced intensification of the range of one's interests and existence, all of which May sees as a diminishing ability to sense one's being, to experience one's identity, in relation to the world, is accompanied by gradual diminution of one's capacity (and willingness) to see and know oneself and one's world clearly and decisively. The neurotic's

time goes out of coordination with that of others, with chronological and social time, with historical time; things may even
become all-equally-crucial (as in compulsion to attend to detail)
or all-equally-unimportant (as in withdrawal). His sense of being
is blurred and his existence may become an ineffectual, frightened, floating awareness of being perilously adrift in confusion
and meaninglessness or of being engulfed by the multifaceted
attack of the fearsome.

    Although, for May, anxiety is inalienable and cannot be
permanently allayed, it is also the measure of one's awareness of
possibility, which, in an integrated response, is not characterized solely by increasingly implosive negativity. Indeed, the
greater potentiality for creative existence, the greater sensitivity
to existence as finite. Such sensitivity can, however—and must—
be reconstituted in the light of courageous, creative willing and
mature, enduring, thoughtful loving, if the challenge of existence is to be taken up and met in an integrated way. Implied in
such integrated response are also mature judgment and responsibility, that is to say, understanding of and decisive, ethical
response to the challenge inherent in self-consciousness, embodied being-in-and-toward-the-world and the sense of that
being.

    To be a self and to have a world are at once the challenge
of integrated existence, for authentic human existence is neither
automatic nor capricious, but rather an oriented becoming, an
integration of freedom and destiny. It is a continuous attempt
at reconciliation of what we are with what we sense we could
be, or would like to be, or should be. Neither participation nor
individuation is possible without "co-inherence" of structure,
order, purpose, and resolution. Hence, May's reflections on
human existence can be properly envisioned and appreciated
only in terms of his enduring commitment to the fundamentality of integration and structure, that is, in terms of his understanding of human sensitivity to, and concern and responsibility
for, oneself and one's world, which sensitivity and concern are
animated by human vitality or being-toward, and are constructively channeled by creative decision. For May, love that is
ephemeral is not love, but anxious dependence and hopeless

whim. He decries, too, "surface willing" or forcible adherence
to a blindly accepted set of conventions, or conformism in place
of mature decision and assent to a thoughtfully chosen order of
values together with the implications and obligations that those
values carry. Love, creative human vitality, cannot be allowed
to waste and dissipate itself, but must endure in order to grow
and deepen. Creative decision and commitment, born in a
strong sense of being, a responsible, self-assertive surging of
one's power to be fully oneself in the world, infuses, informs,
and guides the direction of one's loving, vital response to existence.

Enriched rather than threatened by mortality, deepened
and honed by his tragic consciousness to a greater awareness of
his time as duration, historically formed and yet susceptible of
change and growth, courageous man, as May envisages him,
reaches out in vital, decisive concern to mold and form himself
and his world, to give and receive in a strong, joyous response to
the deep perception of himself as alive. For May, it is precisely
in the explicit realization and intense awareness of the inalienable fact that "I am" that the human being takes hold of and
begins to direct his own existence. Thus, May's understanding
of anxiety, love, and will cannot be separated from his envisioning of them as integrally grounded in the sense of one's being.
Anxiety is double-edged, a trembling before the vulnerability of
human existence and yet a perceiving in that threatened existence the very potentialities for change, growth, union, development, fulfillment, and peace, toward which love or creative
vitality reaches out, while human will, understood as intentionality or orientedness (and orientation) toward meaning, decisively constitutes purposeful, structured expression and responsible existential realization of one's own unfolding in time.

In his theoretical reflections, May seeks to understand and
clarify the meaning of what he has found to be the fundamental
structures of human existence: the sense of one's being-in-the-
world; the six ontological characteristics, namely, centeredness,
individuation, participation, awareness, (self-)consciousness, and
anxiety; care; love as creative vitality or Eros; and will as intentionality (orientedness and orientation). In the light, too, of his

continuing concern for psychotherapeutic inquiry and practice, May seeks to elucidate how these structures can go awry in imbalance, can be distorted, frustrated, overemphasized, twisted, misunderstood, or defectively realized in a painful, disintegrative misinterpretation of what it is to be a person. May's reflections, he states, are oriented to contributing to a comprehensive understanding, a *working* science of man that may be brought to bear in the therapeutic hour.

Therapist and patient do not meet *directly* on the level of concern for the identification and naming of unequivocal, abstract psychotherapeutic or psychoanalytic categories, nor on the level of isolating clinically particular symptoms, even though, in many cases, as May and others of his colleagues have pointed out, the patient may be very well acquainted with the technical terminology of psychiatry and counseling. It is also possible in some instances that the naming of the patient's illness or symptoms may help to relieve his mind of fears of worse conditions. On the other hand, it may only serve to confirm his worst fears or to shatter him with guilt or shame. Primarily, nevertheless, therapist and patient meet in the dimension of encounter, of pretheoretical, intersubjective concern and compassionate support in the healing process of elucidating and reconstituting the patient's whole existence. This emphasis on encounter is not, however, a substitute for disciplined, thorough training or experienced, clear-sighted envisioning of the patient's actual condition, which, for May, are the necessary complement of existential care and understanding. Concern is neither exclusive of nor incompatible with clear vision and clinical observation of particular symptoms and mechanisms, but involves the recognition and acknowledgment of the whole patient as person suffering, in need of help in understanding his own existential predicament. As such, therapeutic concern should subsume and illumine the clear vision, the trained powers of clinical observation, and the objective overall view by which the psychotherapist hopes to be of real, lasting help to his patient in his attempt to reconstitute his existence in an integrated manner.

May's emphasis on encounter, on genuinely "meeting" the patient and exploring with him the meaning and purpose of his existence, serves rather to relocate the project of psychotherapy, to shift its scope from the narrower aim of "why" he has become as he is, to the broader reach of "what" it is that he is and is becoming, of how he senses his being and of how he constitutes his world. An exposure of past factors alone (such as family structure and environment) according to rigidly preset theories and relationships or fixed formulations generates merely mechanical explanations. A concentration on progressive aspects gives one an insight into the future hopes of the patient for himself and his world. The relocation of the whole project in terms of existential encounter, however, attempts to subsume both of these aspects, to explore with the patient his *whole* existence from *his* standpoint, his past and future, their meaning and relationship for him, their grip on his present, and what he is making of them, the predominant mode of his response to his world and to reach the point where his response, his knowing, and his doing are integrated and consistent with each other and with his sense of himself.

May's belief is that the psychotherapist must participate with the patient in guided clarification (guided clarification in the sense of squarely finding and facing the facts with the support of the psychotherapist) of his overall intentionality, the way in which he senses his being as a whole, and how he experiences, expresses or frustrates, denies or works out in his life both past factors and future orientation as he relates to them now. Thus, therapy is a living relationship between therapist and patient, not an automatic diagnosis and cure, but a shared process of concern for and gradual disclosure of the possibilities and difficulties of the patient's existence as an embodied, conscious being-in-the-world. This gradual disclosure involves, too, increasing awareness of and responsibility for the manner in which the patient is acknowledging or frustrating, accepting or rejecting those possibilities and difficulties. Encounter thus becomes the close bond of dependable, trustworthy, utterly confidential working together in concern for the patient's achievement of a stronger sense of his being and of greater ability courageously and thoughtfully to respond to the demands of human existence.

Toward a Working Science of Man

The purpose of this book has been a concentrated, comprehensive, detailed inquiry into the philosophical reflections of Rollo May on the theoretical foundations of psychotherapy. I have undertaken fundamental reconstruction and integration of May's seminal insights, which in his work remain, for the most part, scattered and without sustained, detailed explication or grounding, whether those insights be considered separately or as oriented to integrational understanding. The structure and development of this book were neither immediately suggested by nor easily discernible in May's writings, but had to be formulated on the basis of making explicit what was only implicit throughout May's work. I have sought at all times to respect May's implicit assent to a realist philosophy, his preoccupation with a *working* science of man, and the overall tenor of his work.

A close examination of the citations and references will reveal that systematic presentation, clarity of definition, and sustained development are not always the most outstanding features of May's work. It has more than once been necessary to remark how frequently he seems to hasten to descriptive examples or illustrations without always giving clear and consistent theoretical exposition of central conceptions—for example, centeredness and awareness (Chapter One, Section Four); intentionality, will as organizing capacity (Chapter Four, Section Three). Occasionally, too, these illustrations were found to be inappropriate—for example, the analogy of sympathetic resonance to encounter and agape (Chapter Three, Section Five); incomplete—for example, the description of Umwelt (Chapter One, Section Three); or inconsistent with an ontological understanding ("ontological" here in May's second sense of "characteristic of all *living* beings," Introduction and Chapter One, Section Four) and with the spirit of May's overall thinking—

such as, examples of centeredness, the tree growing a new branch that becomes a "new center," or the well-grown tree whose "balance and unity" were deemed to illustrate well the concept of centeredness (Chapter One, Section Four). Occasionally, references made by May to confirm his view were found to lapse into circular reasoning, as in the case of the Adam and Prometheus myths (Chapter Four, Section Three); or could not sustain the role of being "evidence" from "mythical consciousness" of fundamental, inevitable, psychological processes, as in the case of May's overemphasis on conflict in individuation and his supportive citing of the Oedipus and Orestes dramas (Chapter Four, Section Three), and in the case of social prohibitions of murder, rape, and incest as fundamental, universal, archetypal consciousness of ethical imperatives (Chapter Four, Section Two). Where terminological confusion or theoretical difficulty was detected, however, as in the case of the six ontological characteristics (Chapter One, Section Four) and in the case of May's unclear expression of his understanding and conception of intentionality (Chapter Four, Sections Three and Four), constructive elucidation and restatement were offered, always bearing the overall tenor of May's work in mind.

Some references made for the sake of illustration, however, were found to be extremely apt, as in the case of the references to the values essential to one's being, any threat to which gave rise to anxiety—such as, ability to support family, to fulfill chosen role of life (Chapter Two, Section Four); in the case of the interrelationship in loving of spontaneity and purpose—for example, the patient whose case, for May, illustrated the "union of Eros" (Chapter Three, Section Four); and finally, in the cases of the citing of patients' dreams or conversations in therapy—for example, the "I am" experience (Chapter One, Section Three), the cave symbol (Chapter Four, Section Three), Preston's references to himself as a "self-seal tire" and as a "stage-manager" (Chapter Four, Section Four).

Such references were not only found to be appropriate in illustrating the theoretical discussion in each case, but were also found to reveal May's keen eye for the significance of detail, of the least allusion, and to reveal his ability to single out and understand the import of such details in the whole intentionality or orientation of the patient (for example, the salient symbols in the case of Susan, Chapter Four, Section Four), from the double viewpoint of seeing the detail "from outside" as a trained observer-counselor, and also of entering into the meaning of it in the patient's whole existence. This ability to focus on and understand key moments in therapeutic exchanges and to grasp the place of the particular phenomenon in the overall orientation of the patient, substantially furthers May's whole enterprise of an integrated understanding and a *working* science of man.

In the final analysis, of course, May's concern is primarily concrete and psychotherapeutic and his theoretical deliberations derive from and are secondary to his basic aim of understanding better his patient for the purpose of reaching, guiding, and counseling him. Further, the noted deficiencies of theoretical exposition can be, and have been in this book, clarified and May's theoretical position constructively restated and elucidated without doing violence to his overall thinking and concrete psychotherapeutic concern. It would seem that May undertakes theoretical exploration primarily for the purpose of enrichment of perspective and deepening of concrete understanding of the challenge of existence, most particularly in the content of therapeutic encounter.

The need for psychotherapy arises out of the greater or lesser failure of some human beings to cope with the radical demands of being a coexistent individual. May's real, concrete concern, then, is not merely to throw light on the basic structures of human existence, but to do so in a manner that will also serve to illuminate and understand the ways in which those structures can go awry or be distorted, in a specific existence (when he discusses a particular patient's difficulties, Preston or Susan, for example) or in general (as when he points to common misunderstandings about human freedom or love—for example, freedom confused with license, or love confused with clinging dependence—and to the concrete results of such misunderstandings).

In North American psychotherapy, Rollo May stands out

as a leading representative of the existential attitude and is also to be recognized for the accessibility of his writings, particularly to the interested, educated, but nonspecialist reader who may be unfamiliar with or even wary of obviously technical monographs, articles, and books. While May's two introductory articles in *Existence* (both articles, as has been shown, of fundamental importance in his own development) evince a more involved, theoretical approach, his other books are couched in a simpler, more readable, congenial style and contain frequent references to current affairs and to art and literary work that, in May's view, exemplify, render more directly, or even serve to confirm the particular point that he seeks to make at a given time.

An author of undoubted appeal within as well as outside of professional psychological circles, Rollo May might well be said to offer some considerable help with the difficulty of comprehension that sometimes seems to hinder the contemporary mind (more oriented as it is to positive-scientific, unequivocal, neat formulation and statistical argument, and tending as it does to aver that each "problem" admits of "only one *right* answer") from grasping the import and relevance for oneself of the existential, humanist approach in psychology. It cannot be overstressed that the existential approach does not (nor could) seek to render superfluous or outdated all other approaches or methods in psychiatry, psychotherapy, and psychology, but rather seeks to subsume and illumine them by grounding the whole enterprise in a more faithful, true-to-life understanding of existence, by emphasizing the actual being of the patient, *his* situation, and the degree of his responsibility to and for himself and his world, and by keeping firmly in mind the complexity, multiformity, and individuality of human existence in coexistence. With such an integration of approach and of technique in mind, May has sought, from the outset of his writing career, to render his own approach understandable not only to himself and his colleagues, but also to his patients and his readers in general, and to disclose in a fundamentally pertinent manner the structural bases of his ontologico-empirical approach to human existence.

From his earliest work, May has evinced a notable and deep-rooted concern for what one might call the *reinstatement* in psychological science (that is, reinstatement or rehabilitation as a serious conception requiring proper elucidation and concern) of human freedom and responsibility. These he sees as inalienably arising out of the structure of human existence as embodied, conscious coexistence-in-situation, and he constantly emphasizes the relevance and importance of a clear conception of human freedom and responsibility in the everyday life not merely of his patients but of every person.

May's emphasis on intentionality as decisive, predominant orientation to existence and on love or Eros as vital, inalienable being-toward-others, is not only of fundamental importance in his elucidation of a working science of man, but would seem to have some crucial implications for contemporary psychotherapy and counseling generally, in such areas as marriage guidance, drug and alcohol addiction, unmarried motherhood, and abortion and birth control. Such emphasis on inalienable, free, responsible commitment and concern for self and world as characteristic of mature, integrated, creative existence, applied to drug addicts, alcoholics, neurotic patients, the unmarried pregnant woman, the syphilitic, the marital partners who claim that "*they* tried hard but *it* didn't work," would seek to face them with the dimension of their *personal* responsibility for what "had happened" to them. May's insistence on the polar relationship of self and world, which he sees as an ontological structure of human existence, cannot comprehend any notion of finding *total* excuse for one's situation by blaming society, parents, bad luck, or any of the myriad of efficient, mechanical, so-called causal explanations so often advanced.

Now, one can deduce from May's work that he will not disagree that circumstances play a very strong role; self and world are, for May, intimately correlated. In his discussion of the polar relationship of self and world, and of the modes of that world, he speaks of the person's range of freedom being extended gradually but steadily as he learns to know, accept, and assess, for what they are, the given situation, the determining influences, and the inevitable conflicts that challenge the person in his struggle toward maturity. Thus, while circumstances, for some people, may have seemed difficult even to the point of apparently overwhelming pressure, May still holds for the intentional structure of human existence as inalienable and fundamental, and that in every situation a degree, however slight, of human choice, decision, and commitment has been involved and the person remains in some measure responsible in and for the situation. May would ask, In what predominant manner does the person sense his own being-in-and-toward-the-world? What is his overall intentionality, his decisive orientation?

The whole series of decisions (for example, of assent in weakness, of negative withdrawal, of refusal to accommodate the other or refusal to acknowledge danger or impropriety), which underlies addiction, neurosis, and twisted personal relationships, carry for May an aura of personal responsibility denied, misunderstood, frustrated, or minimized. Such minimizing or denial is made possible by a primary orientation to self-preoccupation or to overconcern with social acceptance; in either case, an imbalance of the person's self-world relation and therefore a stunted sensing of his being, are at the basis of his actions. No matter how many "determining" or strongly influential factors, or how many given conditions of existence tend to circumscribe his options, the individual alone can know intimately his own being, he alone can choose the direction in which he intends to orient his actions, intentionally to build and form his own life. He can—and must, therefore—in direct proportion to his freedom and sensitivity, be held responsible for what he makes of himself and his world.

May has written a considerable amount about freedom exercised; about the structures of human existence; about man's capacity to be self-conscious; about the interrelationship between individual strength and the balanced sensing of one's being as being-in-and-toward-the-world, vitally and intentionally oriented to individuation and participation; and about mature integration as the increasingly reflective, decisive response to the challenge of existence. It is also noteworthy that he holds that with each exercise of freedom, the individual's range of freedom or his capacity for decisive, constructive response to existence, extends a little more. Correspondingly, May holds that denial of freedom in a similarly related way reduces and constricts the person's existence. Although he is an active psychotherapist, May says little else about the *limits* of responsibility, about the reduction through no fault of one's own or even quite unwittingly, of the dimension of responsibility for one's existence. For instance, the drug addict whose addiction is entirely caused by having been treated with a narcotic drug over a long period in hospital can hardly be held to be responsible for his addiction, without at least some degree of knowledge and acquiescence on his part. The same case cannot, however, be made for the person whose addiction is caused by having "tried drugs on just a few occasions to get me over some bad times"; clearly, there is here an element, however slight in some individual case or under whatever pressure, of personal knowledge, choice, and hence of responsibility.

A personal relationship under stress from outside influences or personal weakness of the partners, whether those weaknesses be psychological or physiological or both, remains an intersubjective relationship having its existence in the partners' mutual constitution of each other as related. Hence, to speak of an unhappy marital or other personal relationship in terms such as *"we* tried hard, *we* gave *it* our best efforts, but *it* didn't work" is to constitute that relationship as a thing apart, a *third* element, a defective part in a threesome. Such confused thinking, unnoticed and unexamined for the most part, has become normal and such "explanations" are then constituted, in a self-deceit that is all the more effective as it is more unwitting and increasingly current, as excuse for pleas of incompatibility or impossible situation.

This is not to say that the individual carries the *sole* weight of responsibility for all of his actions; rather, it is to face him squarely with the dimension or share or proportion of responsibility that is his to carry, before as well as during the difficulties that face him in his ordinary existence. This attitude strips away the softening cushion of generally accepted ideas and values and makes the person aware of himself, of his power to choose and his corresponding responsibility, of the intentional, decisive orientation of his whole existence, and of how his primordial response to existence has been decisive in his molding and forming of the "materials" of heredity and environment and in his choice of goals and values.

The degree of the person's responsibility, then, is directly related to the degree of his freedom and responsiveness to existence. The sense of humor, the genuine ability to see the funny side, to withdraw oneself momentarily from intense, serious, subjective involvement and to envisage self and world as comical, perhaps even as ridiculous, is a healthy ability to move from self-preoccupation and attain perhaps a more clear-sighted balance and perspective in one's self-world relationship. The neurotic's problem, whether of overconstricted, intense self-preoccupation or of anxious, chameleonlike conformism to social demands, is thus magnified, because it generally admits of few, if any, genuine moments of humor or relaxation that would help the person attain a less intense, less reduced view of self and world.

May speaks mainly of people whose problems, while admittedly genuine and not susceptible of simple solutions, are at base problems of meaning, of orientation, of lives twisted but not out of control. The people of whom May speaks are people who bring to him questions of meaning, questions about the goal and purpose of their existence and about the problems that they have encountered in their continuing efforts to understand what will for them constitute fulfillment, meaning, purpose, and happiness. In none of May's books will one find a comprehensive, phenomenological exploration of such severely neurotic or pathologically disordered states, nor analyses of such case histories as are explored in detail from the existential point of view by Ludwig Binswanger and Medard Boss, for example. Nor does May at any time deal with the very fundamental question of how the person is to know whether the possibilities of his existence are, in fact, real, spurious, or even hallucinatory. Nor does May deal with the related difficulty of deciding what is the real world as opposed to the world as hallucinatory, or of what in the person's world has been transformed by his intentional orientation, whether constructively or destructively, or of whether his view of the real world is a "true" one, a proper understanding or merely a misunderstanding, or even a deliberate transformation (or change) for the worse.

As must be inferred from even the most superficial reading of his work, May begins from a realist point of view—a presupposition that he never questions or examines—and since he holds that one answers that most fundamental question on the basis "of one's assumptions," he does not then raise or give any evidence of being aware of the problem of the real and the apparent. He does not question whether "the world we see" (the persons, the objects) is, in "fact," the "real" world. His attempt has been to attain or contribute to the attainment of a *working* science of man that will "study man. scientifically and still see him whole," and his method has fundamentally been that of elucidation of what he holds to be the basic structures of human existence as embodied, conscious being-in-and-toward-the-world (*Questions,* p. 199; *Existential Bases,* pp. 72, 83; *Origins,* p. 36). In his elucidation of his understanding of these structures is implied a realist metaphysic, but although in *Love and Will* he declares himself an "inbred realist," he never explicates this position fully, even in his discussion of the six ontological characteristics and of the modes of world.

However, with his conception of human existence as intentional, of the fundamentality and significance of will, and his example of the house in the mountains (Chapter Four, Section Three), May does introduce—whether unwittingly is not obvious—the allied question of the perspectivity of perception, and the multiformity and complexity of modes of human presence to the world.

In his attempt to understand the structures of human existence and to offer light and perhaps help in cases of difficulty with the unfolding and interrelationship of those structures, May begins from a simple, pretheoretical assent, based in common experience, to man as being-in-the-world, together with what May sees as basic, common-sensical recognition of the importance of free, creative coexistence in the world, of authenticity in the three modes of that world. Perhaps his par-

ticular mode of procedure and his unquestioned and fundamentally unexamined assent to a realist position are largely
caused by a fact that has been pointed out several times in the
course of this study: besides his undoubted gifts of understanding, May's most primary orientation is to the concrete; his commitment is not to the imposition of understanding in terms of
mechanisms or abstract, aspectual formulations, but has been
stated to be one of starting from experience, seen as "given
reality," to understand and grasp that reality, and then to find
the terms that best express that reality, as May says, and thence
to achieve a working science of man on which to base psychotherapy. That is to say, his most primary aim is to help his patients and, more widely, those people who seek in his books
help in understanding and coping with the demands of their
own existences. Further, the patients of whom May has spoken
in his work are not spoken of as *pathologically disturbed,* nor as
what is commonly considered insane, unbalanced, irrational, or
completely devoid of rational control of and responsibility for
their lives; perhaps this fact may account for the lack of explication and treatment of the problem, in therapy at least, of the
real and the apparent, for example, and, more broadly, may
account in part for the *unquestioned* presupposition of a realist
metaphysic.

May's aim, as has been said, is to contribute to the formulation of a working science of man; that is, he pursues his philo
sophical reflections in order to grasp, express, and communicate
his understanding of man "on the deepest levels of ontological
reality." His concrete purpose and concern are for the attainment of a true understanding of what man is in order to return
to psychotherapy with that true understanding. To this end he
has chosen those terms that for him best express that reality as
he understands it, and, insofar as he is studying the being of
man and the structures underlying his behavior, some of those
terms have necessarily been ontological ones, useful for comprehensive integration because of their universality, their applica-
bility to all men (van Kaam, 1969, pp. 224, 230-231).

Such borrowing of philosophical concepts does not of
itself constitute an inquiry on the absolute philosophical level,

however, any more than the use of mathematical concepts would of itself constitute a mathematical inquiry. May's reflections, while using an ontological terminology, constitute rather a *relatively* philosophical inquiry. Nonetheless, his approach is validly called *ontological*. A relevant and helpful distinction is made by Ludwig Binswanger between theoretical reflections on man conducted on the ontologico-phenomenological level and those conducted on the empirico-phenomenological level (Binswanger, 1967, pp. 192-193, 206). Now, even while employing an ontological terminology and concentrating on man in terms of ontological characteristics or the structures of his being, May's reflections are both firmly rooted in the experiential order and oriented to returning with greater understanding to that order. In terms, then, of the Binswanger formulation, May's work might well be characterized as empirico-phenomenological, although it employs an ontological terminology and examines the meaning and practical scope of that ontological terminology. His approach is more problem centered than method centered, it is oriented toward concrete understanding of man, in particular of each patient, rather than toward elucidating the ultimate ground of his ontological approach or to developing a precise psychotherapeutic methodology based therein. While his aim is a science of man, or a psychology relevant to the distinguishing characteristics of man, his reflections cannot be said to constitute purely and simply a scientific act, for he does not use philosophical concepts *purely* as working hypotheses, but appeals rather to facts that belong to common experience, elucidating and attempting to integrate his own understanding of these facts, which he considers ontological characteristics of human existence. He has stated himself to be, and has been seen to be, concerned precisely with elucidating his own philosophical presuppositions and, as has also been seen and examined, his enterprise radically broadened and deepened according as his natural, existential, implicitly ontological position grew into a reflectively, explicitly ontological one, with the varying meaning of the word *ontological* as it has been seen in his work. Therefore, while he shares and emphasizes in his own approach the concrete, pragmatic, humanistic concern and criterion of the scientific theorizing psychologist, that is, the consistent and meaningful integration of empirical data concerning *concrete* human behavior in *concrete* life situations (and this has been constantly borne in mind and emphasized throughout this study), May has been seen to be deeply concerned also with gaining insight into the *nature* of man in the light of what for May is a living fact, namely, man as individual being-in-the-world.

May's ultimate philosophical matrix, however, which arises out of his grasp of common experience or everyday life, is what he himself has termed "inbred realism," that is, assent to the world and to man as really present to each other, interrelated, interdependent, and mutually influential. This matrix, for May, is not a mere theoretical concept but a given *fact,* known and accepted in common experience or everyday human existence. The question, for May, is not whether this is so, but rather what is the character, structure, and predominant tonality of that relationship in general and in particular. His concrete and practical concern, as has been seen, is that of exploring the interrelated, essential structures in which this relationship expresses itself, and, given that individually this relationship is a challenge, of exploring what constitutes an integrated response or an unbalanced one in terms of those interrelated structures. May's work thus has an empirical basis, although it proceeds from a philosophical approach based on common experience or everyday human existence and popular understanding rather than on scientific data resulting from special experience, such as controlled experimentation and investigation. May tends to view such special experience, such as aspectual clinical data, as corroborating and supporting his realistic acceptance of man as being-in-the-world and, correspondingly, of world as present to and formed by man.

Philosophy, however, is a radical enterprise, encompassing ultimate questions and interpretations. Were May's reflections to be pursued on the absolutely philosophical, radically ontological level, he would have to examine and justify not only his philosophical borrowings but also his ultimate philosophical matrix of "inbred realism" and his presuppositions—freedom, centeredness, and intentionality, for example. Now, May appeals to facts that belong to common experience or everyday existence (such as consciousness of individuality), the deeper understanding of which is relevant to philosophy, because it is philosophy, rather than science, that is concerned with the understanding of the structures of existence itself. Further, May uses the facts or evidences of common experience as illuminating or integrating principles in the light of which derivative phenomena (such as anxiety and love) are to be understood and their meaning clarified. This is properly a philosophical activity, for philosophy explains not by deducing new facts from premises (as in geometry, for example) but rather by seeking to interpret common experience and to disengage and understand its fundamental underlying structures. It is, then, properly a philosophical activity to examine how a particular attribute is related to the essence or being of the reality under investigation.

Yet although he examines, defines, describes, illustrates, and gives the connotations for him of his own version of each ontological conception, May does not radically question them but simply assumes them on the basis that they are given in common experience, giving his assent to these as unquestionable *facts.* The basic image of man, the "inbred realistic" acceptance of man and world as mutually present, influential and interdependent that is May's ultimate philosophical base, is never questioned, explicated, or justified in the light of a metaphysical or *radically* ontological approach, namely in the perspective of being as such. May gives no evidence of being aware of a need to explicate or justify radically his own position, which emerges simply as a concern in particular with the *human* being, with what structures constitute man as man, and how those structures can go awry, necessitating psychotherapeutic encounter and care, and this despite his awareness of the "broad" meaning of *ontological* as "having to do with being as such."

May's asserted position of "inbred realism," then, remains unquestioned, unexplored, and unjustified. Correspondingly, his understanding of knowing remains simply an acceptance of "intentional presence," as commonly experienced, and without ontological justification of the presence of the other, whether object or person. There is in May's work no formally constituted, reflective theory of knowing, but only a concern for the limited question of the perspectivity of knowing and of individual bias, and these only within an uncritical assent to the being of objects experientially and existentially independent of perspectivity. Given his realistic, pretheoretical acceptance of self and world and his concrete, humanistic concern for human development, integration, and happiness, May assents not merely to the *being* of the other but also to his *importance,* emphasizing ability, possibilities, participation, and "communion of consciousness." Yet his ethics remain highly relative and undifferentiated, reducible simply to a question of individual choice of what should be of ultimate concern, bearing in mind, as May sees it, that if one professes to love the other, one should be as concerned for his being, value, and development as much as for one's own. The ultimate ethical criterion of any act, for May, however, and his criterion of truth, would appear to depend simply on an after-the-fact judgment of pragmatic success, which might be simply stated as "if it has worked, it was the right course of action," a criterion that, if socially applied, could emerge as statistical argument alone.

An *absolutely* philosophical examination of his presuppositions, or a *radically* ontological approach, would have necessitated for May the exploration of his ultimate philosophical matrix in the light of being. This exploration, if conducted May gives no evidence of being aware of the necessity for such an inquiry on his part, or the pursuit of absolute questions— would have confronted May with the choice of espousing either an explicitly idealist or an explicitly realist interpretation of being and of man's relation to or place in being as a whole. That is, May would have had to choose between an ontology grounded in a transcendental subject or an ontology of being *as* being. It has emerged, however, that May is prepared to accept the world as given, to subscribe to a polarity of individuation and participation and hence implicitly and simply to subscribe to an uncritical, common-experience, realist position that is never finally grounded. Ultimately, then, one remains uncertain whether, for May, it is man who creates or discloses meaning in the universe or whether perhaps it is the life process that works through man, who discovers a preexisting, meaningful world; and one is further uncertain whether May would allow that this question should be broached at all and whether the question of an ultimate ontology should be answered in an explicit manner. May's reflections, therefore, are conducted on the *relatively* rather than on the radically or absolutely philosophical level. Even while employing an ontological terminology and concentrating on man in terms of ontological characteristics or the basic, inalienable structures of his being, May's reflections have been disclosed as both firmly rooted in the experiential order and oriented to returning with greater understanding to that order. Further, his approach, as has been seen, is more problem centered than method centered; that is, oriented toward concrete understanding of man, in particular each patient, rather than toward elucidating the ultimate philosophical ground of his ontological approach or to developing a precise scientific, psychotherapeutic methodology based thereon.

There is, then, no reflective, formally constituted philosophical anthropology in May's work, no formulation of the relation or orientation of man to being. The sense of being, anxiety, love, and will, which emerged as the central conceptions in his work (the sense of being as the basic integrating principle), are really only modes of presence to the world. Not only is there no explicit grounding of these conceptions, but it has also emerged clearly that, for May, the sense of being is itself the *ground* and *goal* of the other central modes of presence. Although May's concern is with the awakening, deepening, and intensification of the sense of being (the "task of human being" is, for May, the heightening of awareness, the deepening of consciousness, and so on), there is, in May's work, no further *reflective* examination of the that-toward-which this intensified sense of being-in-the-world is to be oriented.

There is in May's work a constant dialectic between experience and theory, as he reflects on and confirms for himself what he intuits of the being of man. In the light of his pragmatic, problem-centered orientation, his criterion of truth has been seen to be simply to accept as true what would be most coherent with a realistic, synoptic view of experience, as it can be reasonably and meaningfully assented to by the individual. His findings, resulting from this realist, integrational view, such as the intentional character of man, human freedom, and responsibility, have been brought out clearly in their meaning and importance according as each central conception was examined.

The *limits* of May's thinking result precisely from the fact that he did not conduct his reflections on an absolutely or radically philosophical level; that is, the limits of his work result from the ambiguity of his unquestioned, unexamined, realist approach and lack of epistemological foundations. The next step in May's philosophical examination of his presuppositions should be to proceed to the absolute or radical level, in order thereby to elucidate his integrational science of man. Should May be prepared to pursue his reflections to the absolute level, his next step would clearly have to be to confront the question of deciding what his explicit, reflective, ultimate ground is (that is, man's ultimate relation to being, both at the absolute onto-logical level and at the philosophico-anthropological level). This decision and reflective explication should then be related to the explicit formulation of a reflective, formally constituted epis-temology and thereafter a precise scientific methodology for psychotherapy. Only then could his work be said to have at-tained a fully integrated science of man, or to have made such possible. These steps, however, have not been taken by May who has always stated that he "seeks to *contribute*" to the attainment or elucidation of a science of man, without, how-ever, explicating how he envisages the integration of his particu-lar contribution with that of other researchers, scientific or philosophic.

May's practical, concrete concern and psychotherapeutic context must also be borne in mind in any analysis of his work. This point was made with particular reference to his brief treat-ment of philia and agape; in the summary of Chapter Three, I observed that it was entirely possible, given May's concrete orientation toward reaching and helping people in need, that questions of philia and agape probably merited less attention in

May's eyes, because people who are capable of experiencing close friendships and self-transcending concern are more likely to be those with a strong sense of being and therefore less likely to be in need of or enter psychotherapy. While the line between "normal" and "neurotic" may be variable, even in a single person, the patients of whom May speaks bring to him not so much questions of their sanity or of the *reality* of the world or of their experience, but rather questions of their search for meaning, fulfillment, and help in fighting depression, anxiety, dullness, apathy, boredom, uncertainty, and raw, painful sensitivity. They seek guidance in their attempts to attain clear and decisive vision of self and world, of their meaning and purpose. Confused and dissatisfied, rather than totally disoriented as to what exists or does not, May's patients seek counsel as to what they are to do with their lives in order to cope with existence, to extricate themselves from the muddled morass of unhappy, inconstant lives.

The same point might also be recalled in any appreciation of May's recent book, *Power and Innocence,* wherein his whole approach is oriented to examining and exposing the distortion of the structures of existence, the distortion that underlies the contemporary phenomena of violence, power, hostility, and innocence misconstrued as ignorance or as simple noninvolvement in direct action. Such distortion has, of course, already been treated and more than adequately disclosed in May's study of ontological anxiety in the form of a cultural or group phenomenon, and of the violent results and hostility arising out of hidden anxiety and frustration and its relation to the restricted, intense, reduced sense of being (Chapter Two, Section Four).

A final question that arises out of May's attempted *rapprochement* (restoration of relationship) of existential philosophical understanding and psychotherapy is that of the right of the psychotherapist to "guide" the patient. Understood in the sense of the therapist prescribing courses of action or of "imposing" his own viewpoint on the patient, such guidance is rejected as repugnant, not only by May but by many of his colleagues. The psychotherapist, they hold, must be careful to maintain the balance between concerned, supporting encounter and trained, scientific observation and diagnosis, without all of which he cannot really effect any "meeting" with the patient during the therapeutic hour. The psychotherapist, then, does not seek to apply an automatic cure, for this would be to solely treat the patient as a "case" of something; nor does he seek simply to offer friendly understanding and a sympathetic ear, for this would prevent the genuine diagnosis and recognition of the symptoms for what they are. Thus, May will not have the supplying of the patient with a ready-made goal, nor does he articulate specific goals or values from which the patient may "select" a goal or value. Existential analysis, rather, for the existential therapist like May, is regarded not as a method, nor as *the* method of treatment, but a seeking *with* the patient to see the individual patient as individual, as a person for whom existence is difficult and who needs help to clarify for himself his own understanding of himself and his world and their interrelationship; the several ways that are open to him; and the implications of the various ways for his existence as a whole.

The final decision, however, as May sees it, rests with the patient, because the goal of psychotherapy is the steady development of the person's freedom, of his awareness of himself and his world, and of his ability to make self-responsible choices. Psychotherapy must not seek to make the human machine work smoothly again, to overhaul and tune up the human "motor," although some conditioning therapies advocate something very close to such dehumanizing of patients. For May, existential psychotherapy seeks to free the person to develop in his own way; to take his existence seriously as worthwhile, although limited in length and possibilities; to know and accept his being as a being-in-and-toward-the-world, to sense his possibilities and to judge and choose between them in a loving, willing, happy, responsible, strongly individual response to the challenge of integrating one's own existence.

APPENDIX ONE

Rollo May:
A Biographical Note

Note: Sources for this biographical note are (1) May's own writings and those books edited by him, see Bibliography, Part One, for full details of cited publications; (2) Harris, T. G., "The Devil and Rollo May," in *Psychology Today*, 1969, *3*, 13-16; (3) Lawrence, N., and O'Connor, D. (Eds.), *Readings in Existential Phenomenology* (Englewood Cliffs, N.J.: Prentice-Hall, 1967), "Biographical Notes," p. 410; (4) Ruitenbeek, H. M. (Ed.), *Psychoanalysis and Existential Philosophy* (New York: Dutton, 1962), pp. 179 n., 185-186; (5) Sahakian, W. S. (Ed.), *Psychotherapy and Counseling: Studies in Technique* (Chicago: Rand McNally, 1969), biographical note on May, pp. 249-250; (6) Spiegelberg, H., *Phenomenology in Psychology and Psychiatry: A Historical Introduction* (Evanston, Ill.: Northwestern University Press, 1972), pp. 158-164; (7) *Who's Who in America, with World Notables,* Vol. 36 (Chicago: Marquis, 1971), p. 1483; (8) Woodworth, R. S., and Sheahan, M. R., *Contemporary Schools of Psychology,* 3rd ed. (New York: Ronald Press, 1964), pp. 323-327.

Rollo Reese May was born to Earl Tittle and Matie Boughton in Ada, Ohio, on April 21, 1909, and grew up in Marine City, Michigan. In 1938 he married Florence De Frees; they have two daughters and a son. May now resides in Tiburon, California.

May holds an A.B. degree (1930) from Oberlin College, Ohio; a B.D. degree *cum laude* (1938) from Union Theological Seminary, New York; and a Ph.D. degree *summa cum laude* (1949), the first Ph.D. in clinical psychology awarded by Columbia University, New York.

Early in his life Rollo May became interested in art and artistic creativity, an interest that has never left him. Following his studies at Oberlin, he went to Europe where, with a group of artists, "he roamed the backwoods of Poland, to paint primitive people and study their indigenous, non-academic art" (Harris, 1969, p. 16; see also Spiegelberg, 1972, p. 159). He remained in Europe from 1930 to 1933, teaching at the American College at Salonika (Thessaloniki), Greece, and traveling widely throughout Greece, Poland, Rumania, and Turkey. During this time May also attended the summer school of Alfred Adler, with whom he "had the privilege of studying, associating, and discussing intimately" (*Art of Counseling,* p. 8; see also p. 233, n. 19). While greatly admiring Adler, May was later to express some reservations about Adler's "oversimplifications and generalities" (*Meaning of Anxiety,* p. 135; see also *Art of Counseling,* p. 198; *Nature of Creativity,* pp. 55-57). His European experience, however, awakened in May an awareness of the tragic side of human being and kept him, says Harris, "from ever accepting the mechanistic notion of man" (Harris, 1969, p. 16).

Having returned to America, May worked from 1934 to 1936 as a student adviser at Michigan State College, where he also edited a student magazine. Enrolling at Union Theological Seminary, New York, in order, as he declared in retrospect in 1969, "to ask questions, ultimate questions, about human beings—not to be a preacher" (Harris, 1969, p. 16), he was given his first access to existential thought, in particular to that of Kierkegaard and Heidegger, by Paul Tillich, a recent refugee from Germany, whose courses May attended regularly (Spiegelberg, 1972, p. 159). In fact, May did actively serve in a parish in Montclair, New Jersey. It is noteworthy that Tillich became May's lifelong friend, to whom May more than once expresses his appreciation of helpful discussions (*Art of Counseling,* p. 8; *Existence,* p. vii; *Love and Will,* p. 9). Indeed, May's terminology frequently recalls that of Tillich—for example, *centeredness, courage, intentionality, vitality, anxiety of meaninglessness,* and the four kinds of love. A notable exception is May's use of *daimonic* (*Love and Will*) with his emphasis on its being normally both creative and destructive, both integrative and disintegrative, while Tillich's use of the adjective *demonic* clearly and constantly associates it with the meanings of "destructive," "disintegrating," "evil," and "satanic" (*Love and Will,* p. 123; Tillich, 1967, Vol. 1, p. 134; Vol. 3, pp. 174-176). In May's books preceding *Love and Will,* the adjective "*demonic*" appears with the connotations of destructive and disintegrative only. In the second footnote to his article "On the Phenomenological Bases of Psychotherapy," May explicitly acknowledges indebtedness to Tillich for the "philosophical formulation" of his "ontological characteristics." In the same footnote, the reader is directed to treatment of the same points "in greater detail" in *Existential Psychology* (*Existential Bases,* pp. 74ff). Here, however, May states simply that in his work as a psychotherapist he has found characteristics or processes "which can as well be called *ontological characteristics*" (*Existential Bases,* p. 74) and he speaks of Tillich (p. 76) only in connection with self-affirmation and the cogency and fertility for psychotherapy of his emphasis on "the courage to be." In an earlier article, in 1959, proposing six ontological principles, May acknowledged without detail "their relation to the thought of Paul Tillich and Kurt Goldstein," quickly adding that "they are also imbedded in, and arise directly out of, my insights and experience in immediate psychotherapy as well as my own thinking" (*Toward the Ontological Basis,* p. 5). May's use of terms would appear to owe more to his own psychological and psychotherapeutic understanding than to Tillich. Indeed, May himself seems to regard his conception of these principles and other terms as decidedly his own, as when, for example, he speaks of "my prin-

ciple of centeredness" and "my redefinitions of unconsciousness" (*A Phenomenological Approach,* pp. 118, 126). May's
brief mentions of Tillich's work are usually only for the purpose
of illuminating, paralleling, or supporting a point he himself
wishes to make and which arises out of his psychotherapeutic
experience and his own reflective understanding.

It was also during this early part of his life that May came
to know another refugee scholar, Kurt Goldstein, who acquainted May with Goldstein's idea of self-actualization and
with his theory of anxiety as a catastrophic reaction of the
organism (Spiegelberg, 1972, p. 159). In his references to Goldstein's neurological work, in particular concerning manifestation
of anxiety in brain-injured patients and the relation of anxiety
to consciousness and self-actualization, May indicates clearly
that basically he regards such clinical studies and neurological-
biological data as supporting and corroborating psychological
and philosophical insights, and thereby confirming, broadening,
and integrating progress in the attainment of an overall understanding of man (*Meaning of Anxiety,* p. 48; *Man's Search,* p.
192; *Contributions,* pp. 50, 72-73; *Significance of Symbols,* p.
20).

In 1938, May took his B.D. degree and was married in the
same year. In 1939, he published *The Art of Counseling,* which
was based on lectures originally given during the summers of
1937 and 1938 to student workers at Methodist-Episcopal semi-
nars on Counseling and Personality Adjustment (*Art of Counseling,* p. 8). This book, introduced by Dr. Harry Bone, was originally subtitled *How to Give and Gain Mental Health;* the
subtitle was deleted without acknowledgment when the book
was reissued (with no other changes) in 1967 (see Bibliography,
Part One). He also served in a parish in Montclair, New Jersey,
where, he says, "the funeral services were the one point where
there was some reality" (Harris, 1969, p. 16). Judging by the
book *The Art of Counseling,* Spiegelberg (1972, p. 159) states
that May seemed as a counselor "[to have] adopted on the
whole the approach of liberal theology."

Only a year later, in 1940, May published *The Springs of
Creative Living: A Study of Human Nature and God,* a book

very similar to and repetitious of its predecessor in line, tone, content, terminology, and conclusions, except that it links more explicitly May's conception of personality health and his Judeo-Christian beliefs. In his brief survey of May's work, Spiegelberg makes no mention of this book. In personal correspondence with the present writer, May has indicated that he has refused to allow the reappearance of this book. It is not surprising, then, that it is rarely if ever mentioned in bibliographical material on May.

Both books, *The Art of Counseling* and *The Springs of Creative Living*, assert the relationship of personality development, problems, and adjustment to affirmation of "the ultimate meaning of life" or "an ultimate structure." True (healthy, sound) religion, as May sees it (in contrast with neurotic, unhealthy, unsound religion or dependence) is defined as "belief in purpose, and therefore meaning, in the total life-process. . . . Not . . . the religion of . . . any dogmatic sect, but religion as a basic attitude as man confronts his existence" (*Art of Counseling*, p. 217). This broad approach to creative or healthy personality development as inalienable from affirmation of meaning and purpose in life as a whole, and thereby necessitating and even "proving" the existence of an "ultimate structure of meaning," remains characteristic of May's work as a whole (*Love and Will*, pp. 300-302). In *The Springs of Creative Living*, however, May seems to assume a close link between such affirmation and the Judeo-Christian God (even proposing a conception of Christ as "therapist for humanity" and of religion as "the stream of meaning" (pp. 19-24; 134) without grounding this link and while repeating with less development many of the ideas from his first book. On the other hand, in *The Art of Counseling*, a "picture of personality," or view of human being as such, and an exploration of therapeutic attitudes and encounter are undertaken and explored. Thus, *The Art of Counseling* offers a more explicit and broader view of May's presuppositions in germ at the earliest stage, while foreshadowing the ontological approach that later emerged from obscure awareness to be stated in the reflectively conscious attitudes expressed from 1958 (*Existence*) onward.

Continuing to work as a counselor to male students (1943-1944) at the College of the City of New York (Sahakian, 1969, p. 249), May studied psychoanalysis at the William Alanson White Institute of Psychiatry, Psychoanalysis, and Psychology in New York (*Dangers,* pp. 185-186). Note that Harry Stack Sullivan was president from 1933 to 1943 of the William Alanson White Foundation, the Institute being the foundation's training school, espousing a cultural, interpersonal approach to psychoanalysis and therapy and numbering both Erich Fromm and Rollo May among its present associates (Woodworth and Sheahan, 1964, pp. 323-327; *Love and Will,* pp. 19, 84, 318). It would, then, seem clear that at least some Sullivanian conceptions, such as the therapist as a participant-observer, would have been influential in the formation of May's general orientation. Later on, in the 1960s, speaking of himself, May said, "I identify myself as a psychoanalyst of this approach (the W. A. White Institute)—which does not make me any the less existential in my presuppositions" (*Dangers,* pp. 185-186).

Having opened his private psychotherapeutic practice in 1946 and having become a member of the faculty of the W. A. White Institute in 1948 (*Who's Who,* 1971, p. 1483), May prepared his dissertation on anxiety for Columbia University's first Ph.D. in clinical psychology, which he obtained in 1949 (Harris, 1969, p. 16). This was published in 1950 as *The Meaning of Anxiety* (see *Love and Will,* p. 326, n. 14), and is a broadranging descriptive study with what Spiegelberg calls "a keen eye for the varieties of the experience" (Spiegelberg, 1972, pp. 159-160). Interestingly, Spiegelberg concludes that, for May, who had studied philosophers, biologists, psychologists, psychiatrists, and sociologists, Freud and Kierkegaard emerge as those with the deepest and finest insight into anxiety, and that in *The Meaning of Anxiety* May does not give any impression of identifying with the existentialist movement—conclusions that I have reached independently.

During this period of his life, May contracted tuberculosis and lived for some years at Saranac Sanitarium in upstate New York. As drugs to combat the disease had not yet been developed, he was, he says, constantly aware of the grim possibility of death or, should he survive, of lifelong invalidism. Having eventually recovered his health, however, he frequently attests in his writings to the great teacher that this experience of ultimate threat proved to be in his life (*Emergence*, pp. 2-3; *Existential Psychotherapy*, pp. 59-60; *Man's Search*, pp. 92-95). It was during this illness, also, he says, that he studied Freud and Kierkegaard on anxiety and first drew the conclusion that while Freud had brilliantly analyzed the effect on and reactions of the anxious person, Kierkegaard had known and seen what anxiety is, namely the threat of becoming nothing.

In 1952, May became a fellow of the William Alanson White Institute (*Who's Who*, 1971, p. 1483), and in 1953 published *Man's Search for Himself*, a further step in his personal effort to clarify the sources of guidance and strength in the long development of creative personality or mature self-realization. The book attests chiefly to May's belief that apathy is the greatest enemy and that man's self-realization reaches its highest peak in greater self-awareness and self-consciousness, together with a mature affirmation of significant other persons. Spiegelberg speaks of this book as containing and exploring "May's pre-existentialist attempt to meet the problem stated in the title" (Spiegelberg, 1972, p. 160).

From 1955 to 1960, May lectured at the New School for Social Research, New York (Sahakian, 1969, p. 249), and 1958 also brought the publication of *Existence* (subtitled *A New Dimension in Psychiatry and Psychology*—the word order is noteworthy here), which May coedited with Ernest Angel and Henri F. Ellenberger. This book has been widely received as an important event in the development of American phenomenological existentialism, offering as it did access to some considerable European thinkers. At the same time, it reveals May's own adoption and assimilation of some of the main insights and emphases of existential thought—in particular, being-in-the-world, sense of being, time, and the three modes of world. In fact, a reading of May's two contributions to *Existence*, viewed from the perspective of his earlier work, and a reading of the other articles presented in *Existence*, together suggest to me that May may perhaps owe these existential concepts themselves mainly to Binswanger (time and the three modes of world) and Marcel (sense of being, function, and ontological awareness). I have, in this book, sought to clarify in internal critique the more fundamental issue of the role and significance of such concepts in May's work as a whole, and their contribution in giving clearer expression to May's preexistentialist thinking.

In 1959, May became a supervisory and training analyst at the William Alanson White Institute, and also an adjunct professor of psychology at the Graduate School of Arts and Sciences, New York University (*Who's Who,* 1971, p. 1483).

In Cincinnati in 1959, together with Abraham Maslow, Gordon Allport, Carl Rogers, and other notable psychologists and psychotherapists, May participated in a special Symposium on Existential Psychology in conjunction with the annual convention of the American Psychological Association (*Existential Psychology,* pp. vii-viii). The symposium papers later appeared (1961) in book form as *Existential Psychology,* edited by May and containing two papers by him. In the first, he gives his view of the emerging movement of existential psychology; already expanded for its appearance in book form, this article was later revised and expanded once again by May for the second edition in 1969. In the second paper, May offers briefly his own view of psychotherapy's existential bases in the ontological processes or characteristics of the human being, as he envisages them illustrated in a condensed case description, that of Mrs. Hutchens. Interestingly, in his contribution to the symposium, Gordon Allport expresses some reservations about May's "conceptualiz[ation] in the familiar Freudian manner involving the theory of reaction formation, displacement, sublimation and projection" and he adds that, in his opinion, "Mrs. Hutchens' unconscious is filled with Freudian, not existential, furniture" (*Existential Psychology,* p. 97).

Some of the essays that May had published in journals and so forth from 1951 to 1965 (the material also appearing in his books; see Bibliography, Part One, Item 7, and Section D), were collected by May in book form in 1967 under the title of *Psychology and the Human Dilemma.* Initially, in his Foreword (p. iii), May introduces *Psychology and the Human Dilemma* as essays having a common theme, and clearly intends, as evidenced by his careful grouping of the essays, that they be taken as forming a book, and later refers to his thinking "throughout this book" (p. 220). Only four of the fourteen chapters actually antedate *Existence* (1958), being material on anxiety, freedom, and distinguishing characteristics of man, material that had previously appeared in *The Meaning of Anxiety* (1950) and *Man's Search for Himself* (1953), while the remaining ten chapters are listed by May himself mostly as having appeared between 1961 and 1965. As chapters collected in book form by the author himself as late as 1967, these essays, then, offer a fairly broad overview of May's continuing efforts to present his view of man, psychotherapy, and various existential insights.

The common theme of these essays, as May presented them in this book, is the "human dilemma," or dialectical oscillation between being subject and object or seeing oneself as subject in a world of objects, and so on, the goal of such awareness being "the deepening and widening of consciousness." In exploring this dilemma, polarity, or paradox, May's hope, as set down in his Foreword (*Psychology and the Human Dilemma*, p. iii), was to make some contribution to the attainment of a science of man or a true understanding of man's total experience in all its richness.

Also in 1967, May's six radio talks for the Canadian Broadcasting Corporation's program series *Ideas*, given during the autumn of 1966, were published by CBC Publications in book form under the title of *Existential Psychotherapy*. In their compressed style, these talks present a succinct statement of most of May's central ideas.

Meanwhile, May had also been a visiting professor at Harvard (1965) and Princeton (1967) (*Who's Who*, 1971, p. 1483) and had begun, in mimeographed form, the journal *Existential Inquiries*, which later became the *Review of Existential Psychology and Psychiatry*, edited by Adrian van Kaam (Spiegelberg, 1972, p. 165). Also in 1960, May had edited the book *Symbolism in Religion and Literature*, a collection of papers by Tillich, Kahler, Richards, Heisenberg, and others. May's introductory article on the significance of symbols discussed again the creative development of self-identity, this time from the point of view of the role of symbols and of decision in the direction of that development. And, applying the same conception in greater detail, with Leopold Caligor, a fellow psychoanalyst trained also in the early 1950s at the William Alanson White Institute, May coauthored *Dreams and Symbols* (subtitled *Man's Unconscious Language*). Of interest, perhaps, is the fact that Caligor's supervisory analyst while in training at the Institute was Harry Bone (*Dreams and Symbols,* p. 131 n.), who had written the introduction to May's *The Art of Counseling* (1939). May's part of the book *Dreams and Symbols* (pp. 3-128) was a study of a patient's dreams, with the basic object of ascertaining her overall intentionality and the dominant mode of her sense of being, while Caligor provided the record of the case for which Bone had been his supervisor.

With each publication, May's emphasis on creative human being as free, responsible, social becoming was emerging more and more clearly, and, in the publication of *Love and Will* in 1969, May's declaration of his belief in the vitality and intentionality of human being and in the psychotherapeutic importance of these concepts was the most emphatic of all. Once again, some of the terminology of *Love and Will* (for example, *courage, intentionality, vitality, responsibility,* and *Eros*) recalls that used by Paul Tillich, particularly in *The Courage to Be* and his three-volume *Systematic Theology,* and reminds one again of May's long acquaintance with Tillich. *Love and Will* also shows clearly May's awareness of and preoccupation with mortality and his appreciation of the tragic side of human existence, and is, according to the author himself, "the first comprehensive statement (he has) made out of (his) own heart" (Harris, 1969, p. 14).

In his critico-biographical note on May, in speaking of *Love and Will,* Dr. Spiegelberg says that it "is perhaps [May's] most original, outspoken and constructive [book] in therapeutic and cultural respects" but suggests that "seeming quotations based on secondary sources . . . may account for some of the misunderstandings" (Spiegelberg, 1972, p. 161). While calling May's Chapter Nine, on intentionality "climactic," Spiegelberg expresses some reservations about May's conception of intentionality ("far from clear and consistent throughout the book") and about his "puzzling distinction" between intention and intentionality (p. 161). On the basis of this and the earlier books, Spiegelberg concludes that "phenomenology is not May's primary interest" and that May's main concern "is a new existentialism of man capable of supporting a therapy that can strengthen the self" (p. 163), and offering support and guidance in facing modern life and its anxieties.

Since 1969, *Love and Will* has become a national best-seller in America, and has been chosen for the Ralph Waldo Emerson Award given by Phi Beta Kappa. May's ability to write in a congenial manner about contemporary society has been further attested to by the choice of both *Love and Will* and *Power and Innocence* by the American Book of the Month Club. The latter book is an insightful, descriptive exploration of the questions of individual power and strength, their constructive and destructive uses, and of man's capacity for harm and evil to his fellow man through hostility, apathy, and alienation. The term *daimonic* recurs, interestingly, but is not defined or clarified beyond its contextual occurrences, as though it is by now a wholly familiar concept. As in his earlier work, May's main concern in this book is for understanding through an ontological approach, the deeper level of inquiry whose object is the structure or characteristic underlying, in this case, violent action, hostility, or apathy (*Power and Innocence*, pp. 44-45). May has recently completed his personal memoir of Paul Tillich, published under the title *Paulus,* and has also collected some of his articles on creativity under the title of *The Courage to Create.* Both books attest once again to May's consistent faith in courageous self-affirmation, the power of the unconscious and the significance of existential striving in meeting the challenge of existence.

The work of a man of wide reading and of broad, interdisciplinary interests, May's writings abound with allusions to and illustrations from art and literature, both ancient and modern, and with references to psychological and psychoanalytic work. His preferences seem to be those artists and authors who

offer a direct insight into man's contemporary predicament and
into the psychological and cultural pressures of modern living.
He cites Sophocles, Aeschylus, Auden, Eliot, and Ibsen, for
example. He sees illustrations of the tragic, destructive side of
human existence in Picasso and sends the reader to study form
and space in the paintings of Cézanne. He shows that he is all
the while concerned that readers, in particular those involved in
psychological studies or therapy, should try to see deeply into
the meaning, richness, and breadth of human being, into what it
is that responsible human becoming is at its best and most
creative. Indeed, May says that when students who wish ultimately to become psychotherapists write to him for advice on
how to proceed, he advises them to study "literature and the
humanities" as there is, in his opinion, "time enough in the specialized graduate school to learn one's science and the special
forms of scientific method" (*Significance of Symbols,* p. 13 n.).

In 1961, in an article later reproduced in *Psychology and
the Human Dilemma,* May attempted to make clear the relation
of his views and orientation to existential psychology and
psychiatry (*Context,* p. 87); the importance of such a statement
for understanding May's work would seem to warrant quotation
in full:

> *I am trained in psychoanalysis in the neo-
> Freudian interpersonal school, but all my life I
> have been one who believes that the nature of man
> himself must be understood as a basis for our sci-
> ence and art of psychotherapy. The existential de-
> velopments in our culture, whether in literature,
> art, philosophy or science, have precisely as their*
> raison d'être *the seeking of this understanding of
> man. Therefore I valued these developments long
> before I heard about contemporary existential
> psychiatry in Europe. But I am not an existentialist
> in the cultist European sense. I think that we in
> America have to develop approaches that are indig-
> enous to our own experience, and that we must
> discover what we need in our own historical situa-*

tions—an attitude in itself which, in my judgment,
is the only "existential" one.

In addition to his private practice as a psychotherapist
and his considerable lecturing and supervisory duties, May's professional associations include membership on the Board of
Trustees of the American Foundation for Mental Health; co-
chairmanship of the Conference on Psychotherapy and Counseling; New York Academy of Sciences; fellowship in the American Psychological Association; emeritus fellowship and membership on the faculty of the William Alanson White Institute;
fellowship in Brantford College, Yale University; membership
on the Board of Directors of the Manhattan Society for Mental
Health; sometime presidency of the William Alanson White
Psychoanalytic Society; and fellowship in the National Council
of Religion in Higher Education (*Who's Who,* 1971, p. 1483;
Sahakian, 1969, pp. 249-250).

APPENDIX TWO

A Comprehensive Compilation of the Definitions and Connotations of Central Terms as Given in the Writings of Rollo May

Note: The reader is referred to the location of the cited definitions and connotations of May's terms by means of a list of initials and abbreviations of the titles of the main writings of Rollo May (see Bibliography note). This list in alphabetical order, is provided below. For example, the designation MA:100 signifies that the cited phrase or phrases preceding that designation can be found in *The Meaning of Anxiety* on page 100. Italics cited are May's.

It is the purpose of this appendix to convey most comprehensively the connotations for May of each term, especially where a connotation has undergone conceptual growth or change, for example, *daimonic.* Cross-references are also offered in order to highlight some close relationships of terms, such as *self-awareness, self-consciousness, self-relatedness,* and so on. This appendix is doubly useful as it is also, in effect, a comprehensive index of the central concepts in May's main writings. Such an index is needed as some of May's books are not indexed and others have indices that do not always offer references to the philosophical terms under close examination here.

The reader is referred to the Bibliography, Part One, with cross-references, for full publication details of the writings listed below, and is also reminded that in the Note opening the Bibliography it is pointed out that the best and most integrated access to May's thinking is through his books, and those edited by him, since all of the material has appeared in these, a few times over in some cases.

AC: *The Art of Counseling* (1939).

DS: *Dreams and Symbols* (1968).

ECBC: *Existential Psychotherapy* (1967).

E.Con.: "Contributions of Existential Psychotherapy," in *Existence* (1958).

E.Or.: "The Origins and Significance of the Existential Movement in Psychology," in *Existence* (1958).

EP.1: "The Emergence of Existential Psychology," in *Existential Psychology* (1961 and 1969, paging of 1969 edition).

EP.2: "Existential Bases of Psychotherapy," in *Existential Psychology* (1961 and 1969, paging of 1969 edition).

LW: *Love and Will* (1969).

MA: *The Meaning of Anxiety* (1950).

MS: *Man's Search for Himself* (1953).

PD: *Psychology and the Human Dilemma* (1967).

S: "The Significance of Symbols," in *Symbolism in Religion and Literature* (1960).

Agape: Not a sublimation of eros but a transcending of it in enduring tenderness, lasting concern for others (PD:119); esteem for the other, the concern for the other's welfare beyond any gain that one can get out of it; disinterested love; analogy . . . but not identity [with natural parental love and protection] (LW:319).

See *Eros, love, philia.*

Anxiety: The apprehension cued off by a threat to some value which the individual holds essential to his existence as a personality (MA:191), as a self (PD:72); some new possibility of being, threatened by nonbeing (E. Con.:50-52); the state of the human being in the struggle against that which would destroy his being (EP.2:81); losing the sense of one's self in relation to the objective world (PD:41); anxiety of death—prototypically the basic source of all anxiety (LW:301).

Apathy: Apathy and lack of feeling [experience of inner emptiness, powerlessness] are also defenses against anxiety (MS:22); the withdrawal of will and love, a statement that they "don't matter," a suspension of commitment (LW:33); the antidaimon is apathy (LW:123).

See *daimonic, self-assertion.*

Awareness: The more awareness one has—that is, the more he experiences himself as the acting, directing agent in what he is doing—the more alive he will be. . . . Like self-awareness itself, this experiencing of the quality of the present can be cultivated (MS:228); the subjective side of centeredness is awareness (EP.2:77; PD:124); awareness and consciousness should not be identified; I associate awareness . . . with vigilance (EP.2:77); *self-consciousness,* the distinctive form of awareness in human beings (PD:95); the human being's range of freedom increases with the range of awareness, that is, the range of possibilities in relating to the world (PD:95; LW:262-263); generalized awareness, a capacity we share with animals (DS:5, EP.2:77).

See *consciousness, self-awareness, self-consciousness, self-relatedness.*

Being: Not a static word, but a verb form, the participle of the verb "to be"; ontology, the science of being (*ontos,* from Greek "being") (E.Or.:12); ontology, literally the "science of being"; "why is there something and not nothing?", the question which puts one on the ontological level (LW:112).

When used as general noun, "being" means *potentia,* the source of potentiality; "being" is the potentiality by which the acorn becomes the oak or each of us becomes what he truly is; particular sense, *a* human being, means the person being something; *becoming,* more accurate meaning in this country (E. Con.:41).

Man, the being who can be conscious of, and therefore responsible for, his existence; this capacity to become aware of his own being distinguishes him from all other beings (E.Con.: 41); being in the human sense, not given once and for all; does not unfold automatically as the oak tree does from the acorn (E.Con.:41-42).

Being, the individual's unique pattern of potentialities (EP.1:19); "being" must be assumed in psychotherapy; to analyze it is parallel to repressing it; yet a far different thing from analyzing ontology (PD:156-157).

See *being-in-the-world, centeredness, essence, existence, identity, ontological characteristic, ontology, person, self.*

Being-in-the-World: Man as a being interrelated with his world; the two poles, self and world, are always dialectically related; each is understandable only in terms of the other (E.Con.:59).
See *Dasein, world.*

Care: Ontological; refers to a state of being; the source of both love and will; a state in which something does *matter*; the opposite of apathy; the *psychological* side of Eros; a particular type of intentionality (LW:289-293).

Centeredness: All human beings are potentially centered in themselves; not automatic, the human being's centeredness depends upon his courage to affirm it (EP.2:74; PD:94); if the organism goes out too far, it loses its centeredness, its identity (EP.2:76); neurosis, the method the individual uses to preserve his own center, his own existence (EP.2:75), to preserve his own being (PD:95), to preserve his own centeredness, his own existence (PD:117).

See *being, essence, freedom, identity, neurosis, self, self-affirmation.*

Concepts: The orientation by which perception occurs (PD:154; EP.1:21-22); the inner process of *conceiving* the object so that I may *perceive* it; I cannot *per*ceive something until I can *con*ceive it (LW:236).

Conscience: Something more than a residue of one's parents' teachings, more than an expression of social solidarity; it reaches far back into the mysterious sources of our being (AC: 60); guilt feeling is the much broader aspect of human experience of which conscience is one expression (AC:71); one's capacity to tap one's own deeper levels of insight, ethical sensitivity and awareness, in which tradition and immediate experience are not opposed to each other but interrelated; etymology, close to "consciousness" (MS:184).

The daimonic is not conscience, for conscience is largely a social product, related to the cultural mores and, in psychoanalytic terms, to the power of the superego (LW:124).

See *consciousness, daimonic, guilt.*

Consciousness: The uniquely human form of awareness (EP.2: 77; LW:267); consists of our ability to differentiate between subject and object, also involves simultaneously our ability to deny awareness, potentialities and desires (PD:96; DS:6); a process of oscillation between being subject and object (PD:9); refers to the central ontological characteristic that constitutes the self in its existence as a self, namely, the experience that I can be aware that I am the being who has a world (PD:96); etymologically, "knowing with"; strictly speaking, "self-consciousness" in the normal sense in which we are using the term here, is a redundancy; consciousness itself includes my awareness of my role in it (LW:266; ECBC:39).

See *awareness, self-awareness, self-consciousness, self-relatedness.*

Creativity: Readjustment of personality tensions is synonymous with creativity (AC:40); the more sensitive the inward balance of tensions, the greater the creativity (AC:41); infinite creativity of the life-process, unique creativity of own self (AC:192); Prometheus, the symbol of creativity, the bringing of new ways of life to mankind (MS:158); creativity of the spirit gives birth to the values that direct man's technical power; anxiety in creativity inescapable (ECBC:42).

Courageous living within the dilemma (capacity of man to view himself as subject and as object) is the source of human creativity (PD:20).

Eros, original creative force (LW:79); destroys as he creates (LW:100).

The daimonic, can be creative or destructive, is normally both (LW:123).

Creativity is the result of a struggle between vitality and form; it is the nature of creativity to need form for its creative power (LW:320).

The daimonic—that often nettlelike voice which is at the same time our creative power (LW:324).

See *daimonic, Eros, intentionality.*

Daimonic (Daemonic; Demonic): Vicious, demonic, unscrupulous (AC:87); demonic forces in instinctual drives, aggressiveness or the death instinct—which tends to attack and destroy (AC:199); destructive and demonic values (MS:153); demonic, cruel, vindictive (MS:158); man as pushed by demonic, tragic and destructive forces (EP.1:30); the tragic, demonic aspects of power (PD:205).

Tremendously demonic and destructive forces, partial structure, must rest upon hate and venom and demonry (AC: 198).

Daemonic, powerful, primitive, cruel, angry (ECBC:27-28); man cannot obliterate the daemonic aspects of his emotions, and he should not repress them, [but should] take them into consciousness, [constructively reconciling the antinomies or opposites in his psychological and spiritual experience] (ECBC:27).

[*Spelling:*] demonic, popularized form; daemonic, medieval-poetic form; daimonic, the derivative from ancient Greek word *daimon,* unambiguous in its including positive and negative, divine and diabolical (LW:123n).

Eros is a daimon; identification of Eros with the daimonic; the antidaimon is apathy (LW:122-123); the daimon is correlated with *eros* rather than libido or sex as such (LW:127).

The daimonic is any natural function which has the power to take over the whole person. Sex and eros, anger and rage, and the craving for power are examples; can be either creative or destructive and is normally both; all life, a flux between these two aspects of the daimonic; the urge in every being to affirm itself, assert itself, perpetuate and increase itself; not an entity, but refers to a fundamental archetypal function of human experience (LW:123); violence is the daimonic gone awry (LW:130).

The daimonic arises from the ground of being rather than the self as such; not conscience; shown particularly in creativity (LW:124).

Gives individual guidance in particular situations (LW:125); to be guided by your daimon requires a fundamental humility; your own convictions will always have an element of blindness and self-distortion (LW:157).

A blind push, needs to be directed and channeled (LW:127).

In its right proportion, the daimonic is the urge to reach out toward others, to increase life by way of sex, to create, to civilize (LW:146); part of eros and underlies both love and will (LW:164).

Not to recognize the daimonic itself turns out to be daimonic; it makes us accomplices on the side of the destructive possession (LW:131); "diabolic" (*dia-bollein*), "to tear apart," and antonym "symbolic" (*sym-bollein*), "to throw together," to unite; tremendous implications for an ontology of good and evil, both present in the daimonic (LW:138).

The integrated daimonic pushes the person toward some universal structure of meaning; daimon possession requires that the daimonic remain impersonal (LW:157); the Word, the *logos,* the meaningful structure of reality, gives man a power over the daimonic (LW:176).

We are always pushed by the "irrational," daimonic, dynamic forces of the "dark" side of life (LW:233).

See *conscience, creativity, Eros, intentionality, self-assertion, sex, sexuality.*

Daimonic, Stages of the: The daimonic begins as *im*personal. I am pushed by the clamor of gonads and temper. The second stage consists of a deepening and widening of consciousness by which I make my daimonic urges *personal*. I transform this sexual appetite into the motivation to make love to, and be loved by, the woman I desire and choose. . . . The third stage consists of the more sensitive understanding of bodies as body (to use a physical analogy) and of the meaning of love in human life (to use a psychological and ethical analogy). The daimonic then pushes us toward the logos. The more I come to terms with my daimonic tendencies, the more I will find myself conceiving and living by a universal structure of reality. This movement toward the logos is *trans*personal. Thus we move from an impersonal through a personal to a transpersonal dimension of consciousness (LW:177).

Dasein: The existence of this particular being sitting opposite the psychotherapist (E.Con.:37); the term the existential therapists use for the distinctive character of human existence; composed of *sein* (being) plus *da* (there). *Dasein* indicates that man is the being who *is there* and implies also that he *has* a "there" in the sense that he can know he is there and can take a stand with reference to that fact. The "there" is moreover not just any place, but the particular "there" that is mine, the particular point *in time* as well as space of my existence at this given moment (E.Con.:41).

See *being, being-in-the-world, person.*

Death: The one absolute fact about life; individualizes man; awareness of death sharpens our sense of being; capacity to face death, courageous awareness of the fact that *I* will die, is the means by which we gain freedom (ECBC:51-57).

Love is not only enriched by our sense of mortality but constituted by it (LW:102); death is the symbol of ultimate impotence and finiteness; sexual activity is the most ready way to silence the inner dread of death and, through the symbol of procreation, to triumph over it (LW:106).

See *anxiety.*

Decision: Orientation of commitment, the attitude of *Dasein,* the self-aware being taking his own existence seriously; decisive orientation, a necessary prerequisite for seeing truth (E.Con.: 87-88); precedes insight and knowledge (PD:134; S:16); creates out of wish and will a pattern for acting and living which is empowered and enriched by wishes, asserted by will, and is responsive to and responsible for the significant other-persons who are important to oneself in the realizing of long-term goals (LW:267; ECBC:40).

See *freedom, responsibility, will wish.*

Dream: A highly significant process, translogical and prelogical, protentive and intentional; reflects one's deepest concerns; is within the sphere of one's intentionality, though not one's conscious control; connected with man's distinctive capacity for transcendence, or the capacity to break through the immediate objective limits of existence and bring together into one dramatic union diverse dimensions of experience (DS:4; S:15-20; LW:235); the purpose of the dream is to enable the person to *experience,* rather than to *explain,* symbols and myths (DS:9).

See *myth, symbol, unconscious.*

Encounter: The grasping of the being of the other person occurs on a level different from that of knowledge of specific things about him (E.Con.:38); one expression of being (EP.1:16); in the therapeutic hour, a total relationship between two people involving four levels, of real persons, of friends, of esteem or agape, and of erotic attraction (EP.1:16-17; PD:122-123); to *experience* the phenomena, not merely to observe (EP.1:21).

Epistemology: How we know reality (LW:225); a way of knowing reality (LW:226).

See *intentionality, knowing.*

Eros: [In Freud] "eros" or love—which tends to unite living substances and builds up (AC:199); "eros"—the sexual drive toward the other, which is part of the individual's need to fulfill himself (MS:204); one level in therapy, frankly *erotic,* in the general sense of having a sexual tone (EP.1:17, 17n.).

A state of being (LW:73); the drive toward union with what we belong to—union with our own possibilities, union with significant other persons in our world in relation to whom we discover our own self-fulfillment; Eros seeks union with the other person in delight and passion, and the procreating of new dimensions of experience which broaden and deepen the being of both persons (LW:74-75).

Not a god in the sense of being above men, but the power that binds all things and all men together, the power *informing* all things (LW:78).

The power in us yearning for wholeness, the drive to give meaning and pattern to our variegation, form to our otherwise impoverishing formlessness, integration to counter our disintegrative trends; an eternal reaching-out, a stretching of the self, a continuously replenished urge; the binding element par excellence; the bridge between being and becoming; binds fact and value together; the original creative force . . . now transmuted into power which is both "inside" and "outside" the person; much in common with intentionality (LW:78-79).

Eros pushes toward self-fulfillment, but it is not at all the egocentric assertion of one's subjective whims and wishes on a passive world (LW:80); the daimon Eros (LW:102); Eros is a daimon; identification of Eros with the daimonic; the anti-daimon is apathy (LW:122-123).

Eros has to do not simply with love but with hate also, it has to do with an energizing, a shocking of our normal existence; our daimonic tendencies and our feelings of tenderness, two aspects of the same thing (LW:148-149).

The daimonic, which is part of eros and underlies both love and will, acts as a gadfly to our consciousness (LW:164).

See *daimonic, intentionality, self-assertion, sex, sexuality.*

Essence: Essence refers to the greenness of this stick of wood, let us say, and to its density, weight, and other characteristics which give it substance (E.Or.:13).

Existence requires essence; essence requires that it be

made real by our existential efforts; we live in a constant interaction between the two (EP.1:7).

See *centeredness, polarity*.

Ethics: An ethical act must be an action chosen and affirmed by
the person doing it, an honest act expressive of his inward motives and attitudes (MS:188); the essence of human ethics—
one's sensitive awareness of the unique relationship with the
other person, and the working-out, in some degree of freedom
and personal responsibility, of the creative relationship
(MS:162); not simple obedience nor conformity (MS:161-162).

Ethics begin with, have their psychological base in, this
capacity of the human being to transcend the self-oriented wish
and desire and to live in the dimensions of past and future, to
live in terms of the welfare of persons and groups upon which
his own fulfillment intimately depends (ECBC:40; LW:268);
the actions of a living, self-aware human being are never automatic, but involve some weighing of consequences, some potentiality for good and evil (PD:199).

A new morality not in appearance and forms, but of
authenticity in relationship. . . . The error . . . is the lack of content; every answer sells us short; it does not do justice to the
depth of the question but transforms it from a dynamic human
concern into a simplistic, lifeless, inert line of words. Hence,
there "probably aren't any answers." . . . The only way of resolving—in contrast to solving—the questions is to transform
them by means of deeper and wider dimensions of consciousness (LW:306-307).

See *being, Dasein, essence*; also *care, decision, responsibility*.

Existence: Becoming static is in this realm synonymous with
death (AC:29); to stand out, to emerge; it is always in the
process of becoming, always becoming in time, and is never to
be defined at static points (E.Con.:66).

See *being, essence*.

Existential Approach in Psychology: It seeks theory not in the
realm of abstraction but in the realm of the concrete, existing,

human being (E.Or.:10); not a movement back to the armchair of speculation but an endeavor to understand man's behavior and experience in terms of the presuppositions that underlie them—presuppositions that underlie our science and our image of man. It is the endeavor to understand man as experiencing (EP.1:9).

The existentialist emphasis in psychology does not . . . deny the validity of conditioning, the formulation of drives, the study of discrete mechanisms, and so on. It only holds that we can never explain or understand any *living* human being on that basis; rather, the "mechanism" has meaning in terms of the person (EP.1:14; E.Or.:13).

Existential Psychotherapy: The movement which, although standing on the scientific analysis owed chiefly to Freud, also brings back into the picture the understanding of man on the deeper and broader level—man as the being who is human; assumes the possibility of a science of man which does not fragmentize man and destroy his humanity at the same moment as it studies him; unites science and ontology (E.Or.:36); fundamental contribution, its understanding of man as *being* (E.Con.: 37).

Not a system of therapy but an attitude toward therapy; a concern with the understanding of the structure of the human being and his experience that must underlie all techniques (EP.1:15; PD:156).

Existentialism: The endeavor to understand man by cutting below the cleavage between subject and object which has bedeviled Western thought and science since shortly after the Renaissance (E.Or.:11); basically concerned with ontology; dynamic approach (E.Or.:12); not a comprehensive philosophy or way of life, but an endeavor to grasp reality (E.Or.:19); centers upon the existing person and emphasizes the human being as he is emerging, becoming (EP.1:11); existentialism is an *attitude,* an approach to human beings, rather than a special school or group. Like any philosophy, it has to do with the *presuppositions* underlying psychiatric and psychoanalytic technique (PD:156).

Freedom: Man's capacity to take a hand in his own development; the other side of consciousness of self (MS:138); freedom and will consist not in the abnegation of determinism but in our relationship to it (LW:269).

See *sense of being, responsibility.*

Goal of Therapy: To free the individual to develop according to his own unique form (AC:40); that the patient experience his existence as real, that he become aware of his existence fully, which includes becoming aware of his potentialities and becoming able to act on the basis of them (E.Con.:85); that the person discovers his being, his *Dasein* (E.Con.:87).

Guilt (Guilt Feeling): Actually a positive, constructive emotion; [guilt feeling] is a perception of the difference between what a thing is and what it ought to be; a normal element of it compatible with, and even necessary for, personality health (AC:70); when the person denies his potentialities, fails to fulfill them, his condition is guilt; an ontological characteristic of human existence (E.Con.:52).

See *anxiety, conscience, ethics, responsibility.*

Identity: It takes a strong self, a strong sense of personal identity, a strong sense of self, to relate to nature creatively (MS:64-65); experience of one's own identity, or becoming a person; consciousness of one's identity as a self; we experience ourselves as a thinking-intuiting-feeling and acting unity (MS:80; see MS:74); anxiety, threat of diminution or loss of personal identity, or self, in relation to one's world (PD:40-41); to be able to question is the beginning of one's experience of identity; function of questioning, distinguishes self from world (PD:215).

Centeredness, identity, self-affirmation (EP.2:74-76); identity, self, self-image (S:22; PD:120).

See *being centeredness, Dasein, individuation, self.*

Individuation: The person has only himself through which [sic] to live and face the world; his self is different from every other self; it is unique and healthiness of mind depends upon his accepting this uniqueness (AC:53); becoming a self (PD:68).

Individuation . . . since the original breaking-out is from the actual womb of the mother, every subsequent act is a re-enactment both of fighting against the mother who now represents one's own fear of moving ahead, and an expression of anger and hostility at her for having ejected one in the first place (S:39).

We all begin life not as individuals, but as "we," created by the union of male and female; individuality emerges *within* this original "we," and by virtue of this "we" (LW:316); no one of us would actualize himself at all if he did not, sooner or later, become an individual, did not assert his own identity against his mother and father; individual consciousness is essential for that (LW:317); as the "we" is original *organically,* the "I" is original in human *consciousness*; the original "we" is always a backdrop against which we conduct the pilgrimage (toward full consciousness) (LW:317); my body is an expression par excellence of the fact that I am an individual; my will is an embodied will (LW:240).

Intention: A psychological state; I can set myself voluntarily to do this or that; conscious purpose (LW:234); a turning of one's attention toward something (LW:236); encompassed in intentionality (LW:253).

See *intentionality, knowing.*

Intentionality: A dimension which cuts across and includes both conscious and unconscious, both cognition and conation (LW:222); the structure which gives meaning to experience (LW:223); the structure of meaning which makes it possible for us, subjects that we are, to see and understand the outside world, objective as it is (LW:225); gives meaningful contents to consciousness (LW:226).

Intentionality contains both our knowing and our forming reality and these are inseparable from each other (LW:230); a form of epistemology (LW:233); not solipsistic, intentionality is an assertive response of the person to the structure of his world (LW:233).

Intentionality in therapy, the patient's intentionality, his way of relating to (the therapist) as a whole (LW:258); psychoanalysis requires that we should not rest with intentions, or conscious rationalizations, but must push on to intentionality (LW:270).

The structure by which experience becomes meaningful (LW:302); intentionality, itself consisting of deepened awareness of one's self (LW:325).

See *decision, Eros, intention, knowing, will.*

Knowing: Knowing another human being, like loving him, involves a kind of union, a dialectical participation with the other (E.Con.:38); in therapy, as the patient gets more and more knowledge and insight about himself, he will make decisions; the second half of that truth, the patient cannot permit himself to get insight or knowledge until he is ready to decide, takes a decisive orientation to life, and has made the preliminary decisions along the way (E.Con.:87).

Intentionality begins as an epistemology, a way of knowing reality; it carries the meaning of reality as we know it; understanding itself is constitutive of its world; intentionality gives meaningful contents to consciousness (LW:226).

Meaning has no meaning apart from intention. Each act of consciousness *tends toward* something, is a turning of the person toward something, and has within it, no matter how latent, some push toward a direction for action (LW:230); cognition, or knowing, and conation, or willing, go together; if I do not *will* something, I could never *know* it; and if I do not *know* something, I would never have any content for my willing; intentionality contains both our knowing and our forming reality and these are inseparable from each other (LW:230); we are unable to give attention to something until we are able in some way to experience an "I can" with regard to it (LW:232).

See *epistemology, intentionality, meaning, truth.*

Logos: New Testament, universal structure; a term taken from Hellenistic philosophy meaning "the reasonable, meaningful structure of life"; more accurate translation than "the Word," this Logos, which we can term the mind of God, is in the world from the beginning, yet it comes in special form in the person of Christ, the Logos, the very mind of God speaking to man; the ultimate structure (AC:200-201).

Ontology, Greek *onto-* (being) and *logos* (science), the science or study of being (PD:92-93).

Logos, speaks not only in objective laws but subjectively, through the individual person (LW:157).

The "Word," the logos, the meaningful structure of reality, which is man's capacity to construct form, and underlies his capacity for language as well as for dialogue; the Word discloses the daimonic, forces it out into the open; the Word gives man a power over the daimonic (LW:176).

See *daimonic, intentionality, ontology, meaning.*

Love: A delight in the presence of the other person and an affirming of his value and development as much as one's own (MS:206).

Four kinds of love, sex, eros, philia and agape; every human experience of authentic love is a blending, in varying proportions, of these four (LW:37-38); the nature of love as separation and reunion (LW:113); the romantic and ethical basis for love is not available to us any longer; we must seek to start from the beginning, psychologically speaking, with feelings (LW: 304); the paradox of love is that it is the highest degree of awareness of the self as a person and the highest degree of absorption in the other (LW:311); love pushes us toward a new dimension of consciousness, a oneness (LW:316).

Love as desire becomes personal and involves will, self-conscious freedom, and choice (LW:310).

The fact that there are men and women—the polarity of loving—is ontologically necessary (LW:311).

See *agape, Eros, participation, philia, sex.*

Meaning: True religion, a fundamental affirmation of the meaning of life (AC:212); personality health requires belief in some purpose in the total life-process as well as in his own life; for one cannot live on an island of meaning surrounded by an ocean of meaninglessness; if the universe is crazy, the parts of it must be crazy too (AC:216).

Meaning has no meaning apart from intention; . . . in [a]

sense, man makes his own meaning; I do not say that he *only* makes his meaning, or that it is not dialectically related at every instant to reality; I say that if he is not engaged in making his meaning, he will never know reality (LW:230); intentionality, the structure by which experience becomes meaningful (LW: 302).

See *intentionality, knowing, myth, truth.*

Myth: More inclusive than symbol, myths develop and elaborate symbols into a story; same function psychologically, man's way of expressing the quintessence of his experience, his way of see- ing his life, his self-image and his relations to the world of his fellow men and of nature; myths carry the vital meaning of man's experience (S:34); we find our myths all about us in the unconscious assumptions of our culture; we use them as images, as guides to our way of life (ECBC:22).

See *symbol.*

Neurosis: Lack of adjustment of tensions within the individual (AC:28).

Distortion of the need for centeredness, is *precisely an adjustment to preserve centeredness,* to preserve one's being, a way of accepting nonbeing in order that some little being may be preserved (EP.2:75; PD:95, 117); from the ontological ap- proach, sickness (PD:95).

See *anxiety, centeredness, self-affirmation.*

Ontological Characteristics: The distinctive qualities and charac- teristics that constitute the human being as human; the char- acteristics that constitute the self as a self, without which this being would not be what he is: a human being (EP.2:75); con- stitute man as man (LW:290; EP.2:83; LW:20, 292; PD:96, 192).

Ontology: The word "ontology" comes from the Greek *onto-* (being) and *logos* (science) and is the science or study of being (E.Con.:37; PD:93; LW:112); being, to be understood, when used as a general noun, to mean *potentia,* the source of poten- tiality; "being" is the potentiality by which the acorn becomes the oak or each of us becomes what he truly is (E.Con.:41).

"Why is there something and not nothing?" This is the question which puts one on the ontological level; must ask the ontological question directly, examining the being of the thing at hand; ontology seeks to discover the basic structures of existence—the structures which are given to every one at every moment (LW:112).

The existence of maleness and femaleness, seen ontologically, is one expression of this fundamental polarity of all reality (LW:112; see PD:124).

Ontological, constitutes man as man (LW:290); care, ontological, refers to a state of being (LW:292).

See *being, ontological characteristics, polarity.*

Participation: The person, like all beings has the need and possibility of going out from his centeredness to participate in other beings; always involves risk (EP.2:76; PD:94-95); eros is our capacity to participate in a constant dialogue with our environment, the world of nature as well as persons (LW:87); one pole of the fundamental polarity of all reality (LW:112-113).

See *Eros, intentionality, social integration.*

Person: Not a collection of static substances nor a set of mechanisms and patterns but a human being emerging, becoming (ECBC:2); a trajectory moving toward a future; always existing, always emerging, always becoming something (ECBC:8); embodied, conscious (MC:91-93; LW:238-240).

See *being, essence, existence, self.*

Phenomenology: The first stage in the development of existential psychology (EP.1:9); the endeavor to take the phenomena as given; the disciplined effort to clear one's mind of other theories and systems, to experience, not merely observe, the phenomena in their full reality; requires openness and readiness to hear (EP.1:20-21); the finding and description of what the thing is as a phenomenon—the experience, as it is given to us, in its "givenness"; this is not to rule out causation and genetic development, but rather to say that the question of *why* one is what one is does not have meaning until we know *what* one is (PD:88).

We psychotherapists look to phenomenology to give us a road to an understanding of the fundamental nature of man (PD:115).

See *existential approach in psychology, existentialism.*

Philia: Eros cannot live without philia, brotherly love and friendship. The tension of continuous attraction and continuous passion would be unbearable if it lasted forever. Philia is the relaxation in the presence of the beloved which accepts the other's being as being; it is simply liking to be with the other, liking to rest with the other, liking the rhythm of the walk, the voice, the whole being of the other. This gives a width to eros; it gives it time to grow; time to sink its roots down deeper. Philia does not require that we do anything for the beloved except accept him, be with him, and enjoy him. It is friendship in the simplest, most direct terms (LW:317).

The importance of philia is [at least] very great in helping us to find ourselves in the chum period and begin the development of identity (LW:319).

See *agape, Eros, love, participation, sex, sexuality.*

Polarity: Self and world are correlates, each understandable only in terms of the other (E.Con.:59).

Polarity, capacity of man to view himself as subject and as object, both necessary; in the dialectical process between the two poles lies the development, and the deepening and widening, of human consciousness; the courageous living within this dilemma is the source of human creativity (PD:20).

Rhythm of separation and reunion; eternally repeated participation and separation into individual autonomy (LW:113); the polarity which is shown ontologically in the processes of nature is also shown in the human being; the continuous rhythm of each moment of existence in the natural universe is reflected in the pulsating blood stream of each human being; polarity of loving—the fact that there are men and women—ontologically necessary (LW:311).

Personality cannot be understood apart from its social setting. For this social setting—the community of other persons

—gives personality a world without which it would have no meaning (AC:61).

See *existence, ontology, participation, subject-object.*

Possibilities: As the person gains more consciousness of self, his freedom and range of choice proportionately increase (MS: 139).

Achieving of possibilities is a continual venturing into new areas, in individual development and in deepening relations with our fellows (PD:67); potentialities for knowledge and action (PD:97).

See *task of human being, values.*

Presence: The relationship of therapist and patient is a real one, the therapist being not merely a shadowy reflector but an alive human being who happens, at that hour, to be concerned not with his own problems but with understanding and experiencing as far as possible the being of the patient (E.Con.:80).

The significance of the personal relation between therapist and patient is . . . that it gives the patient a new personal world, characterized by stable concern, in which he becomes able to take a decisive orientation to his own existence (PD:135).

See *decision, encounter, existential approach in psychology.*

Psychotherapy: Through this immediate interaction in psychotherapy, we achieve a quality of information and understanding of human beings that we could not get in any other way (EP.1: 11).

The art and science of assisting people for whom the dilemmas of existence have become especially severe and difficult (PD:85); it is . . . [must be] dynamic; not merely *treatment* in the narrow sense, but an encounter with one's own existence in an immediate and quintessential form (PD:134).

It is essential that we clarify the *ontological* bases on which the dynamisms of psychoanalysis rest (PD:134).

Reveals both the immediate situation of the individual's "sickness" and the archetypal qualities and characteristics which constitute the human being as human (LW:20).

See *existential psychotherapy, goal of therapy, ontological characteristics, presence, transference.*

Religion: The belief in purpose, and therefore meaning, in the total life-process (AC:217); whatever the individual takes to be his ultimate concern; shown in one's total orientation to life; the assumption that life has meaning; psychologically religion is to be understood as a way of relating to one's existence (MS:180).

Not all religious traditions are equally constructive; may be destructive (as were the Nazis and the Inquisition); the problem always remains for theology, philosophy and ethics with the aid of the sciences and history of man to determine what beliefs are most constructive and most consistent with other truth about human life (MS:180; see PD:213).

See *ethics, values*; also *logos, meaning.*

Repression: A way of behaving; conflict grounded in patient's difficulty in accepting or rejecting his own potentialities (E.Con.:79; see EP.1:17; PD:97).

See *resistance, unconscious.*

Resistance: An outworking of the tendency to slip back into the anonymous mass, to renounce one's potentialities (E.Con.: 79); a broader, structural phenomenon [than in Freudian elucidation]; we are unable to give attention to something until we are able in some way to experience an "I can" with regard to it; [necessity] to block the world out at times (LW:232).

See *intentionality, repression, unconscious.*

Responsibility: Interrelated with freedom, essence of human ethics, sensitive awareness of self, of unique relationship with the other person (MS:162; AC:35); free acceptance of self as an autonomous being-in-the-world (MS:148); involves being responsive to, responding; decision and responsibility are the distinctive forms of consciousness in the human being who is moving toward self-realization, integration, maturity (LW:267; ECBC:40; see MS:235-236).

Our human responsibility is to find a plane of consciousness which will be adequate to (the new world) and will fill the

vast impersonal emptiness of our technology with human meaning (LW:308-309).

See *decision, ethics, participation, task of human being.*

Science: Has been preoccupied with those aspects of nature which
were susceptible to mathematical treatment; its methods: isolation, tabulation, measurement and experimentation (MA:100);
the essence of science is that reality is lawful and therefore understandable; in our day, often uncritically identified with methods
of isolating factors and of observing them from an allegedly detached base (E.Or.:8-9); Western science has largely been *essentialist* in character, emphasis on immutable principles, truth,
logical laws, and so forth; in psychology, the endeavors to see
human beings in terms of forces, drives, conditioned reflexes
. . . illustrate the approach via essences (EP.1:12).

Psychology, sociology, anthropology, etc., "cultural sciences" (PD:183; see PD:188).

Science of Man: Should yield an understanding of the reality
underlying all situations of human beings in crises (E.Or.:7); the
scientific challenge is to find a concept, a way of understanding,
which does not do violence to reality, even though it may be
less precise (E.Or.:47n.).

A structural base for psychotherapy (EP.2:83).

A working theory which will enable us to understand and
clarify the specific, distinguishing characteristics of man (PD:183;
EP.2:72-73); requires no less rigorous thought and wholehearted
discipline than the pursuit of experimental and natural science
at their best, but it will place the scientific enterprise in a
broader context; to study man scientifically and still see him
whole (PD:199).

Must have as its fulcrum the unique, distinguishing characteristic of man, namely, his capacity to relate to himself as
subject and object at once (PD:198).

See *ontology, psychotherapy, science.*

Self: The organizing function within the individual and the
function by means of which one human being can relate to
another (MS:79); consciousness of one's identity as a self; we
experience ourselves as a thinking-intuiting-feeling and acting

unity; the self, not merely the sum of "roles," but the capacity by which one *knows* he plays these roles; it is the center from which one sees and is aware of these "sides" of himself; experience of one's own identity or becoming a person (MS:80); personal identity, individual experiences himself as a self in terms of symbols (S:22); self, being, centeredness (PD:94-96); self, identity (LW:313).

See *centeredness, identity, self-awareness, self-consciousness, self-relatedness.*

Self-Affirmation: The need to preserve one's centeredness (PD:94; EP.2:75); the particular name we give this self-affirmation in human beings is "courage" (EP.2:75).

See *centeredness, individuation, self-assertion.*

Self-Assertion: Eros pushes toward self-fulfillment, but it is not at all the egocentric assertion of one's subjective whims (LW:80).

The daimonic is the urge in every being to affirm itself, assert itself, perpetuate and increase itself (LW:123).

There is required a self-assertion, a capacity to stand on one's own feet, an affirmation of one's self in order to have the power to put oneself into the relationship (LW:146).

No one of us would actualize himself at all if he did not assert his own identity against his father and mother (LW:317).

See *Eros, daimonic, intentionality, self-affirmation.*

Self-Awareness: Self-awareness, consciousness of self, awareness of self as an "I," experience of own identity (MS:73-74); makes possible self-directed individual development (PD:68); the conscious intellectual aspect of self-relatedness (PD:196).

The paradox of love [as personal] is that it is the highest degree of awareness of the self as a person and the highest degree of absorption in the other (LW:311).

Self-Consciousness: Knowledge felt inwardly (PD:96); refers to the fact that I am the being who has a world (LW:266; PD:96); strictly speaking, "self-consciousness," in the normal sense . . . is a redundancy; consciousness itself includes my awareness of my role in it (LW:266).

See *consciousness, self-awareness, self-relatedness.*

Self-Relatedness: Man's capacity to stand outside himself, to know he is the subject as well as the other of experience, to see himself as the entity who is acting in a world of objects (PD:75); not merely a subjective inner experience, but rather the basis on which we see the real world around us; a grasping of what something in the world means to me (ECBC:7).

See *consciousness, self-awareness, self-consciousness, symbol*; also *awareness*.

Sense of Being: An experience of Dasein, realized in the realm of self-awareness; not to be explained essentially in social categories (E.Or.:45); my sense of being is *not* my capacity to see the outside world, to size it up, to assess reality; it is rather my capacity to see myself as a being in the world, to know myself as the being who can do these things (E.Or.:46; see ECBC:4); rooted in one's own experience of existence (ECBC:4).

Sex, Sexuality: [Sex] can, in its daimonic form, hurl the individual into sloughs of despond, and, when allied with eros, it can lift him out of his despondency into orbits of ecstasy (LW:38); whereas sex is a rhythm of stimulus and response, eros is a state of being; a drive, a need, where eros is a desire (LW:73-74; LW:310).

The existence of maleness and femaleness, seen ontologically, is one expression of this fundamental polarity of all reality (LW:112; LW:311-312).

A final ontological fact . . . in sexuality . . . simple and elemental fact; sexuality, procreative, can make a new being, literally a baby, or the birth of some new aspect of one's self (LW:116; LW:314).

Sex is saved from self-destruction by eros; contributes to the deepening of consciousness; can and should provide a sound and meaningful avenue to the sense of personal identity; pushes us toward a new dimension of consciousness (LW:313-317).

The two necessary poles of human existence itself, participation in dual being and separation into individual autonomy, shown in their fullness in sexual intercourse (LW:113).

See *Eros, daimonic, love, polarity*.

Social Integration: Social setting gives personality a world without which it would have no meaning (AC:61).

Social interest and *co-operation* ... mark the healthy individual who realizes and cheerfully accepts his social responsibility; by expressing himself in socially constructive ways he is able to achieve and realize himself (AC:66).

See *being-in-the-world, participation, world.*

Subject-Object: Existential protest against rationalists and idealists who would see man only as a subject—that is, having reality only as a thinking being; also, against tendency to treat man as an object to be calculated and controlled (E.Or.:12); mind-body dichotomy, self-world polarity (E.Or.:57-59); Descartes' dichotomy between subject and object (E.Con.:58).

The human dilemma, capacity of man to view himself as òbject and as subject (PD:8; PD:20); seeing the patient as subject and as object (PD:8-9); consciousness, a process of oscillation between seeing ourselves as subject and as object; time, the experience of a distance between subject and object (PD:9); split between essence and existence (LW:284).

Subject-object polarity, nature "out there" an illusion, "subject" always part of the formula (PD:10); man as subject, open to objective world (PD:11); the split between body and mind, the separation between man and nature, the dichotomy (PD:188-189); the tendency to posit nature and animals as purely objective, "out there" (PD:189).

Intentionality is the bridge between (subject and object). It is the structure of meaning which makes it possible for us, subjects that we are, to see and understand the outside world, objective as it is. In intentionality, the dichotomy between subject and object is partially overcome (LW:225).

See *existentialism, intentionality, science, self-relatedness.*

Symbol: The language of the capacity for self-consciousness, the ability to question which arises out of and is made necessary by the distinction between subject and object; a bridging of the gap between inner meaning and outer existence (S:21-22;

PD:72-76); the quintessence of experience, a "boiling-down" of the most real relationships and satisfaction (PD:76); the *symbolic* is that which draws together; diabolic disintegrates, tears apart, both present in the daimonic (LW:138).

Presents a totality of meaning which "grasps" us, a meaning which contains a union of feeling, willing and thinking (DS:9).

See *daimonic, dream, intentionality, myth, unconscious.*

Task of Human Being: To move from his original situation as an unthinking and unfree part of the mass . . . through the experience of the birth of self-awareness . . . to ever-widening consciousness of himself, and thus ever-widening freedom and responsibility, to higher levels of differentiation in which he progressively integrates himself with others in freely chosen love and creative work; one's goal is to live each moment with freedom, honesty and responsibility . . . fulfilling so far as he can his own nature and his evolutionary task; the ultimate criteria are the honesty, integrity, courage and love of a given moment of relatedness (MS:234-235; see ECBC:62).

Development of decisive orientation, the attitude of Dasein, the self-aware being taking his own existence seriously (E.Con.:88).

Deepening and widening of consciousness (PD:20 and 220; LW:308-309).

To have tried to know our own potentialities honestly; and to some extent, at least, [to] have lived up to them; [to] have listened to the call of being and [to] have responded (ECBC:62).

The relating of love and will, a task; to the extent that it is gained, an achievement. It points toward maturity, integration, wholeness . . . touchstones and criteria of our response to life's possibilities (LW:286).

See *consciousness, ethics, responsibility, values.*

Time: Human time depends upon the significance of the event (MS:220); must learn to live in the present; the past has meaning as it lights up the present, and the future as it makes the present richer and more profound (MS:226-227); time, a continual opening-out (MS:231).

Temporality, future is dominant mode of time for human beings; personality can be understood only as we see it on a trajectory toward its future (E.Con.:68-69).

Time, the experience of a distance between subject and object, a creative void that must be taken account of and filled (PD:9).

We participate in the forming of the future by virtue of our capacity to conceive of and respond to new possibilities, and to bring them out of imagination and try them in actuality (LW:92).

See *being, consciousness, death.*

Transcendence: Capacity to stand "outside," to look at oneself and the situation, to assess and guide oneself by an infinite variety of possibilities (E.Con.:74); to go beyond the immediate, concrete situation (E.Con.:75).

Dreaming has some connection with man's distinctive capacity for transcendence, i.e., his capacity to break through the immediate objective limits of existence and bring together into one dramatic union diverse dimensions of experience (DS:4).

See *possibilities, self-assertion, self-consciousness, self-relatedness, sense of being.*

Transference: Not merely a displacement of feelings (E.Con.: 79), but must be seen in the new context of an event occurring in a real relationship between two people (E.Con.:83; EP.1: 16-17); the distortion of encounter (EP.1:16; PD:119).

See *encounter, neurosis, psychotherapy.*

Truth: To see truth, like other unique characteristics, depends on man's ability to be conscious of himself (MS:214); one experiences truth in moving ahead as a thinking-feeling-acting unity (MS:215); goes with ethical and emotional maturity (MS:216).

There is no such thing as truth or reality for a living human being except as he participates in it, is conscious of it, has some relationship to it (EP.1:14).

Not merely scientific facts alone (MS:211); crucial question in psychology is the chasm between what is abstractly true and what is existentially real for the given living person (E.Or.: 13).

Truth exists in the individual as well as in universal structures, for we ourselves participate in these structures (LW:156).

See *decision, ethics, logos, meaning, science, values.*

Unconscious: A dynamo more than a storehouse, for out of it come the drives and tendencies which consciousness merely directs (AC:58); a series of levels, one's own consciousness, childhood experience, deeper levels of the collective unconscious, and ultimately the source of [one's] mind which is in the very structure of the universe (AC:58-61).

The potentialities for awareness and experience which the individual is unable or unwilling at this time to actualize (DS:6; ECBC:46; PD:125).

Intentionality . . . includes spontáneous, bodily elements and other dimensions which are usually called "unconscious" (LW:234).

See *decision, intentionality, knowing, possibilities, repression, resistance, symbol.*

Values: Term, neutral (MA:230); value, goal, psychological center, core of integration (MS:151); depend very much on age we live in (MS:152); an interpretation in symbolic terms of experience; a "boiling-down" of the most real relationships and satisfactions; the quintessence of experience (PD:76).

Mature values are those which transcend the immediate situation in time and encompass past and future; mature values transcend also the immediate in-group and extend outward toward the good of the community, ideally and ultimately embracing humanity as a whole (PD:82).

Mores, customs; cultural, irrespective of conscious choice of individual value, a pushing forward toward some new form of behavior (PD:212).

[*Content:*] not from science, but from religion, philosophy and other disciplines in the humanities (PD:213).

New morality of authenticity, no content for these values

as yet (LW:306); every answer seems to somehow impoverish the problem; the only way of resolving—in contrast to solving— the questions is to transform them by means of deeper and wider dimensions of consciousness (LW:307).

The problems must be embraced in their full meaning; they must be built upon; and out of this will arise a new level of consciousness. This is as close as we shall ever get to a resolution; and it is all we need to get (LW:307-308).

See *ethics, intentionality, myth, symbol, transcendence.*

Will: Founded on care (LW:290), will is the capacity to organize one's self so that movement in a certain direction or toward a certain goal may take place (LW:218); the generic term for self-conscious intentions (LW:266).

See *intentionality.*

Wish: Founded on care (LW:290), wish is the imaginative playing with the possibility of some state or act occurring (LW:218); occurs on the level of awareness (LW:262).

See *intentionality, unconscious.*

World (Umwelt-Mitwelt-Eigenwelt): The structure of meaningful relationships in which a person exists and in the design of which he participates (E.Con.:59); three modes, three simultaneous aspects of world which characterize the existence of each one of us as being-in-the-world; *Umwelt,* world-around, biological world or environment; *Mitwelt,* with-world, the world of beings of one's own kind, the world of one's fellow men; *Eigenwelt,* one-world, the mode of relationship to one's self (E.Con.:61; ECBC:5).

We love and will the world as an immediate, spontaneous totality; I do not imply that the world does not exist *before* we love or will it; one can answer that question only on the basis of his assumptions and, being a mid-westerner with inbred realism, I would assume that it does exist; but it has no reality, no relation to me, as I have no effect upon it (LW:324).

See *being-in-the-world, polarity, subject-object.*

Reflections
and Commentary
by Rollo May

It is an honor for an author to have and to read such a thoughtful and insightful study of his works as this book. Clement Reeves has brought to bear a penetrating intelligence in treating my ideas, especially the more problematic ones. His criticisms have been generally fair and often point to problems that I need to resolve as best I can. His stated concern is to treat my work with "internal critique," a method by which the philosopher seeks to stand within the work rather than outside it and to explicate the author's work in its own terms—that is, to deal with what the author actually intended to say. This has meant (as a not too minor contribution to me) that Reeves has occasionally redefined my terms in ways more satisfactory not only to philosophers but, for the most part, also to me. It occurs to me that it is not by accident that this philosophical criticism comes from neighboring Canada, where, in contrast to our frenetic life in the United States, one can approximate to a greater extent Sophocles' advice "To see life steadily and to see it whole."

More specifically, reading a work like this one serves the valuable purpose of introducing one to his own past. I have sometimes hesitated to re-read my earliest writings for fear that they would seem hopelessly naive. When Reeves painstakingly traces my development and finds the origins, no matter how naive, in my first book written when I was twenty-seven, I then begin to see, as he points it out, a progressive development into my later concepts, such as will, love, freedom. This affirmation of one's history (especially since history is in disrepute in the United States today, having been supplanted by the worship of change), this reacquaintance with the person one used to be, is a highly replenishing experience.

In this chapter of reflections, I will select for comment and discussion some of the crucial points in Reeves' work, most of them having to do with criticisms of my thought. This, I fear, will give the impression that we disagree more than is actually the fact. Let me reiterate that I feel most of Reeves' points are just and valuable. In relation to the many aspects of this work that I do not mention, the reader may assume that I either agree with them or feel that more discussion would achieve no constructive result.

My appreciation of Reeves' study does not mean that some of the differences of opinion between us are not exceedingly important. The first major problem is to clarify, and to answer as far as possible, the questions: For whom am I writing? And, what am I trying to do in my writing? First, I do *not* write for my fellow psychologists and other colleagues. It always seemed to me a waste of time, and a denial of the wisdom our discipline of psychology should exemplify, to write only for the limited number of one's colleagues. I write for intelligent, open-minded, questioning, motivated lay people. I am, and have been during the major part of my life, a psychotherapist, working in face-to-face relationships with people who need psychological help and are often desperate in their search for it. It is at such times of need—and only, I believe, at such times—that the human being is willing to bare the deeper levels of his motivations and conflicts. To do therapy, therefore, is to be privy to these usually hidden aspects of human nature. My writings are an endeavor to interpret to a larger public—that public which is intelligently concerned with understanding themselves and the place and function of human beings in the world—what I have learned in my journeys into the depth-psychology of human beings. The simile for the therapist's work that always leaps to my mind is Dante's journey into the successive levels of hell in company with Virgil. One cannot brave the rigors of loneliness and desperation of such inward journeys without a companion; and this is the role Virgil plays in the metaphor. The meaning behind this metaphor radically affects the form my writing takes.

Reeves sees my purpose in my writing most of the time; *vide* his many cautions in this study to himself and others not to require my writings to do what they were never intended to do. He correctly writes that my "preferred method must be 'to confront first of all our real experience in psychotherapy, and then find the terms . . . that will most fully express and communicate this experience' " (p. 5). But occasionally, it seems to me, he forgets his own cautions. In referring to *The Symposium*, quoted from *Love and Will*, he remarks that I do not deal adequately with Plato's concept of love and then goes on, to some extent, to do so himself. No, I do not deal adequately with it; nothing could be further from my mind than the explication of *The Symposium* or Plato's view of love as such. I am concerned only with pointing out how persons in psychotherapy can, and sometimes do, integrate as far as it is possible what we call platonic love and Freud's view of love.

Yes, I am more "problem centered," as Reeves charges, than "method centered." I do not aim to write theory for its own sake. I have always asserted this point strongly in arguing that the way for the therapist to be authentically empirical is by trying to keep close to the actual problems of the patient or client. This is often in contrast to the traditional use (or misuse) of the Freudian method to make the patient fit the Procrustean bed of Freudian theory. I do conduct my philosophical inquiries, as Reeves also charges, on a "relative" rather than an "absolute" level. Until fairly recently I have been actively suspi-

cious of any therapist who attempts to use an "absolute" philosophical base for his therapy. This can lead quickly to dogmatism. Many of the errors of traditional psychoanalysis arose
from a lack of flexibility on the part of the therapist, and this
seems to stem at times from the tendency to hold to an absolute philosophical base.

My suspicion of philosophical abstraction has never
meant, however, any lack of interest in philosophy; nor has it at
all decreased my fascination with philosophy. I have often
-stated emphatically that a philosophical base is necessary, albeit
not an absolute, one. As his first sentence in Chapter One,
Reeves rightly quotes from my earliest book, "The effectiveness
of counseling with human beings depends upon our understanding of what those human beings really are" (p. 22). I am sometimes considered a philosopher in contrast to a psychotherapist;
I am honored by the appellation.

But the problem is whether one can be a therapist and at
the same time conduct an "absolutely philosophical inquiry." It
seems that Reeves would be happier if this could be done. But I
strongly doubt that it can be done. One of the reasons the phenomenological method, as portrayed by Husserl and Merleau-
Ponty, has been so important to me is that it is a way of both
being philosophically clear and simultaneously giving full attention, and freedom, to the patient to create and express his own
world. Karl Jaspers, we remember, changed his profession (I
believe rightly) from psychiatry to philosophy when he sought
to make a radical philosophical inquiry. For those of us who
still remain therapists but are cognizant of the necessity of clarifying our philosophical presuppositions, the Gordian knot can
be cut only on a basis that includes a strong respect for the
psychological freedom of the patient. If we genuinely believe in
the other person's own freedom of inquiry and freedom to draw
his own conclusions, then we can pursue with integrity our own
philosophical inquiries and, concurrently, permit our patient to
pursue his own. I believe this is essential for good therapy. The
patient may end up a Platonist, an Aristotelian, a Spinozist; the
particular philosophical type is not the important issue.

I have always believed, however, that the therapist has a

responsibility to clarify his own presuppositions and that this is a philosophical task. My sentence about the effectiveness of counseling depending on our understanding of what the human being is still rings true to me. I was always left cold by observing psychotherapists who uncritically take over the values and the logic of the culture in which they live in its emphasis on "adjustment," "happiness," and the like; I then resolved to do my best to emphasize the importance of the therapist clarifying his own values.

These considerations lead us to Reeves' statement, repeated a number of times in this study, that I assert a position of "inbred realism." He goes on to add at one place, "May's asserted position of inbred realism . . . remains unquestioned, unexplored, and unjustified" (p. 244). I believe this interpretation is an error of emphasis on Reeves' part. He makes too much of the phrase "inbred realism." It occurs in my writing only once to my knowledge, in the sentence on the next to the last page of *Love and Will* (1969) where I am talking about "willing" the world. To quote it,

> *I do not imply that this world does not exist* before *we love it or will it. One can answer that question only on the basis of his assumptions, and, being a mid-Westerner with inbred realism, I would assume that it does exist [p. 324].*

The reader will see that I use the phrase only as a kind of "toss off," so to speak, and it is there as a caution against too strong an assumption of its opposite, the philosophical position of complete idealism, that the world exists only in one's mind. With respect to Reeves insisting that my "inbred realism" remains "unquestioned, unexplored, and unjustified at the radical level," I answer: Yes, because I did not offer it as a philosophical position but as a characteristic of somebody who grew up in the middle West.

The question arises as to whether this "realism," quite apart from a philosophical position, is essential for authentic therapy. "Realism" has more meaning when we observe that the person in therapy regularly experiences the "dawn" of insight as something that makes sense, in contrast to a pattern of behavior that in the past has resulted in just the opposite from what the patient wanted and expected. The latter is experienced as "unrealistic" and the insight which dawns in the patient is experienced as at last "realistic." (This perspective apparently is also why I appear to Reeves to be a pragmatist—a kind of philosophy that I find myself using in therapy but about which I have great doubts on the level of theory.) Lawrence Kubie was referring to this point when he said that in therapy you must accept the patient's saying two times two equals five, no matter how firmly theoretically you believe it to be wrong, until you can see the meaning of this assertion for the patient. Whereas the "assertion of inbred realism" is too strong to suit me philosophically, it is true that in general I do adopt a realistic position in my therapy.

If I do not accept the position of "inbred realism," what then is my philosophical position? Reeves does well to ask this question. But he proposes that, if I were to undertake an absolute and radical philosophical analysis, I would have to be idealist or realist. I do not believe that that exhausts the possibilities. Also it seems to me to commit the Procrustean-bed error in philosophy.

There is also the position of the existentialists. These are the philosophers who seek to go below both idealism and realism and to posit their philosophy on the basis from which both idealism and realism spring. This is why one cannot say whether Heidegger—or Jaspers or Tillich or Sartre or Marcel—is more a realist or an idealist. There are features in the position of each of these existentialists that are idealistic: for example, the phenomenology on which the philosophy rests and is the preferred method of inquiry, and the presupposition of the dignity of human beings. At the same time there are features in each of the above philosophies that relate existentialism to realism; for example, the emphasis on the here and now, and the concern with the problems of daily life, such as death. In one of his books, Tillich calls his perspective "belief-ful realism."

The existential movement in philosophy has always been congenial to me, because there is in it a welcomed freedom from the abstractions of so much modern philosophical thinking. In the United States, sad to say, these abstractions have moved into the fields of logic and linguistics to such an extent that the philosophical results seem to have nothing to do with the immediate problems of our Western world, such as justice, or to do with people's confusion of love and hate; nor do they give any understanding to people about the meeting of anxiety, guilt, and death. The existentialists, on the other hand, saw that the choice between idealism and realism, as in traditional philosophy, occurred because the philosophical task was pegged at too superficial a level. As Jaspers has stated, they seek to go below the level of subject and object to find that level on which thought is based, and out of which both subject and object arise.

A statement by Nicholas Berdyaév has had a great deal of meaning for me, and I used it as the frontispiece for one of my books:

> *Man is the dominating idea of my life—man's image, his creative freedom and his creative predestination . . . But to treat of man is also to treat of God. And that, for me, is the essential point. . . . At the present time it is imperative to understand once more that the rediscovery of man will also be the rediscovery of God.*

The reader will note that most of the sentences in the above paragraphs are in the past or perfect tense. To shift to the present tense, I now state that I recently have been in a period of change in my philosophical position. I have become increasingly what I would call an essentialist. I can do this, I hope, without losing my devotion to existentialism. This essentialism has come out in recent years in my interest in *form* in art. From this it moves to the *form* in Pythagoras, and from that into *form* in mathematics. This concern with form is also basic to my great interest in symbols and myths. I have come more and more to the belief that the closest we will ever get to ultimate truth will be a reflection of truth in form. I was always fascinated by Plato, as an adolescent as well as a college student. I have always thought—if we take the old adage that everyone is born either a Platonist or an Aristotelian—that I was born emphatically a Platonist. This would make me *an idealist in philosophical position but a realist in psychological therapy.*

A problem similar to the one that arises in Reeves' statement that I must be a realist or an idealist also arises in his criticism of me for speaking of the *centering* of the human being. Reeves would prefer to use the word "center," the noun. He adds in his criticism of my use of "centering," "It would . . . be a case of a center endlessly centering *and* affirming itself" (p. 55).

But I ask, why not? This is actually what we see people doing in psychotherapy and the "cure" consists not of finding a regular center, but of the patient *continuously seeking a center in a process of centering.* I think Reeves' criticism rises again from his need to see the world of thinkers as either idealists or realists. As stated above, it may be possible to go beneath both of these points of view and to base one's thinking on the level from which both arise. If this existential position is accepted, then it would be possible to speak of man's nature as being the *process* of centering. I'm aware that Reeves believes my point of view is too fluid, "not solid" enough, too "dynamic." As Reeves holds at one point, "May is effectively overemphasizing the dynamic" (p. 63). Reeves argues, rightly, that we must retain our concern with the *nature* of man. But cannot it be the case that the nature of man is just this *process of becoming*? Man is that creature, if we can paraphrase Sartre, whose nature is continually to become. As Kierkegaard so well said, "The self is only that which it is in the process of becoming." I am definitely in the Heraclitean tradition. I find much meaning in Heraclitus' emphasis on process, as in his famous adage to the effect that you never can step into the same river twice. I can deeply empathize with the Heraclitan idea of *fire* as the basic element in creation because its nature is to be in constant change, constant mutation.

This brings us to the criticism Reeves makes of my ethical formulations—or rather, my lack of them. In his general discussion of my failure to take a stand on realism versus idealism issue, he remarks, "Yet his [May's] ethics remain highly relative and undifferentiated, reducible simply to a question of individual choice of what should be of ultimate concern" (p. 245).

My ethics have not been explicitly stated because I assumed that my books were, in various ways, always elucidations of ethics. Reeves may feel that the ethics should be stated more directly, and in this he may be right. But again, we must look at the task of the therapist and how the patient works out his own ethical beliefs. The therapist has to be particularly careful of asserting a special ethical stance. To the extent that his neurotic patterns enter into the relationship with the therapist— and they surely will—the patient will continuously try to get from the therapist, sub rosa, some ethical rules or creed. The tendency to take over the ethical system of the therapist arises from the patient's anxiety at his having to work out his own ethics. It is of the greatest importance that the therapist not succumb to the seductive and flattering temptation proposed by the patient. Only as the patient himself asserts some code or standard based on his own inner promptings, his own knowledge and conscience, will his ethical standard endure.

Reeves also states, "The ultimate ethical criterion of any act, for May, however, and his criterion of truth, would appear to depend simply on an after-the-fact judgment of pragmatic success, which might be simply stated as 'if it has worked, it was the right course of action' " (p. 245). Pragmatism arose in the United States out of the thinking of the philosopher-psychologist William James. As he formulated pragmatism, it was a way of transcending the split between idealism and realism and a way of avoiding the abstractions of academic philosophy. It is a respectable form of philosophy and ethics. I do not regard myself, however, as a pragmatist.

Reeves' challenge gives me an impetus to formulate my own ethics, or as much as I can at this moment. I believe in a teleological approach—that each person, by virtue of his being a person, has certain potentialities that he is required, by life it-self, to live out. The oak is in the acorn, to give a simple anal-ogy. Failure to live out these potentialities is neurosis; this is why some therapists think that every neurosis is at base an ethi-cal problem. Each of us is required by life (again at peril of neurosis) progressively to explore and to know the form within himself. In my ethics there is something of the ideal of ancient Greece, *areté*, meaning moral excellence. I have always assumed a sense of destiny in individual persons. Each has his or her par-ticular form, and the discovery of this form and the actualizing of it are the central challenges of anyone's life.

I am strongly opposed to the ethical conformism in our day and its various derivations (hence my surprise at being termed an ethical pragmatist by Reeves). This pragmatism, in my judgment, would skate on the edge of conformism and "ad-justment," neither of which I like in this sense. I am firmly indi-vidualistic in my ethical assumptions. The ethics of Nietzsche have always appealed to me, if one can assume that we can infuse these ethics with a sense of love as a part of our participa-tion in being. What seems most important to me is described in this study by Reeves himself: "if one professes to love the other, one should be as concerned for his being, value, and de-velopment as much as for one's own" (p. 245).

I need now to clarify the concept of the "daimonic." My original reason for developing this concept was to enable readers to relate to the presence of evil. I also wanted to show the rela-tionship between evil and creativity. I believed that the com-mon personalized term which has been used historically, namely the *devil*, is unsatisfactory because it projects the power outside the self and opens the way for all kinds of psychological projec-tion. Furthermore, it always seemed to me a deteriorated and escapist form of what needs to be understood about evil. Espe-cially in the American mood is there a lack of capacity and a lack of vocabulary to relate to evil. This goes along with the lack of the tragic mood in this country.

We confront this paradox: Evil is surely very prominent in our day and is at the same time generally ignored by American humanistic systems. Carl Rogers has no place for it. Abraham Maslow has no clear statement of the relation to evil, although I am told that at the end of his life he was studying evil intensively. In some few psychologies in the present day it has become a subject of real concern: the book *Sanctions for Evil,* * is one example. Stanley Milgram's experiments and his book entitled *Obedience to Authority*† is another; Philip Zimbardo's "prison experiment also illuminates human destructiveness. These outcroppings show the need for some concept that will deal adequately with evil.

I use the term *the daimonic* as a noun to include these many aspects of evil. It refers to any capacity which has the power to push the individual into disintegrative behavior, such as sex, rage, power needs, and so on. When the daimonic is used integratively, it produces creativity. But whether it is used disintegratively or creatively, the daimonic (1) is powerful, (2) is dynamic, (3) changes the status of the person and what he creates, (4) involves some choice on the part of the individual. Evil is certainly not exclusively within the self—it is also the result of our social interrelationships—but the participation of the self in evil cannot be overlooked.

In the daimonic I wish to retain a decisive element, that is, the choice the self asserts to work for or against the integration of the self. I also want to state the problem of evil in such a way that psychologists will not be able to derogate it simply as a *lack* of something, for example, a lack of growth or as simply immaturity; or as a process which depends always on something else, such as the doctrine of the shadow in Jungianism. The perennial presence of evil is the aspect of consciousness that makes it destroy itself. In the case of Mrs. Hutchins, cited in the chapter I wrote for *Existential Psychology* (1961), I have described this patient's experience as follows (p. 81): after finding a baby that she had been hunting for at some length, she was

*Nevitt Sanford, Craig Comstock, and associates, *Sanctions for Evil: Sources of Social Destructiveness* (San Francisco: Jossey-Bass, 1971).
†Stanley Milgram, *Obedience to Authority* (New York: Harper & Row, 1974).

greatly relieved. But then immediately she had the impulse, "Shall I kill it?" This reaction seems perverse, and indeed it is; but I believe it is also an inseparable part of human consciousness. Evil has one of its sources in the fact of consciousness. *The daimonic* is used as a term that requires us to confront in consciousness our own evil.

Ever since Roman times, the relation of the concept of the daimonic to the word *genius* is very significant. Gregory Bateson has told me that in Bali the dragons are not killed at the end of the drama, but, like the erinys in Orestes, they live to have some good influence on the society.

The daimonic process is characteristic of all human activity. Eros is a particular way of relating to other human beings as well as other aspects of life; the daimonic certainly overlaps with eros, that is, some of eros is the daimonic. But I do not believe that all eros is. I hope these remarks clarify to some extent the concept of the daimonic.

In reference to Reeves' criticism of my double use of the word *intentionality*, I also would like to make a few comments. Reeves holds that I first use the term *intentionality* as a description of the general relationship between the subjective world of living human beings and the objective world, and then I use the term to apply to the particular way each person relates to his world. In the examples of therapy, I spoke of "the patient's intentionality."

This criticism is certainly justified. It was an error on my part to apply intentionality to the particular way each person reacts to his own life. One cannot say "*my* intentionality." Strictly speaking, as I look back on writing the chapter on intentionality in *Love and Will*, I realize that I was aware of the distinction then but I got carried away by the attractiveness of the term, and I overused it. I was also trying to put the matter as persuasively and clearly as possible so that other people, including therapists, would certainly understand the meaning of intentionality. Actually, however, my misuse makes the word harder to understand rather than easier.

With reference to my use of myth, Reeves holds that I confuse drama with mythology. He argues that my quotations from the dramas of Sophocles and Aeschylus are made because of the psychological elaboration of their characters rather than because their dramas present various myths. For example, he would hold that I quote from *Oedipus Rex* as illustrating my points because Sophocles so skillfully elaborated the subjective aspects of the conflict of Oedipus and Jocasta rather than because of the underlying myth itself. There I believe he is mistaken. I refer in my writings to many myths that are not psychologically or subjectively elaborated. One of these is the myth of Adam and Eve, which is present in some form in practically all of my books; but it is not elaborated at all as it is given in Genesis. Neither is the creation myth, to which I also refer often. Other writers, such as Homer, do not subjectively elaborate their myths, but that does not mean the myths lack power as a consequence. It is obviously good that Aeschylus and Sophocles have psychological and subjective insight into their characters, but I do not believe this changes the pregnant qualities of the genre of myth itself.

Another issue that Reeves brings up is that I do not develop *philia* and *agape* as forms of love equal to eros and libido. He goes on to hold that I understand philia in a "reduced way." I think the situation is somewhat different. My purpose in not discussing philia and agape, as Reeves elsewhere rightly avers, is that I was not writing for people who have pronounced problems about philia. Similarly, a discussion of agape would not, I believe, be relevant to their lives. The problems that patients bring to the therapist in our culture are chiefly problems of confusion of eros and libido. As I have said earlier, my work is predicated on meeting, so far as it is possible, the questions and problems of human beings who encounter the therapist.

In discussing my belief that both Platonic and Freudian attitudes toward love are necessary and present in a relatively integrated person, Reeves points out that I am trying to integrate two points of view which cannot be integrated. Plato and

Freud come, he holds, from two radically different sets of presuppositions about human beings and life. This is true. But my mistake here, I believe, is of a different nature. It arises from a strange relation I detect in myself toward authority: a carry-over of a curious kind of "perpetual apprenticeship." There is a tendency in me to hide behind such authorities as Plato and Freud in espousing a particular idea that arose in my mind quite apart from their ideas. Actually Plato and Freud only illustrate the two sides of the human being that I am trying to bring together in my patients. This integration would still be necessary and of moment if no one had ever heard of Freud or Plato. I have tried to communicate that the physical and idealistic aspects of love are two necessary poles of the dialectic that occur in human beings at all times. I was glad to have Reeves' confirmation of my personal problem in this regard, and with his caution I think I will make progress in overcoming this habit. I was glad to read in Reeves' discussion the following summary paragraph:

> For May, then, Freud's preoccupation with the biological life of man is rejected, as is Plato's insistence on the higher worth of man's intellectual nature and the consequent devaluation of embodied existence. Now, grounding the two thrusts is the assertion of man as an embodied conscious being, as constituting meaning in his world, and as intersubjective in reciprocal relations freely chosen [p. 117].

I accept this entirely.

Another minor cavil is in the reference Reeves makes to *The Art of Counseling*. I wrote that book when I was twenty-seven years old, when I was obviously naive about these problems. One justification for its contents is that everyone in the country was naive about counseling when the book was published (1938). I myself believe that *The Art of Counseling* ought to be used merely to state the original basis of my ideas and theories, rather than (as I thought was the case in Reeves' longish discussion) as a basis for disputation. Yet, it was replenishing and refreshing to me to notice how expertly Reeves draws out from this book the concept of will, for example, and then proceeds to trace the concept in its growing sophistication from that early book through to my latest writings.

There are several parts of Reeves' study of my work that I wish specifically to single out for appreciation. His discussion of the ontological characteristics that inform and constitute my writing is insightful and constructive. He rightly sees that this ontological emphasis, assumed or specifically stated, is critical from my first writing to my last. He rightly points out that the search for understanding of what we "human beings really are" is the cause to which my life is devoted. Reeves' discussion of the ontological characteristics ranges widely, with the specific questions of whether "will" should be included in such a list and also whether "care," as a concern about the values of human beings, should also be included. I have asked myself the same questions. But Reeves rightly sees that the important thing is not so much what the philosopher-therapist would include or omit from his list of ontological characteristics; it is whether or not the philosopher-therapist sees and experiences the *need* for such a conception of ontological characteristics to begin with. Reeves and I both answer yes, it is critical that the philosopher-therapist see this need.

I also wish to state my appreciation of his emphasis on the phrase *sense of being*, which he makes the central theme of his first chapter. I agree entirely that this, as a statement of the ontological concern from the experiential aspect, is central throughout my books. Reeves remarks, anent this "sense of being," that there is in my writings "no confusion as to its import nor as to its foundational role and significance" (p. 38). To understand and appreciate this sense of being has always been my passion, even before I became a psychoanalyst; and this passion has surely underlain my work as a therapist. This *sense of being* is the central concern of my life, and everything else is subsumed under it.

Bibliography

Note: At the outset of preparing this book, in personal correspondence with the present writer, Rollo May offered to compile and send a complete bibliography of all of his published writings to date, but has since written to say that, due to pressure of work, he has after all been unable to prepare the promised bibliography. In the absence of such an authorized bibliography, every effort has here been made to compile as complete and accurate a bibliography as is possible in the case of a living author. In each entry, also, the publication data given first is that of the edition used in the preparation of this book.

Part One of the bibliography is devoted entirely to the writings of Rollo May, while Part Two contains the secondary sources for this study. For the convenience of the reader, the primary sources presented in Part One are divided into sections, as follows:

A. Books written by May.
B. Books edited and coedited by May.

C. Books coauthored by May.

D. Articles collected in *Psychology and the Human Dilemma*.

E. Other articles and papers (including one coauthored with Adrian Van Kaam).

To facilitate reference, the order of presentation is alphabetical, except in Section D, where the order is that of the articles' appearance as chapters in *Psychology and the Human Dilemma,* in deference to May's expressed intention that this material be construed as having an organic unity and as centering around the title theme.

Entries in Part One are continuously numbered through the sections in order to facilitate cross-referencing. The word *Item* and a number, sometimes between parentheses, e.g., *Item 22* or *(Item 22),* indicates that the reader's attention is directed to the entry bearing that number where the same material is to be found. Such indications are the result of the present writer's own original careful scrutiny and, in some isolated cases, references or acknowledgments by May. In Section D, the phrase "as indicated by May," refers specifically to listings given in the author's own note of acknowledgments in *Psychology and the Human Dilemma* (p. iv). For the researcher, the present writer suggests that the most integrated access to May's thinking, as evidenced by the extensive cross-referencing here given, is through his books and those edited or coedited by him, since all of the material has appeared there in some form and sometimes several forms.

Part One: Primary Sources, Rollo May
(with Cross-References)

A. Books Written by May

1. *The Art of Counseling.* Introduction by H. Bone. Nashville: Abingdon (Apex Books), copyright renewed 1967, 247 pp.

Reissue; only change, omission (unacknowledged) of subtitle. First published as *The Art of Counseling: How to Give and Gain Mental Health*, introduction by H. Bone (Nashville: Abingdon-Cokesbury, 1939), 247 pp.

A consideration of theory of personality and its relevance for the practice of counseling or psychotherapy. Early emphasis in May's work on the counselor's need for a properly based understanding of man.

See also Items 8, 33, 36, 40, and 46.

2. *Existential Psychotherapy*. Toronto: Canadian Broadcasting Corporation Publications, 1967, 62 pp.

Text of talks given during the fall of 1966 in the CBC program series *Ideas*. This material appears in extended form in some of May's other books, notably *Existence* (Item 9), *Symbolism in Religion and Literature* (Item 11), *Existential Psychology* (Item 10), *Psychology and the Human Dilemma* (Item 7), and *Love and Will* (Item 3).

This book provides a compressed statement of most of May's central ideas.

See also Items 3, 7, 11, 24, 27, 29, 31, 32, 34, 38, 41, and 44.

3. *Love and Will*. New York: Norton, 1969, 352 pp.

New York: Dell (Delta Books), 1973, 352 pp.; and New York: Dell (Laurel Books), 1974, 363 pp.

A discussion of the person as situated in the contemporary world, as characterized by anxiety, love, and will. Presentation of May's view of Eros, the daimonic, intention and intentionality, and their relation to therapy.

See also Items 2, 15, 24, 32, 34, 36, and 44.

4. *Man's Search for Himself*. New York: New American Library (Signet), 1967, *viii*, 239 pp.

First published New York: Norton, 1953, 281 pp.

May's view of the existential predicament of twentieth-century man, the crisis of meaning and the goals of integrated selfhood and responsible maturity.

See also Items 13, 14, 16, 23, 24, 25, 26, 28, 35, 36, 39, 40, and 41.

5. *The Meaning of Anxiety*. New York: Ronald Press, 1950, *xvi,* 376 pp.

Material originally May's Ph.D. dissertation in clinical psychology, Columbia University, New York, 1949.

Part One, "Modern Interpretations of Anxiety," offers an examination of theories of anxiety in their cultural, historical, biological, and psychological dimensions, together with May's summary and synthesis of their composite meaning for him. Clinical individual cases of anxious patients are integrated with May's overall view of anxiety, in Part Two, "Clinical Analysis of Anxiety."

See also Items 13, 14, 16, 17, 33, and 40.

6. *Power and Innocence: A Search for the Sources of Violence.* New York: Norton, 1972, 283 pp.

May's basic view of man and the contemporary crisis of meaning, focusing on the interrelationship of apathy, frustration, violence; the pseudoinnocence of noninvolvement; the need for individual power (or strong sense of being); and ethical solidarity (or participation). Basic theme is development of "integrated self-assertion."

This book appeared too late to have been available for detailed analysis within this study, but its themes have already been dealt with in some measure in the context of our discussion of ontological anxiety, guilt, apathy, and hostility.

7. *Psychology and the Human Dilemma*. New York: Van Nostrand Reinhold, 1967, 221 pp.

Simultaneously, student edition, Princeton, N.J.: Van Nostrand, 1967; and Toronto: Van Nostrand, 1967, 221 pp. Collected essays from 1951-1965, but mostly in the last four years of that period; chosen and integrated by the author around the title theme and having an organic unity. May himself speaks of it as a book rather than as discrete essays.

See also this bibliography, Section D, Items 13-26 inclusive, special section devoted to the material of this book. See also Items 29, 31, 35, 40, 41, and 43.

8. *The Springs of Creative Living: A Study of Human Nature and God.* Nashville: Abingdon-Cokesbury, 1940, 271 pp.

Very similar to and repetitious of *The Art of Counseling* (1) in line, tone, content, terminology, and conclusions, but, unlike its predecessor by only a year, this book does not offer (1) a systematic personal view of human being, healthy and neurotic, or May's "picture of personality," nor (2) an exploration of psychotherapeutic attitudes and encounter. The earlier book, containing May's views in germ at their simplest stage, was deemed more pertinent and more informative for the present study. (See also this book, Introduction, and Appendix One, "Rollo May: A Biographical Note.")

B. Books Edited and Coedited by May

9. *Existence: A New Dimension in Psychiatry and Psychology.* Coedited with E. Angel and H. F. Ellenberger. New York: Simon & Schuster (Clarion), 1967, x, 446 pp.

First published New York: Simon & Schuster (Basic Books), 1958, x, 446 pp.

Part One, "Introduction," contains two articles by May: "The Origins and Significance of the Existential Movement in Psychology" (Item 38), pp. 3-36; and "Contributions of Existential Psychotherapy" (Item 27), pp. 37-91.

See also Items 2, 18, 20, 27, 29, 30, 38, and 42.

10. *Existential Psychology* R. May, Ed. (2nd ed., rev.; Studies in Psychology PP 19). New York: Random House, 1969, x, 117 pp.

First edition, New York: Random House, 1961, 126 pp. See also "Introduction" of this book for comment on changes in second edition, largely reorganizational.

This book consists of papers presented at the Symposium on Existential Psychology, annual convention, American Psychological Association, Cincinnati, Ohio, 1959. Two papers by May: "The Emergence of Existential Psychology" (Item 29), pp. 1-48; and "Existential Bases of Psychotherapy" (Item 31), pp. 72-83. Page numbers of second edition used in the present study.

See also Items 2, 18, 19, 21, 29, 31, and 37.

11. *Symbolism in Religion and Literature.* R. May, Ed. New York: Braziller, 1960, 253 pp.

Introductory essay by May entitled "The Significance of Symbols" (Item 41), pp. 11-49.

See also Items 2, 18, 35, 38, 41, and 43.

C. Books Coauthored by May

12. *Dreams and Symbols: Man's Unconscious Language.* Coauthored with L. Caligor. New York: Basic Books, 1968, *x,* 307 pp.

Part One, "Dreams and Symbols," pp. 3-128, is by May, while Part Two, "The Case of Susan," pp. 131-300, is by Caligor, and consists of his original record of the case. Introductory and concluding material of May's section is also to be found compressed in *Existential Psychotherapy* (Item 2), Ch. 3, "The Healing Power of Symbols and Myths," pp. 21-30.

D. *Articles Collected in* Psychology and the Human Dilemma

13. Ch. 1, "What is the Human Dilemma?" pp. 1-22.

Written for the volume (1967). See also *Man's Search for Himself* (Item 4), Ch. 2, "The Roots of our Malady," pp. 41-69, and *Love and Will* (Item 3), pp. 222-231. Also recalls introductory material in *The Meaning of Anxiety* (Item 5), pp. 3-22.

14. Ch. 2, "Modern Man's Loss of Significance," pp. 25-39.

See also *The Meaning of Anxiety* (Item 5), pp. 203-223; and *Man's Search for Himself* (Item 4), Part One, "Our Predicament," pp. 13-69. Also, as indicated by May, given as "Modern Man's Image of Himself," an Alden Tuthill Lecture, Chicago Theological Seminary, University of Chicago, 1962.

15. Ch. 3, "Personal Identity in an Anonymous World," pp. 40-52.

See also *Love and Will* (Item 3), Ch. 1, "Introduction: Our Schizoid World," pp. 13-33. Also, *Man's Search for Himself* (Item 4), Ch. 1, "The Loneliness and Anxiety of Modern Man," pp. 13-40. Also, as indicated by May, lecture, "Anxiety Among Students and its Relation to Education," annual convention, New England Association of Colleges and Secondary Schools, Boston, 1964, and in their *New England Association Review.*

16. Ch. 4, "Historical Roots of Modern Anxiety Theories," pp. 55-71.

See also *The Meaning of Anxiety* (Item 5), Ch. 1, "Introduction," pp. 3-16, and Ch. 2, "Philosophical Predecessors to Modern Theories of Anxiety," pp. 17-45. Also, *Man's Search for Himself* (Item 4), Part One, "Our Predicament," pp. 13-69. Also, as indicated by May, paper, thirty-ninth annual convention, American Psychopathological Association, June 1949, and in *Anxiety,* P. H. Hoch and J. Zubin, Eds. (New York: Grune & Stratton, 1951 and New York: Hafner, 1964), pp. 3-26.

17. Ch. 5, "Anxiety and Values," pp. 72-83.

See also *The Meaning of Anxiety* (Item 5), pp. 215-234. Also, as indicated by May, lecture, annual convention, American Psychiatric Association, 1956, and in *Progress in Psychotherapy* (New York: Grune & Stratton, 1957).

18. Ch. 6, "The Context of Psychotherapy," pp. 87-110.

Also published in M. I. Stein (Ed.), *Contemporary Psychotherapies* (Glencoe, Ill.: Free Press, 1961), pp. 288-304. Also, excerpts in M. Friedman (Ed.), *The Worlds of Existentialism: A Critical Reader* (New York: Random House, 1964), pp. 442-446; see also Item 19. Also in *Existence* (Item 9), *Existential Psychology* (Item 10), and *Symbolism in Religion and Literature* (Item 11); see also Items 27, 31, 41, and 43. As indicated by May, also given as lecture to University of Chicago graduate psychology department.

19. Ch. 7, "A Phenomenological Approach to Psychotherapy," pp. 111-127.

Also (with peripheral changes), as "On the Phenomenological Bases of Psychotherapy," in E. Straus (Ed.), *Phenomenology: Pure and Applied* (Item 37); and in N. Lawrence and D. O'Connor (Eds.), *Readings in Existential Phenomenology* (Item 37). Portions modified also within *Psychology and the Human*

Dilemma (Item 7), Ch. 6, "The Context of Psychotherapy" (Item 18); and in *Existential Psychology* (Item 10), "Existential Bases of Psychotherapy" (Item 31). Also see "Toward the Ontological Basis of Psychotherapy" (Item 43).

20. Ch. 8, "Existential Therapy and the American Scene," pp. 128-137.

Also, modified, in "Contributions of Existential Psychotherapy" (Item 27) in *Existence* (Item 9). Also, as indicated by May, in *Topical Problems of Psychotherapy,* Vol. 3 (Basel, Switzerland: S. Karger, 1960), and as address, Third International Conference on Psychotherapy, Barcelona, 1959.

21. Ch. 9, "Jean-Paul Sartre and Psychoanalysis," pp. 138-146.

Also, modified, in "The Emergence of Existential Psychology" (Item 29) in *Existential Psychology* (Item 10). Also, as indicated by May, as introduction to paperback edition of J. Sartre, *Existential Psychoanalysis* (Chicago: Regnery, 1963).

22. Ch. 10, "Dangers in the Relation of Existentialism to Psychotherapy," pp. 147-157.

Also in H. M. Ruitenbeek (Ed.), *Psychoanalysis and Existential Philosophy* (New York: Dutton, 1962), pp. 179-187; and, as indicated by May, in *Review of Existential Psychology and Psychiatry,* 1963, *3,* 5-10. Also, compressed, in "The Emergence of Existential Psychology" (Item 29) in *Existential Psychology* (Item 10), pp. 45-48; and excerpts in M. Friedman (Ed.), *The Worlds of Existentialism: A Critical Reader* (New York: Random House, 1964), pp. 453-454.

23. Ch. 11, "The Man Who Was Put in a Cage," pp. 161-167.

Also, compressed, in *Man's Search for Himself* (Item 4), pp. 125-128; and as indicated by May, in *Psychiatry: Journal for the Study of Interpersonal Relations,* 1952, *15.*

24. Ch. 12, "Freedom and Responsibility Re-examined," pp. 168-181.

Also in *Man's Search for Himself* (Item 4), Ch. 5, "Freedom and Inner Strength," pp. 125-249, and Ch. 6, "The Creative Conscience," pp. 150-190; portions also in *Love and Will* (Item 3), "Intentionality in Therapy," pp. 262-272; and in *Existential Psychotherapy* (Item 2), Ch. 4, "Will and Decision in Existential Psychotherapy," pp. 31-40. Also, as indicated by May, in Lloyd Jones and Westervelt (Eds.), *Behavioral Science and Guidance: Proposals and Perspectives* (New York: Columbia University, Teachers' College, Bureau of Publications, 1963). See also Item 45.

25. Ch. 13, "Questions for a Science of Man," pp. 182-200.

Also, at greater length, in *Man's Search for Himself* (Item 4), Ch. 2, "The Roots of our Malady," pp. 41-69, Ch. 3, "The Experience of Becoming a Person," pp. 73-102, and Ch. 8, "Man, the Transcender of Time," pp. 217-236. Also, as indicated by May, address to the New York Society of Clinical Psychologists, New York, 1955.

26. Ch. 14, "Social Responsibilities of Psychologists," pp. 201-221.

Also, expanded, in *Man's Search for Himself* (Item 4), Ch. 3, "The Experience of Becoming a Person," pp. 73-102, and Ch. 6, "The Creative Conscience," pp. 150-190. Also, as indicated by May, paper presented at Symposium on Social Responsibilities of the Psychologist, annual convention, American Psychological Association, September 1963.

E. Other Articles and Papers

27. "Contributions of Existential Psychotherapy." In *Existence* (Item 9), pp. 37-91.

Pages 76-91 of this article are reproduced in W. S. Sahakian (Ed.), *Psychotherapy and Counseling: Studies in Technique* (Chicago: Rand McNally, 1969), pp. 261-275. Also, in *Existential Psychotherapy* (Item 2), Ch. 1, "Existential Psychotherapy," pp. 1-10. See also Items 30 and 42.

28. "Creativity and Encounter." *American Journal of Psychoanalysis*, 1964, *24*, 39-45.

Also, in *The Art of Counseling* (Item 1), pp. 71-74, pp.

189-194; and in *Man's Search for Himself* (Item 4), pp.
120-122, pp. 181-184; and in *Existential Psychotherapy* (Item
2), Ch. 5, "Creativity and the Unconscious," pp. 41-50; and in
Love and Will (Item 3), pp. 78-80, pp. 170-177; and in "The
Nature of Creativity" (Item 36); and in "The Significance of
Symbols" (Item 41) in *Symbolism in Religion and Literature*
(Item 11). See also *Dreams and Symbols* (Item 12).

    29. "The Emergence of Existential Psychology." In *Exis-
tential Psychology* (Item 10), pp. 1-48.

    And in "On the Phenomenological Bases of Psychother-
apy" (Item 37); and in *Psychology and the Human Dilemma*
(Item 7), Ch. 6, "The Context of Psychotherapy" (Item 18),
and Ch. 7, "A Phenomenological Approach to Psychotherapy"
(Item 19), and Ch. 9, "Jean-Paul Sartre and Psychoanalysis"
(Item 21); and in "The Origins and Significance of the Existential Movement in Psychology" (Item 38) in *Existence* (Item 9).

    30. "The Existential Approach." In S. Arieti (Ed.), *Amer-
ican Handbook of Psychiatry* (Vol. 2). New York: Basic Books,
1959, pp. 1348-1361.

    And, as indicated by May in two footnotes to this article,
this material consists of compressed form of material of his two
articles in *Existence* (Item 9): see Items 27 and 38. See also
"Some Comments on Existential Psychotherapy" (Item 42); see
also Items 29, 42, and 43.

    31. "Existential Bases of Psychotherapy." In *Existential
Psychology* (Item 10), pp. 72-83.

    Also, in "On the Phenomenological Bases of Psychother-
apy" (Item 37); and in *Psychology and the Human Dilemma*
(Item 7), Ch. 6, "The Context of Psychotherapy" (Item 18),
and Ch. 7, "A Phenomenological Approach to Psychotherapy"
(Item 19); and in "Toward the Ontological Basis of Psychotherapy" (Item 43); and excerpts in M. Friedman (Ed.), *The Worlds
of Existentialism: A Critical Reader* (New York: Random
House, 1964), pp. 440-446.

    32. "Existential Theory and Therapy." Coauthored with
A. van Kaam, in J. H. Masserman (Ed.), *Current Psychiatric*

Therapies (Vol. 3). New York: Grune & Stratton, 1963, pp. 74-89.

The first two sections of this article, pp. 74-77, briefly offer van Kaam's view of comprehensive theorizing and foundational integrational constructs as presented in his book, *Existential Foundations of Psychology* (see this bibliography, Part Two), in particular pp. 156-160, and his "Introduction," pp. 11-14. The remainder of the article, pp. 77-81, offers in compressed form the material later presented in May's *Love and Will* (Item 3), Chs. 8-10, on wish, will, and decision, both as stages in therapy and as foundational theory; see in particular pp. 262-272. Also in *Existential Psychotherapy* (Item 2), Ch. 4, "Will and Decision in Existential Psychotherapy," pp. 31-40.

See also Items 34, 44, and 45.

33. "Historical and Philosophical Presuppositions for Understanding Therapy." In O. H. Mowrer (Ed.), *Psychotherapy: Theory and Research.* New York: Ronald Press, 1953, pp. 9-43.

Also in *The Meaning of Anxiety* (Item 5), Ch. 1, "Introduction," pp. 3-16, and Ch. 2, "Philosophical Predecessors to Modern Theories of Anxiety," pp. 17-45. Also in *Psychology and the Human Dilemma* (Item 7), Ch. 4, "Historical Roots of Modern Anxiety Theories" (Item 16); and in "A Psychologist looks at Mental Health in Today's World" (Item 40); and in "The Work and Training of the Psychological Therapist" (Item 46).

34. "Intentionality, the Heart of Human Will." *Journal of Humanistic Psychology,* 1965, *5* (2), 55-70.

Consists of excerpts (acknowledged without details in the author's footnote to the title) from *Love and Will* (Item 3), Ch. 8, "Wish and Will," pp. 202-222, and Ch. 9, "Intentionality," pp. 223-245. Also in *Existential Psychotherapy* (Item 2), Ch. 4, "Will and Decision in Existential Psychotherapy," pp. 31-40.

35. "The Meaning of the Oedipus Myth." *Review of Existential Psychology and Psychiatry,* 1961, *1,* 44-52.

Also in *Existential Psychotherapy* (Item 2), Ch. 2, "Oedipus and Self-Knowledge," pp. 11-20, and Ch. 3, "The Healing

Power of Symbols and Myths," pp. 21-30; and in "The Significance of Symbols" (Item 41), in *Symbolism in Religion and Literature* (Item 11); and in *Man's Search for Himself* (Item 4), pp. 212ff.; and in *Psychology and the Human Dilemma* (Item 7), Ch. 6, "The Context of Psychotherapy" (Item 18).

See also Items 28 and 36.

36. "The Nature of Creativity." In H. H. Anderson (Ed.), *Creativity and its Cultivation.* New York: Harper, 1959, pp. 55-68.

Also in *The Art of Counseling* (Item 1), pp. 40-41; 51-52; 71-72; 161-162; and in *Man's Search for Himself* (Item 4), pp. 120-122; and in *Existential Psychotherapy* (Item 2), Ch. 5, "Creativity and the Unconscious," pp. 41-50; and compressed in *Love and Will* (Item 3), pp. 78-80; and in "Creativity and Encounter" (Item 28).

See also Items 35 and 41.

37. "On the Phenomenological Bases of Psychotherapy." In E. Straus (Ed.), *Phenomenology: Pure and Applied.* Pittsburgh: Duquesne University Press, 1964, pp. 166-184.

And in N. Lawrence and D. O'Connor (Eds.), *Readings in Existential Phenomenology.* Englewood Cliffs, N.J.: Prentice-Hall, 1967, pp. 365-376; and in *Review of Existential Psychology and Psychiatry,* 1964, *4* (1), 22-36; and in *Psychology and the Human Dilemma* (Item 7), Ch. 7, "A Phenomenological Approach to Psychotherapy" (Item 19); and in "Existential Bases of Psychotherapy" (Item 31) in *Existential Psychology* (Item 10); and in "Toward the Ontological Basis of Psychotherapy" (Item 43).

38. "The Origins and Significance of the Existential Movement in Psychology." In *Existence* (Item 9), pp. 3-36.

Also in "The Emergence of Existential Psychology" (Item 29) in *Existential Psychology* (Item 10); and in "The Existential Approach" (Item 30); and in "Some Comments on Existential Psychotherapy" (Item 42).

39. "A Preface to Love." In I. Schneider (Ed., Intro.), *The World of Love* (Vol. I, *The Meanings of Love*). New York: Braziller, 1964, pp. 279-284.

Consists of excerpts (acknowledged without details, in editor's footnote) from *Man's Search for Himself* (Item 4), pp. 204-210.

40. "A Psychologist looks at Mental Health in Today's World." *Mental Hygiene,* 1954, *38,* 1-11.

Address, Spring Conference, New York State Society for Mental Health, New York, N.Y., May 6, 1953. And in *The Meaning of Anxiety* (Item 5), Ch. 1, "Introduction," pp. 3-16, and in Ch. 6, "Summary and Synthesis of Theories of Anxiety," pp. 215-234; and in *Man's Search for Himself* (Item 4), Part 1, "Our Predicament," pp. 13-69; and in *Psychology and the Human Dilemma* (Item 7), Chs. 1-5; see also Items 13, 14, 15, 16, and 17; and in *Love and Will* (Item 3), Ch. 1, "Introduction: Our Schizoid World," pp. 13-33.

41. "The Significance of Symbols." In *Symbolism in Religion and Literature* (Item 11), pp. 11-49.

Also in *Existential Psychotherapy* (Item 2), Ch. 2, "Oedipus and Self-Knowledge," pp. 11-20, and Ch. 3, "The Healing Power of Symbols and Myths," pp. 21-30; and in "The Meaning of the Oedipus Myth" (Item 35); and in *Man's Search for Himself* (Item 4) pp. 212-216; and in *Psychology and the Human Dilemma* (Item 7), Ch. 6, "The Context of Psychotherapy" (Item 18).

42. "Some Comments on Existential Psychotherapy." In M. Friedman (Ed.), *The Worlds of Existentialism: A Critical Reader.* New York: Random House, 1964, pp. 446-453.

Although Friedman acknowledges this material as "written expressly for this anthology" (see his "Acknowledgements," p. vii), the material actually antedates this publication, having appeared previously in "The Origins and Significance of the Existential Movement in Psychology" (Item 38), and in "Contributions of Existential Psychotherapy" (Item 27), both in *Existence* (Item 9), originally published in 1958. Material also in "The Existential Approach (Item 30), compressed form of May's articles in *Existence,* and appearing in 1959.

43. "Toward the Ontological Basis of Psychotherapy." *Existential Inquiries,* 1959, *1,* 5-7.

Also in "Existential Bases of Psychotherapy" (Item 31), in *Existential Psychology* (Item 10); and in *Psychology and the Human Dilemma* (Item 7), Ch. 6, "The Context of Psychotherapy" (Item 18), and Ch. 7, "A Phenomenological Approach to Psychotherapy" (Item 19); and in "On the Phenomenological Bases of Psychotherapy" (Item 37).

44. "Will, Decision and Responsibility: Summary Remarks." *Review of Existential Psychology and Psychiatry,* 1961, *1,* 249-259.

Also in *Existential Psychotherapy* (Item 2), Ch. 4, "Will and Decision in Existential Psychotherapy," pp. 31-40; and in *Love and Will* (Item 3), Ch. 8, "Wish and Will," pp. 202-222, Ch. 9; "Intentionality," pp. 223-245; also within Ch. 10, "Intentionality in Therapy," in particular pp. 262-272; and in "Existential Theory and Therapy" (Item 32), coauthored with Adrian van Kaam; and in "Intentionality, the Heart of Human Will" (Item 34); and in *Psychology and the Human Dilemma* (Item 7), Ch. 12, "Freedom and Responsibility Re-examined" (Item 24).

45. "Wish and Intentionality." In W. von Baeyer and R. M. Griffith (Eds.), *Conditio Humana: Erwin Straus on his 75th birthday.* Berlin: Springer, 1966, pp. 233-240.

Also (as acknowledged without details in author's footnote) in *Love and Will* (Item 3), Chs. 8-10, in particular Ch. 10, pp. 262-272. Also *Existential Psychotherapy* (Item 2), Ch. 4, "Will and Decision in Existential Psychotherapy," pp. 31-40; see also Items 24, 32, 34, and 44.

46. "The Work and Training of The Psychological Therapist." *The Psychological Service Center Journal,* 1950, *2,* 3-23.

Also in *The Art of Counseling* (Item 1), Ch. 3, "Empathy —Key to the Counseling Process," pp. 75-97, and Ch. 8, "The Personality of the Counselor," pp. 165-178; and in "Historical and Philosophical Presuppositions for Understanding Therapy" (Item 33); and in "Contributions of Existential Psychotherapy" (Item 27) in *Existence* (Item 9), pp. 76-91.

Part Two: Secondary Sources

Allport, G. W. *Becoming: Basic Considerations for a Psychology of Personality.* New Haven: Yale University Press, 1969, x, 106 pp.

A systematic, structured inquiry into personality theory with emphasis on "oriented becoming" and self-appropriation.

Binswanger, L. "The Case of Ellen West: An Anthropological-Clinical Study." W. M. Mendel and J. Lyons (Trans.). In R. May, E. Angel, and H. F. Ellenberger (Eds.), *Existence: A New Dimension in Psychiatry and Psychology.* New York: Simon & Schuster (Clarion Books), 1967, pp. 237-364.

An extremely complex and detailed exploration of the life history of Ellen West, phenomenologically described and analyzed, and elucidating the problem of the fundamental key to and existential forms of her whole being-in-the-world.

Binswanger, L. "Existential Analysis and Psychotherapy." In H. M. Ruitenbeek (Ed.), *Psychoanalysis and Existential Philosophy.* New York: Dutton, 1962, pp. 17-23.

A brief exploration of the basic conceptions and relationship of exitentialism and psychotherapy. Very helpful in outlining the context of our inquiry.

Binswanger, L. "The Existential Analysis School of Thought." E. Angel (Trans.). In R. May, E. Angel, and H. F. Ellenberger (Eds.), *Existence: A New Dimension in Psychiatry and Psychology.* New York: Simon & Schuster (Clarion Books), 1967, pp. 191-218.

An examination of the nature, method, and goals of Binswanger's existential analysis.

Boss, M. " 'Daseinsanalysis' and Psychotherapy." In H. M. Ruitenbeek (Ed.), *Psychoanalysis and Existential Philosophy.* New York: Dutton, 1962, pp. 81-89.

A brief appreciation of the decisive influence of Daseinsanalysis or existential analysis on therapy and the therapist.

Boss, M. In L. B. Lefebre (Trans.), *Psychoanalysis and Daseins-analysis.* New York: Basic Books, 1963, *viii,* 295 pp.

    A major discussion of the therapeutic application of Daseinsanalytic insights and approach. Cogent inquiry into the basic assumptions implicit in contemporary psychoanalytic theory.

Caligor, L. See this bibliography, Part One, Primary Sources, Item 12, *Dreams and Symbols: Man's Unconscious Language,* coauthored with R. May.

Ellenberger, H. F. "A Clinical Introduction to Psychiatric Phenomenology and Existential Analysis." In R. May, E. Angel, and H. F. Ellenberger (Eds.), *Existence: A New Dimension in Psychiatry and Psychology.* New York: Simon & Schuster (Clarion Books), 1967, pp. 92-124.

    Presentation of the context and methods of phenomenological observation and analysis, together with brief discussion of some therapeutic implications. Useful distinctions on the modes of world.

Freud, S. In J. Strachey (Ed.), J. Riviere (Trans.), *The Ego and the Id* (rev. edition). London: Hogarth Press, and the Institute of Psychoanalysis, 1962, *xvii,* 67 pp. Originally published in 1923.

    Offers elucidation of the Freudian conception of Eros.

Freud, S. In J. Strachey (Trans.), *Beyond the Pleasure Principle.* New York: Bantam (Matrix), 1967, 121 pp. Originally published in 1920.

    This book offers elucidation of Freud's understanding of Eros.

Freud, S. *A General Introduction to Psychoanalysis* (rev. ed., authorized trans. by J. Riviere). New York: Washington Square, 1968, 480 pp. (a). Originally published as a series of lectures in 1916-1917.

    Of particular relevance for the present study are (1) Freud's libido theory as discussed in Lecture 20, "The Sexual Life of Man," pp. 312-328; Lecture 21, "Development of the Libido and Sexual Organisations," pp. 329-347; and Lecture 26, "The Theory of the Libido:

Narcissim," pp. 419-455; and (2) Freud's articulation of his first theory of anxiety in Lecture 25, "Anxiety," pp. 400-418.

For the convenience of the reader referring to the Strachey *Standard Edition* of Freud's work, this series of lectures is there entitled *Introductory Lectures in Psychoanalysis,* and occupies Vols. 15 and 16 of that edition. Freud's second theory of anxiety is found in *Inhibitions, Symptoms and Anxiety* (1926) which has also been translated under the title of *The Problem of Anxiety* and in the papers entitled *New Introductory Lectures in Psychoanalysis* (1933) which two books may be found in Vols. 20 (pp. 75-175) and 22 (pp. 1-182) respectively.

Freud, S. *New Introductory Lectures in Psychoanalysis,* in *The Standard Edition of the Complete Psychological Works of Sigmund Freud* (translated from the German under the general editorship of J. Strachey in collaboration with A. Freud, assisted by A. Strachey and A. Tyson). London: Hogarth Press and the Institute of Psychoanalysis, 1968, Vol. 22, *vi,* 282 pp.

This group of lectures occupies pp. 1-182 (b). First published, 1933.

Giorgi, A. *Psychology as a Human Science: A Phenomenologically Based Approach.* New York: Harper & Row, 1970, *xvi,* 240 pp.

This book gives a useful formulation of the conception of psychology as a human, comprehensive, and integrational rather than a natural or positive science.

Heer, F. In J. Sondheimer (Trans.), *The Mediaeval World: Europe 1100-1350.* New York: New American Library (Mentor), 1961, English trans. copyright 1962, *xvi,* 432 pp.

This book offers a comprehensive description of what might be characterized as the working polarity of self and world in the twelfth-century era of courtly love and social stability in Europe, and in the thirteenth-century decline of cultural values and the rise of intolerance and anxiety.

Kierkegaard, S. In W. Lowrie (Trans.; Intro.). *The Concept of*

Dread. Princeton, N.J.: Princeton University Press, 1969, *xiii,* 154 pp. First published, 1844.

Of seminal importance in the development of May's own theory of anxiety, its source and expression, in particular its relation to nonbeing, possibility, and freedom.

Mullahy, P. *Oedipus Myth and Complex: A Review of Psychoanalytic Theory.* New York: Grove (Evergreen), 1955, author's copyright 1948, *xiv,* 370 pp.

A critical summary of the major interpretations of the Oedipus myth and complex. Excellent contextual and comparative aid to understanding of May's envisioning of the Oedipus myth and drama, and hence to understanding of his conceptions of symbol, myth and dream.

Plato. *Symposium.* In *The Dialogues of Plato* (fourth ed., rev.; trans., analyses, and intro. by B. Jowett; Vol. 1 of four vols.). Oxford: Clarendon, 1953, pp. 479-555.

Of seminal importance in the development of May's own theory of love or Eros.

Ruitenbeek, H. M. "Some Aspects of the Encounter of Psychoanalysis and Existential Philosophy." In H. M. Ruitenbeek (Ed.), *Psychoanalysis and Existential Philosophy.* New York: Dutton, 1962, pp. xi-xxvi.

This introductory essay briefly outlines some of the main contributions of existentialism to psychotherapy such as emphasis on existence, the person, and encounter; understanding of the modes of world and of nothingness; and the absurd.

Spiegelberg, H. *Phenomenology in Psychology and Psychiatry: A Historical Introduction.* Evanston, Ill.: Northwestern University Press, 1972, *xlv,* 411 pp.

This book was not available to the present writer until this study was almost complete. In these circumstances, this book, especially its chapter "The American Scene: Beginnings" (pp. 143-168) provided a helpful critico-biographical note on May (pp. 158-164).

Tillich, P. *The Courage to Be.* New Haven: Yale University Press, 1952 (Yale Paperbound, 1970), *ix,* 197 pp. Originally published in 1952.

Helpful articulation of central conceptions such as anxiety, courage, individuation, and participation. As Tillich taught May in his formative years (see Appendix One, *Rollo May: A Biographical Note*), this book offers some insight into the context of May's thinking.

Tillich, P. *Systematic Theology* (3 vols.). New York: Harper & Row; Evanston, Ill.: University of Chicago Press. Separate copyrights: Vol. 1 (1951); Vol. 2 (1957); Vol. 3 (1963). Published as one volume, 1967; 1967 pagination used here.

Of particular interest and insight on the subjects of love and the demonic.

van Kaam, A. *Existential Foundations of Psychology.* Garden City, New York: Doubleday (Image Books), 1969, 396 pp.

Original copyright 1966, by Duquesne University Press.

This book provides an integrational perspective on the tasks of the theorizing psychologist, as existential, as humanistic, as comprehensive or aspectual (differential) theorist.

Index